T0327739

The Anthology in Digital Culture

The Anthology in Digital Culture

Forms and Affordances

Giulia Taurino

Amsterdam University Press

The publication of this book is made possible by a grant from the University of Bologna, Department of the Arts.

Cover illustration: Woman at Main Reading Room card catalog in the Library of Congress, ca 1930-1950, photograph by Jack Delano
Cover design: Coördesign, Leiden
Lay-out: Crius Group, Hulshout

ISBN 978 94 6372 426 5
e-ISBN 978 90 4855 459 1 (pdf)
DOI 10.5117/9789463724265
NUR 670

Printed and bound by CPI Group (UK) Ltd, Croydon, CR0 4YY

A Daniela e Giancarlo,
per essere stati la mia prima forma di conoscenza.

Consider a future device for individual use, which is a sort
of mechanized private file and library. It needs a name,
and, to coin one at random, 'memex' will do. A memex is a
device in which an individual stores all his books, records,
and communications, and which is mechanized so that it
may be consulted with exceeding speed and flexibility. It is
an enlarged intimate supplement to his memory. [...] Wholly
new forms of encyclopedias will appear, ready made with a
mesh of associative trails running through them, ready to be
dropped into the memex and there amplified.

Vannevar Bush, *As We May Think*, 1945

Now imagine that the forest is a huge information space and
each of the trees and bushes are classification systems. Those
who make them up and use them are the animals and plants,
and the soil is a mix of the Internet, the paper world, and
other communication infrastructures. Your job is to describe
this forest.

Geoffrey C. Bowker and Susan Leigh Star,
Sorting Things Out, 1999

Table of Contents

Preface

Academic writing is about the world as we collectively know it and understand it, but it is also, inevitably, about ourselves and our own systems of knowledge. As such, it is never complete. It always needs to be revised, redefined, rewritten. A palimpsest model would be perfect to erase the original words that we no longer recognize, those sentences that do not match with our present thoughts, with our new discoveries, and with our developing perception of reality. It would be a manuscript, which means it might contain errors. But, then, so does our memory. As needed, the text could be scraped or washed off, resurfaced and the material reused anew. Some traces of earlier versions might be still visible. There might be remains of ancient marks, drafts, and records, like an old magnetic drawing board that no longer functions properly. But the entire primitive text would be lost or corrupted forever. It could be incomplete or unintelligible. The palimpsest model is multilayered, and yet each version lives in some sort of isolation from previous ones. Each narrative exists on the premises of another narrative's erasure. The reasons for overwriting can be tied to the mere diachronic privilege granted by temporality: the most recent text will be the easiest to read. Or, perhaps, it is a way to correct inaccuracies. Or else, in more extreme cases, survival might depend on acts of dominance, authority, recognition, disapproval, even violence. Such record-keeping system would require little or no classification. There would be no complex archival system to keep track of multiple versions of the same text, no *errata corrige* detailing corrections to a published paper, but just a series of writings perpetually striving for permanence. In the lexicon of Italian television, the term *palinsesto* came to be commonly used to define the programming schedule. In a way, linear media do superimpose, day by day, a new broadcasting flow to the former one in a relation of posteriority. In the case of broadcasting, some form of organization or ordering is imposed, via the hourly, daily, weekly, monthly, season-long schedule that articulates mediated time. Yet, this is not quite the model we have chosen for our archives of the future. The digital has shifted oral, ephemeral, transient practices into an incessant process of documentation. The cultural repository continuously grows to satisfy the human impulse to collect and store artifacts as permanent records. In digital culture, the palimpsest model ultimately left space for the anthology model, for the synchronous accumulation and sorting of objects. With it, we have achieved access to the possibility of a deeper understanding: not only can we see the things in between relations, but also the relations between things. This system of kinships came with a higher cognitive load. Forms of knowledge became dynamic entities in an expanding network of associations, categories, and classification schemes. They acquired functions, uses, and affordances. Relations between things can help us understand ourselves, but they can also create barriers to interpreting otherness if not discerned in their appropriate contexts. We now find ourselves questioning not how we may think, but how we already think. The human kind struggles to make sense of the amount of information currently available. Since many contemporary societies have embraced the anthology model, the load of stories, collections, and data has been hard to divide and compute. We require machines, infrastructures, and algorithms to organize the mass of content. In algorithmic culture, texts are not handwritten, but it is difficult to find the errors. Versions are saved into unlimited storage, but we cannot remember. Some artifacts are overly exposed and prominent, others get lost – but we cannot tell which ones – somewhere in the universe of millions of computationally curated categories. I wrote this book to regain our awareness, responsibility, agency, and control over the deep structure (Chomsky 1969) of concepts, thoughts, ideas, as well as our capacity to discern the surface structure of forms that emerge from the internet. In architecture and design, it was said that *"form ever follows function*, and this is the law. Where function does not change, form does not change. The granite rocks, the ever-brooding hills, remain for ages; the lightning lives, comes into shape, and dies, in a twinkling" (Sullivan 1896). But in the information forest of the mind, where plants are narratives and the soil is a mix of communication infrastructures (Bowker and Star 1999), form follows function insofar as function follows form (Weiss et al. 2014). For it is always a form-in-a-medium (Luhmann 2000). In this forest, "wholly new forms of encyclopedias will appear, ready made with a mesh of associative trails running through them, ready to be dropped into the memex and there amplified" (Bush 1945). Much of the work for this book has required me to return to the roots of this forest of interconnected branches, trails, systems, and morphologies, into a genealogy of my own education and upbringing. So I will start from the roots. This book is dedicated to my "forms of knowledge", those I was born into and those I was able to create. To my origins, my family – the close ones and the extended ones, the past ones and the future ones – and to the forms of true and honest kinship I shared. Writing this would not have been possible without you.

Introduction

The anthology is a form of cultural preservation. It can be historical, political, and technological, and can expand into forms of narrative adaptation, experimentation, and organization. Since the origins of writing systems, this editorial structure has provided not only a conceptual shape to oral and written narratives, but also a material means for cultural survival. Traditionally referring to collections of short literary works, anthologies have offered important curatorial frameworks for the development, organization, and retrieval of stories – prose, scripts, epigrams, or poems – contributing to recounting a partial history of human societies through organized arrangements of narrative artifacts. From paper-based media to machine-generated content, throughout a series of discontinued analog and digital technologies, they have adapted to the ubiquitous acts of categorization of knowledge and information that characterize internet culture. In its multiple occurrences, the practice of anthologization has represented more than a pragmatic solution to the need for a systematic classification and storage of documents.

From a critical perspective, anthologies were found to be instrumental to the definition of cultural authority in a comparable way to reading lists or bibliographies. While not all anthologies constitute authoritative canons per se, they contribute to determining canonical principles for the archival of heritage records by enabling a process of exclusion and inclusion and, ultimately, assigning value to a selected collection. With its potential to generate a series of small archives around a range of literary categories, themes, or styles, over time the anthology form transitioned from being a space dedicated to validating the vision of dominant cultures to serving as a literary refuge for marginalized communities seeking to reconstruct their own histories outside of the traditional Western canon. Within this ambivalence, anthologies came to act as tools of power as much as tools for subversion, resistance, and repair. As sites of constant renegotiation between overarching dynamics of cultural imperialism and informal, under-documented cultural movements, they remind us that "canonicity is not a property of the work itself but of its transmission, its relation to other works in a collocation of works" (Guillory 2013, 55).

Taurino, Giulia. *The Anthology in Digital Culture*. Amsterdam: Amsterdam University Press, 2023.
DOI: 10.5117/9789463724265_INTRO

This book is about anthologies as modes of conservation, transmission and mediation of cultural heritage. By observing their multilinear evolution from analog to digital culture, it examines how traditional editorial practices of anthologization intersect with data-driven content classification. More than ten years on, this research complements Milad Doueihi's seminal works, *Pour une humanisme numérique* (2011a) and *Digital Culture* (2011b), in which he describes digital environments as inherently anthological, made of fragmented and yet interconnected records aggregated via a semantic network of tags and labels. In this view, the anthology form stands out as a way to manage cultural memory (Doueihi 2011, 151), allowing for extensive track-recording and content archival practices. While Doueihi's work focuses on digital culture and content production as seen in the early years of online platforms, the present volume expands the conversation to include pre-digital and post-digital (Cramer 2014), algorithmic culture. By doing so, it aims at reconstructing the socio-cultural conditions of existence (Foucault 1972) and techno-cultural histories (Parrika 2012) that lie behind the anthology form. Through a genealogical study (Apprich and Bachmann 2017) that combines the analysis of historical records with new media research, the chapters examine the connection between narrative structures, editorial traditions, and technological forms. In particular, observing media as techno-cultural apparatuses, the anthology is considered at the intersection of technological specificities and cultural commonalities, in the context of "all the organizations and *milieux* in which artistic, intellectual, and scientific work goes on, and by which entertainment and information are produced and distributed" (Mills 2008, 204, his emphasis).

The historical lens serves as the main analytical framework for understanding anthologies as both narrative forms and forms of knowledge in the *longue durée* (Braudel 1982) of cultural structures. Moreover, it draws a connection between curatorial practices for heritage preservation and data-based forms of content organization as common attempts to regain control over the archival uncertainties (Thylstrup et al. 2021) of our time. Given the lack of a comprehensive publication on the anthology form across media, this work inaugurates an interdisciplinary construction site for building a genealogy of anthology series using a hybrid methodology that combines archival research and data collection, with comparative historical analysis and media studies. Drawing upon previous studies on the anthological turn in digital culture (Doueihi 2011), data classification (Bowker and Star 1999), and platform infrastructures (Poell et al. 2021), the book retraces the cultural roots of the anthology form, reconnecting it with contemporary practices of algorithmic curation. The purpose is to investigate the relation between anthological *forms*, distribution *platforms*, and consumption *models* by proposing a comparative approach to the study of anthologies that leverages *cross*-cultural, *cross*-historical, *cross*-media analysis.

Overall, the research behind this volume touches upon several interdisciplinary concepts and approaches. First, a distant reading analysis of the evolution of the anthology in literature, publishing and broadcasting was conducted to better understand the transition that accompanied this editorial form from its early etymological origins to more recent occurrences in television, and, in later years, on digital platforms. This approach led to further observations on how hierarchical and networked industrial dynamics have operated in specific media contexts with consequences on the emergence of anthological narrative features. Thereafter, I have reviewed theories borrowed from the field of design as they intertwine with the history of anthological models and their applications. In particular, I have investigated notions like form and affordance as found in disciplines that examine the role of design in processes of storytelling and content organization (i.e., narrative studies and platform studies). Finally, starting from a preliminary historical overview and conceptual framing, I opted for qualitative cultural and media analysis in order to accompany this research with a thorough case study.

Chapter after chapter, the book engages in a discussion about the historical, formal, infrastructural, platformed components of cultural production and distribution, as the driving forces that contributed to shape contemporary anthological practices and uses. In this process, the notion of anthology is explored through four lenses: history, design, infrastructures, and platforms. Each one of these keywords highlights different aspects that lead us to an updated definition of anthology and outline an anthological approach to the practice of archiving for the future. Chapter 1 focuses on the *history* of the anthology form by considering its etymological and cultural relevance, as well as its cross-media transformations. This first section situates such a form in an evolutionary context that spans from its primordial archetypes in early analog media to its contemporary uses. A genealogy of the anthology model serves as the point of departure for observing recent practices of content organization from a cultural and media studies standpoint. We will notably see how, in their evolution from printed to broadcasting media, anthologies have consolidated new structural features (e.g., a recurring introductory tagline and sometimes a closing line as means of framing a collection of stories). Furthermore, taking a media-ecological standpoint, the paragraphs provide examples of how narrative forms can be both cultural and political in response to the surrounding social and industrial context. The intent is to redirect the attention to the ways the anthology form is actively constructed and designed across a range of techno-cultural scenarios.

To tackle the generative nature of the anthology form, Chapter 2 proposes a *design*-oriented framework for the study of digital culture, one that can explain the epistemological as well as morphological and pragmatic relevance of anthological variations by introducing the concepts of form and affordance. The chapter echoes Caroline Levine's *Forms: Whole, Rhythm, Hierarchy, Network* (2015), which adapts the notion of form to the fields of literature and the arts. Following Levine's work, this section considers the functionalities and potential uses of forms as properties that are not only perceptual (e.g., visual, tactile, auditory), but also social, psychological, and intellectual. Such a perspective is reminiscent of Marshall McLuhan's (1994) definition of media as human extensions with personal, social, cultural, political, economic, aesthetic, ethical, and moral implications. With this reflection on the relation between media forms, affordances and knowledge design (Schnapp 2014), the chapter opens up to an interdisciplinary conversation that will be present all throughout the rest of the book, spanning from narrative theories to media, infrastructure and platform studies.

In the attempt to provide a background for the establishment of the anthology form in algorithmic culture, Chapter 3 provides a brief overview of archival classification strategies and discusses the transition from analog to digital data that led to the current mediascape. Central to the volume, this section tackles the issue of storing digital records and introduces the reader to the complex set of structures and *infrastructures* that lie behind streaming platforms. In doing so, it demonstrates how modern-day anthology-making practices, as they evolved into a diverse array of forms, are grounded in the ecological thinking (Bowker et al. 2016) of media platforms, in that they respond to the organizing urge of digital ecosystems where individual narratives are woven together mimicking ecologies in the natural world. By tackling the ecosystem features of internet environments, this chapter digs deeper into the challenge of online content sorting and retrieval, anticipating some of the themes addressed in Chapter 4 on *platforms* and algorithms.

Covering the platformization of culture and the introduction of algorithmic technologies, the final chapter takes a closer look at forms of classification and indexing of audiovisual records on streaming platforms. As part of the "anthological turn" in digital culture (Doueihi 2011), it observes practices of editorial anthologization online as they interact with computational approaches to content filtering and recommendation. In this process, it guides us through a series of examples and case studies by approaching media platforms as infrastructural organizations for cultural diffusion, or else as techno-cultural apparatuses that produce narratives of their own and can give rise to forms, impose norms, and define standards. Building upon a post-modern and post-structuralist perspective, this research accounts for the complex relation between the anthology form and narratives, industrial and social spheres, temporal continuities/discontinuities, and techno-cultural transitions, which help understand today's coexistence of human and computational practices. With regard to this digital destiny (Floridi 2002), the conclusion returns to the epistemological impacts of anthological and algorithmic forms of content classification, asking just whose canon, whose heritage (Hall 1999), and whose revolution (King 2003) the anthology came to be, and which affordances it acquired in the process of becoming digital.

1. History

Abstract

This chapter considers the anthology form across historical, cultural, and media variations. This process stands somewhere between a conceptual and a pragmatic framing. Supported by literature review, archival research, data collection, and qualitative analysis, this media genealogy (Apprich and Bachmann 2017) analyzes what the anthology is, what it does, and how it is designed, marking a fundamental step for further discussion on its forms and affordances in digital and algorithmic culture. What emerges in this overview of anthologies in literature, radio, television, and digital media is that, from the outset, this narrative device and cultural form establishes itself as a common practice in search of a definition.

Keywords: Anthology; Literary Studies; Media Studies; Digital Culture

1.1. Etymological and Cultural Roots

The anthology form is a cross-historical, cross-cultural, and cross-media phenomenon. As such, it has evolved to include slight variations in its meaning, yet always maintaining a reference to the etymological origin of collection. Traditionally, the Greek word ἀνθολογία— ἄνθος (ánthos, "flower") + λέγω (legō, "I collect") – has been used to describe collectanea of short texts, in prose or verses. As per the *Oxford English Dictionary* definition, the term "anthology" notably indicates a curated selection of "flowers of verse, i.e., small choice of poems, esp. epigrams, by various authors" (Simpson 1989, 510) reunited in a single volume. This definition addresses formal issues of quality, size, multiplicity/plurality, and uniformity of the text, while also mobilizing contextual questions related to the design operations involved in gathering and assembling a group of relevant written records within a given corpus. With its nominal materiality and performativity, embedded in the verbal morpheme of the noun *anthologìa*, this literary form paved the way for modern practices of reconfiguration, recontextualization, and remediation of narratives artifacts. Studying the roots of the anthology form

Taurino, Giulia. *The Anthology in Digital Culture*. Amsterdam: Amsterdam University Press, 2023.
DOI: 10.5117/9789463724265_CH01

therefore requires understanding not only its etymological and conceptual meaning, but also its cultural histories and mediated uses, as they unfolded in contemporary systems of knowledge. This chapter provides a description of the cultural and industrial dynamics that favored or limited the diffusion of the anthology form. It draws a critical portrayal of an often-undervalued history of short narrative forms and of the ways they have built structural relationships and formal patterns, only to converge towards the digital present and future starting from archaic, analog cultural forms.

In theory, the process of constituting an anthology might appear similar to the process of constituting a corpus, in that both anthologies and corpora are concerned with defining a selection principle, a set or subset, and a system of relationships (Lorusso 2015). However, while it can be defined as a collection or as a series of texts, an anthology is not really a corpus in the strict sense of the term. Unlike corpora, anthologies always oscillate between two levels, in ways analogous to the interplay found in rhetoric between sign and text, where the former "operates as a discrete system of coding and forms texts which come together like linear chains of linked segments. [...] In the second system the text is primary, being the bearer of the basic meaning. This text is not discrete but continuous" (Lotman 1990, 36). As such, whether in literature, radio, television, or in digital culture, anthologies have always been constructed on the same fundamental duality. Two structural entities coexist within their nature: the totality of the collection (i.e., a continuous chain of linked segments) and its fragmented narrative units (i.e., the single segments). The combination of these two elements – the whole and its parts – makes the anthology a versatile, dynamic, and resilient form, capable of being constantly reformulated in a continuous process of assemblage and dis-assemblage. Reasoning in terms of a dual system of meaning offers interesting options for the study of the anthology form, both in analog and digital environments. For instance, we could use such a duality to analyze narratives and their interaction with the cultural context, or else to reason about the genealogical evolution of the anthological form in the context of different media landscapes.

Early examples of anthologies can be found in pre-internet cultures, such as in printed translations, and it is even possible to hypothesize the existence of pre-media anthologies in non-recorded oral literatures. A preliminary knowledge of what the anthology is and what it is not is necessary if we aim at investigating the ways the anthology form operates in specific narrative media before and after the digital (e.g., literature, radio, television, online platforms). In 2013, Lieven D'hulst clarified some of the issues encountered in the definition of anthology, by pointing at the connections and differences between anthology, collection, and series. Since its origins, and throughout its evolution in different media, the anthology has been always associated with the concept of seriality. Much like anthologies and collections traditionally refer to ways of arranging and organizing stories, "the term seriality is generally used to mean objects that are arranged in some form of a series, whether temporal, spatial, or conceptual" (Boluk and LeMieux 2012, 17). According to D'hulst, "criteria for defining the 'anthological object' are needed: linguistic, geocultural, generic, historical, thematic. Given the difficulty in drawing borderlines, it might prove useful to offer a prototypical definition of the conceptual core of anthology and neighboring notions (such as collection, or album) as an 'anthological class', a dynamic generic construct [...]" (Seruya et al. 2013, 3).

However, talking about an anthological class at large risks being too broad to be useful when it comes to the actual analysis of practical applications. A distinction between anthology and collection or series can help avoid the chance of a tautological impasse where these terms are adopted interchangeably.

> As stated by Essmann and Frank, the difference between a series or collection and an anthology "is, quite pragmatically, a matter of magnitude: an anthology is what you can carry home in one hand" (Essmann and Frank 1991, 67). A prototypical definition of anthology would require the further consideration of physical, institutional, formal, semantic and functional features, among others.
>
> (Ibid.)

Seruya et al. collectively outlined these characteristics of the anthology form based on occurrences found in literature and printed media. Such a definition is particularly relevant when describing certain publishing practices, but it can also be effective in order to account for the interplay between anthology form and other techno-cultural apparatuses, such as radio or television.

As this chapter shows, linguistic, geo-cultural, generic, historical, and thematic criteria are, indeed, common parameters in the formation of anthologies at large. Similarly, physical, institutional, formal, semantic, and functional features emerge as useful in assessing the multifaceted nature of anthology forms. While the former set of parameters hints at a more theoretical evaluation, the latter stresses the "cultural complexity" (Hannerz 1992) of media apparatuses in which anthologies are produced and circulate. With this scope, the philosopher Milad Doueihi advanced the discussion on the anthology form by considering its evolution in digital culture. In his work, the anthology is treated as both a concept and a practice, a model and a methodology. Recalling previous definitions, he notably designates anthology as any "surreptitious selection and dissemination of apparently unrelated snippets or fragments as meaningful collections, where meaning is largely derived from an apparently arbitrary association of content [...]" (Doueihi 2009, 11). In the context of digital publishing, such a process of collection, whether user-generated or part of a company's strategy, became increasingly present, to the point where we can discuss an anthological property as much as an ontological one, as the core components of the World Wide Web and the linked content—and data – that exists within it (Ibid., 9).

Theorized before the extensive adoption of algorithmic technologies and artificial intelligence for the sorting and retrieval of online content, Doueihi's description of an "anthological turn" is essential for understanding the connection between the structural form of the anthology and the infrastructural organization of data that lies at the basis of digital and algorithmic culture. The extent of the anthological turn and its impact on contemporary media is evident. Anthology-like "digital norms [...] are shaping both the technological development as well as the economic models underlying the deployment of the latest generation of large-scale web hubs" (Ibid., 11). Alternative versions of the pre-digital anthological model can be found on most online platforms, from user-generated labeled playlists to practices of collaborative tagging and automated clustering of personalized content. For instance, the idea of linking data, metadata, and, ultimately, content into anthological streams is at the basis of online recommendation systems used by over-the-top content providers like Netflix. "The anthological model makes it possible to transform collected items into a dynamic and open publication of potentially new knowledge and to present them in their extensibility" (Ibid.). Along with factors related to its length and "magnitude" (Essmann and Frank 1991, 67), which were already present in analog anthologies, extensibility and scalability appear to be significant features in the constitution of digital anthologies. Perhaps a good analogy with the physical ability to "carry something home in one hand" (Ibid.) is given by the way digital anthologies facilitate user interaction and navigation, by filtering the amount of information and content available online and limiting it to easily reproducible, scalable, and extensible lists.

Indeed, in internet-distributed television, where users are granted a seemingly complete autonomy in organizing their own viewing agendas and habits, a shorter narrative, already cut into small narrative pieces, is easier to fit into individual, daily time schedules than longer ones. If early anthology series in television were simply repurposing and remediating older literary, theatrical, or radiophonic traditions, today, anthological practices create self-sufficient narrative modules that actively regulate media consumption. The fragmentation of content into multiple units aligns with the way narrative forms adapted to internet culture, often subjected to cross-platform and transmedia dynamics. By accounting for its affordances in the context of Western culture, the following paragraphs outline a history of the morphological occurrences of the anthology form. This comparative historical analysis of the anthology in literature and press, radio and television will provide a preliminary methodological framework to understand the transition of this form to digital culture. A look at different evolutionary stages in media ecology will demonstrate how anthologies tend to externalize their affordances, potentialities, and functions depending on the industrial system in which they are inscribed. This comprehensive overview will advance cues for further reflections on the intertwining between modes of cultural production, technological advancements, and techniques of preservation.

The present chapter ultimately serves as a starting point to observe the anthology form in both continuity and discontinuity between analog and digital culture, which eventually fostered its reappearance in non-linear platform environments. Beyond a definition of what anthologies are, we will try to understand what anthologies do across different media ecosystems, anticipating subsequent chapters focusing on the design, infrastructures, and platforms of anthological production. With the intent to examine the anthology and its affordances, we will begin with an overview of anthologies as they have established their presence in early world literature, to then undergo a transformative journey towards new forms of storytelling and clas-sification in the Western tradition. So far, we have considered a preliminary definition of anthology based upon its etymological and epistemological roots. In the rest of the chapter, we will consider the cultural implications of its applications and affordances in literature, radio, television, and digital media. We will notice how, while their actual uses have changed, anthologies are still likely to return to the same set of potential functions throughout their evolution over time. After all, "forms are not so historically specific that their operation change radically from place to place" (Levine 2015, 39).

1.2. In Literature

Anthological indexing is a practice that dates back to pre-internet culture. While going through the entire history of world literature would be an unnecessary digression, considering the anthology form in its original appearances in the history of writing and publishing might contribute to highlighting some of its intrinsic affordances. Firstly, literary anthologies are usually built onto several *short stories* grouped into uniform *collections*. An introduction to the anthology form should therefore start from an overview of short narratives, as the microscopic components of editorial processes of anthologization. Edgar Allan Poe, who inaugurated several Western scholarly theorizations on short stories, defined them as "brief tales, or narratives that can be read in a single sitting. [...] Singleness of effect that can be achieved when a story is read straight through, unity of a pre-established design, in which the end controls the beginning and the middle" (Keen 2015, 21). Along with conferring a sense of uniqueness of time, story, and experience, the centrality of a preliminary conceptual curation makes such composition particularly poignant. In an essay published in 1901, the American writer Brander Matthews reiterated that the structural specificity of the modern North American short story is not only one of length – or magnitude, to echo a definition of anthology – but primarily one of "symmetry of design" (Matthews 1901). Descendant of an entirely different literary *genus* (Ibid., 77), with its peculiar design, the short story solicits a discrete set of effects when compared to longer narratives, leveraging a sense of totality, clarity, brevity, and directionality. Although the concept of symmetry in short stories has been discarded by literary scholars (Reid 2017), who lamented the risks of biases towards an arbitrary idea of creative quality as synonymous of structure and symmetry, it is still interesting to remark that many scholarly studies of the short story have moved their attention towards elements of narrative design over content.

World literature yields many examples of brief written compositions across different genres, including Nordic folklore, ancient fables, and other tell-a-tale short stories coming from strong oral traditions in countries as varied as India or Libya. Sometimes forgotten in the analysis of Western literature, which often privileged long narratives while underplaying the value of brief forms of storytelling, short fiction was found to have a solid presence across postcolonial literatures in Canada, the West Indies, South Africa, Australia, and New Zealand, among others. In these countries, short narrative forms became opportunities for indigenous communities to reconfigure their own cultural identity, recover lost heritage, and re-establish a relationship with their native land, as in the case of Caribbean orature (Bardolph et al. 2001). The power of short narratives lies precisely in their ability to permeate interstitial spaces in popular cultures, thus allowing for the emergence of discourses that would otherwise remain untold or at the margins, trapped in peripheral circulation and orality. "A form of the margins" (Hanson 1989, 2), the short story provides a variety of alternative voices to dominant epic narratives, myths, and dramas. By doing so, it opens up windows onto a multiplicity of perspectives, lending itself to "losers and loners, exiles, women, blacks" (Ibid.).

Because of their brevity and the unique way they approach broader topics through a series of microscopic views on human life, short stories are often organized into groups, thus forming collections or anthologies. Standard academic definitions differentiate between the two terminologies: whereas a literary collection is a more suitable term for a group of works from a single author, anthologies are often composed of stories by different authors and gathered together in a single volume based on homogeneity of themes, style, or other indicators of coherence. What is interesting, however, is not determining a single/multiple source for anthological authoriality, but rather discussing the flexibility and resilience of the anthology form in collecting short narratives, allowing them to expand or contract depending on the cultural and media ecosystem in which they are inserted. In a way, anthologies in literature have contributed to elevating brief written compositions to the status of archetypal works and myths. Some examples of anthological collections based on short stories in European literatures range from the Italian *novella* or *racconto* – a separate typology of short story prone to anthologization, with several mimic descendants, including the Spanish *novela corta* – to more recent cycles in the Irish tradition, like James Joyce's *The Dubliners* (1914) or enclosed miscellanies akin to the anthology form born in Germanic cultures, namely, the *rahmenerzählung*, which uses a prolog and epilog structure as a framing device. In literature, a frame story is a technique through which a fictional narrator intervenes as an informative companion to the readers in order to guide them from the main piece into a series of short stories. Popular frame stories include the collection of Middle Eastern folk tales *Alf Laylah wa-Laylah* (Arabic: وَلَيْلَةٌ لَيْلَةِ أَلْفُ, translated as *One Thousand and One Nights*, also known as *Arabian Nights* from the first English edition [c.1706–1721]), *The Decameron* (c.1349–1353) written by Giovanni Boccaccio, which inspired Geoffrey Chaucer's *Canterbury Tales* (c.1387–1400). In these examples, a narrator guides the readers through a series of short stories contained within a larger narrative arc that operates as a frame story.

Generally, literary anthologies always adhere to a principle of uniformity, which can vary depending on each specific case. Examples can be found all over the world as attempts to preserve the memory of ancient oral or written narratives and fix the gaze on a canon of texts. One example is the Chinese poetry anthological collection *Shijing*, also known as *Classic of Poetry*, which brings together some of the oldest odes in Chinese literature, covering a span between the eleventh to seventh century BC (Dobson 1964). Much like more recent literary anthologies, as well as radio and television anthologies, *Classic of Poetry* alternates "elements of repetition and variation" (Frankel 1979, 216), resulting in the presence of "similarities and differences in the formal structure" (Ibid., 51). This collection represents a particularly relevant case. It shows that the actual connotations of the anthology as we know it nowadays – i.e., the alternation of repetition/ variation, an organizing and archiving principle, a selection process with a canonical scope – were born long before the first known occurrences of the Greek terminology in relation to Meleager of Gadara's collection of short compositions – each dedicated to a different "flower" – by several poets. Although discovered as part of a more recent manuscript, the Palatine Anthology, based on a lost collection from circa the tenth century, Meleager of Gadara's older anthology is believed to date back to the first century BC. These circumstances suggest that, both in Eastern and Western culture, the origins of the anthology form need to be traced before its actual definition, as far back as the appearance of the first moveable media tools for writing, whether in the format of a papyrus roll, or *volumen*, or in the form of a codex – the precursor of the modern book.

What makes ancient literary anthologies worth exploring in relation to analogous forms in contemporary culture is not just the coexistence of processes of repetition and variation, one of the main characteristics of anthologies across media, but more importantly the emergence of a core affordance of this form: the presence of an "organizing principle," which returns in analog and digital anthologies alike to provide either a sense of historical validity for the maintenance of past heritage records or an interpretative framework for future reading. To this point, the scholar Martin Kern notices that *Classic of Poetry* as "a body of text came into being [...] as a repository of expressions inherited from the past" or else "[...] an artifact of the past remembered – a canonical curriculum [...]" (Mutschler 2018, 43–44). The anthological form, as a way to archive records into a "repository," an "artifact of the past," or a "canonical curriculum," suggests that, with their inner property of cataloging documents from various sources, anthologies have the potential to turn short stories into foundational texts. While conducting a comparative study of Asian and European traditions, Beecroft (2018) pointed out that "anthologies and anthologizers have long played a major role in the establishment of literary canons" (Ibid., 341).

After early occurrences in ancient literature and before more recent examples, one invention that boosted the production of anthologies was that of the printing press (Doueihi 2011, 162). The introduction of print enabled a revolution of unprecedented scale for the publishing industry, preparing the ground for new workflows and models in the distribution of textual documents at large. Quoting Innis (1950), "we can conveniently divide the history of the West into the writing and the printing periods" (Ibid., 27). As one of the first centralized forms of organized mass production and commodification of literature (McLuhan 1962, 221), Gutenberg's invention fostered new practices of textual aggregation and anthologization whether for preservation, educational, or commercial purposes. In discussing how short story collections have shaped literary canons, Prescott (2016) identifies a list of affordances gained by anthologies with the advent of the publishing industry. On the one hand, in Europe, the printed anthology was initially exploited as a resource for academic learning, for sampling literary works deemed of high intellectual merit that could fit into the "Western canon" (Bloom 1994). On the other hand, as a "commercially oriented" (Prescott 2016, 564) product, it was adopted as a curatorial practice for the organization of short stories into publications, magazines, reprinted volumes for sale and editorial distribution.

Over the years, editorial processes of anthologization became increasingly common among Western publishers, such as in the serialized structure of newspapers and weekly magazines or in more specific strategies for organizing, translating, or simply marketing literary content. In more recent occurrences, the publication of anthologies in newly updated editions became a way to make amends for biased, white male-centric views on literature that have perpetuated hegemonic systems of power. For example, in the North American literary landscape, twentieth-century scholars and anthologizers took a critical stance with respect to the process of text selection, by turning the practice of anthologization into a critical device. Modern literary collections, such as the *Norton Anthology of American Literature* (1979, first edition) or the *Heath Anthology of American Literature* (1989, first edition), marked "a departure from earlier anthologies' dismissal of minority writing" (Bona and Maini 2012, 69), signaling some of the first attempts to open up the canon to "non-canonical" work. In this regard, a study on translation in printed collections posited that anthologies can be used as "tools of static and dynamic canonization," and can therefore be "considered tokens of culture planning, a notion put forth by both Gideon Toury (2002, 2003) and Itamar Even Zohar (2002) and defined as a 'deliberate act of intervention, either by power holders or by 'free agents' into an extant or a crystallizing repertoire' (Even-Zohar 2002, 45)" (Seruya et al. 2013, 5).

As acts of culture planning and literacy, anthologies can be associated with a vast array of different purposes and functions, depending on intra- and intertextual dynamics, as well as on the arbitrary classification that each anthologist has to institute. Other than responding to subjective curatorial choices, the practice of anthology-making may be deployed as a means for cultural preservation, organization, innovation, or dissemination. For these reasons, "anthologies and collections become very important first order objects for the study of the underlying criteria for selection and restructuring, the underlying taste of individual agents or of the community they belong to, of publishing and book-market mechanisms, of fluctuations in cultural importance, as second order objects" (Ibid.). This brief outline of the anthology form in Western literature shows that a discussion on anthologies cannot be complete unless we tie their poetic, literary, and cultural aspects with the technological, industrial, and economic contexts that influenced their uses. As we will discuss over the course of this chapter, whereas early handwritten anthologies resembled literary volumes carefully curated by experts, the introduction of modern processes of formatting, printing, and publishing textual records for mass distribution shifted the affordances of anthologies to include in equal parts a cultural and a technological component. In digital publishing, this shift was brought to the fore by hybrid – i.e., human-driven and data-driven – acts of "editorialization" (Vitali-Rosati 2016). "Editorialization [is] the set of dynamics that produce and structure the digital space. These dynamics can be understood as the interactions of individual and collective actions within a particular digital environment" (Ibid., 1).

Adopting an English neologism derived from the French term *éditorialisation*, Vitali-Rosati notably underlines three main definitions connected to this practice: a restrictive one; a general one; and a combination of the two. On the one hand, a restrictive definition looks at the way content is produced, organized, and distributed on the web, through a "set of technical devices (networks, servers, platforms, CMS, algorithms of search engines), structures (hypertext, multimedia, metadata), and practices (annotation, comments, recommendations via social networks)" (Ibid., 5). On the other hand, a general definition observes the extensive overlapping between non-mediated reality and virtually mediated reality, thus seeing editorialization as a globally diffused digital practice that affects everyday life. Vitali-Rosati synthesizes these two definitions, by outlining a third one that accounts for the technological, cultural, and practical aspects of such a practice. He further explains that "editorialization shapes and structures content in a way that is not limited to a closed, well-defined context (such as a journal) or a group of predetermined individuals (editors and publishers). It involves an opening up of space (several platforms) and time (several different editors unbound by deadlines). This opening up is one of the key differences between curation and editorialization" (Ibid., 6).

These dynamics call for a re-semantization of the notion of anthology in relation to digital literature, where older editorial practices are repurposed to incorporate new ways of "structuring space and authority in the digital age" (Vitali-Rosati 2018). As we argue here, digital practices of editorialization are, in fact, derivatives of early analog processes of anthologization, in the sense that, from pre-digital to post-digital culture, both of these forms of content organization have come to represent the main support for the collection and diffusion of content in mediated environments. In their intent to filter and display digital records, contemporary digital anthologies transitioned from literary content curation in printed editions to content editorialization through a progressive adaptation from analog to digital environments, which involved the emergence of electronic literature. Electronic literature has been pivotal for the transition of textual narratives into digital forms, from electronic formats like DVD-ROMs and emails to websites and online blogs. Not only independent scholars and writers, but also academic-based organizations have promoted e-literature as a way to experiment with narrative forms in the years pre-dating the advent of algorithmic practices. Among others, the Electronic Literature Organization (ELO) was founded in 1999 by Scott Rettberg, Robert Coover, and Jeff Ballowe, as an inter-institutional effort "to promote and facilitate the writing, publishing, and reading of electronic literature as it develops and persists in a changing digital environment."[1]

Over the years, the ELO contributed to the establishment of electronic literature as a field in and of itself, by curating several anthologization initia-tives. For instance, the publication of *Electronic Literature Collections*[2] (2006, 2011, 2016, 2022) in a series of volumes has taken on the definition of new storytelling models, by archiving born-digital works produced using different sets of technologies, methods of transmission, and programming languages. The collections include computer-based works created in HTML, Javascript, Python, css3, Java, C++, and other languages. Some of the works collected in these edited volumes are themselves anthologies, an affordance granted

---

1   https://eliterature.org/about/.
2   https://collection.eliterature.org/.

by electronic media, which can host hypertextual experiences, such as the electronic anthology of poems *Rice*.[3] In other cases, technologies that became outdated, such as Flash, posed issues for the maintenance of projects, as in the case of *Cruising*, a work by Ingrid Ankerson and Megan Sapnar, currently preserved with Ruffle by the Electronic Literature Lab.[4] More recently, the open access online journals *Electronic Book Review* (ebr) and *The Digital Review* (tdr) have supported critical and creative forms of electronic writing through theme-based issues that offer "a curated combination of commissioned work, submitted work, restored past work and re-designed public domain work"[5] along with multimodal projects that use computational methods to produce interactive works and new forms of literary expression. To document this ensemble of digital publishing practices, in *Post-Digital: Dialogues and Debates from Electronic Book Review*, Tabbi (2020) collected the work of scholars, writers, and digital artists in electronic literature in a series of seminal articles chronicling the history, present evolution, and future of the field.

Tabbi's collection shows how, drawing from the print tradition, electronic literature accompanied the move from paper-based to born-digital writing (Hayles 2008) all along the second half of the twentieth century, through a series of computer-based initiatives designed not only for creating increasingly interactive reading experiences, but also for fostering a reprise of older applications of the anthology as a form of heritage preservation. In this scenario, the anthology as a form of rediscovery of undervalued work emerged in printed and electronic literature alike. For example, founded in 2006, the website *The Neglected Books Page* features reviews of literary works that have been "neglected, overlooked, forgotten, or stranded by changing tides in critical or popular taste."[6] *The Neglected Books* website was itself inspired by David Madden's printed collections *Rediscoveries* (1971) and *Rediscoveries II* (1988), where well-known authors revive neglected fictional works. In a similar operation, founded in 1999 and based in the UK, the independent publishing company Persephone Books centers its entire catalog on a seemingly anthological model, by devoting its publications entirely to reprinted works of fiction by women writers of the late nineteenth and twentieth centuries.

In this intermingling of traditional and emerging media practices for the long-term archival of content, the paperless nature of electronic books,

---

3   https://collection.eliterature.org/1/works/geniwate__rice/riceindex.html.
4   https://collection.eliterature.org/1/works/ankerson_sapnar__cruising.html.
5   https://electronicbookreview.com/.
6   https://neglectedbooks.com/.

perhaps even more relevant than its interactive features, led to improvements in the durability of printed works and the acquisition of additional storage capacity via hardware devices. Along with the digitization of printed material, the advent of electronic documents reduced the risks of memory loss, which had affected out-of-print records, old editions, and manuscripts for centuries. Adapting early practices of documentation, editorialization, and anthologization to the digital landscape became fundamental to sustaining the new affordances of the anthology form. Important technological advancements include, among others: the introduction of publishing software and other tools for book manufacturing based on computer programming; the possibility to implement metadata associated with textual artifacts and annotate digital editions with contextual information; and the invention of electronic prototypes, physical supports, and web platforms for accessing and curating reading material on local devices. In the following paragraphs, we will show how the digital turn inspired similar moments of technological disruption across a variety of media, contributing to framing yet another redefinition of the anthology form as a narrative-content host not only in literature, but also in oral and audiovisual storytelling.

1.3. In Radio

After the printing revolution, the discovery of electromagnetic waves and the invention of the wireless telegraph inaugurated another series of major technological developments in the history of narrative media, leading to the establishment of the first modern mode of communication for the long-distance transmission of the spoken word. Three major factors helped frame such a landscape: (1) the evolution of radio into a mass medium; (2) the establishment of international corporations that regulated the extension of airwaves globally; and (3) the large-scale investment in research and patent production (Iriye and Saunier 2009, 871). Along with other technologies for sound recording and archiving introduced during the nineteenth century, such as the phonautograph or the phonograph cylinder, the radio pioneered a new era of reproducible oral storytelling and, long before the internet, it "inaugurated the age of globalization in telecommunications" (Ibid., 872). The aural phase of this medium is particularly useful for understanding the consequent growth of the broadcasting industry as one of the predominant commercial frameworks for the circulation of both spoken and written anthologies for decades ahead. Even though radio and television broadcasting eventually found their own specific positioning in the media landscape,

during the early days of experimentation with sound and audiovisual technologies these modes of communication briefly converged in overlapping
industrial and narrative structures. Since the first regular broadcasts of the
1910s and 1920s, the radio was welcomed in Western countries as, simultaneously, a public utility, a consumer good, and a vehicle for the production of
needs (Hilmes and Loviglio 2002, 23). As the US was about to enter the Great
Depression and European nations were suffering the consequences of being
on the verge of two world conflicts, the first three decades of broadcasting
were largely affected by two contrasting forces: one supporting an ideology
of abundance and one striving in conditions of scarcity. This was a moment
when the US was slowly transitioning from a "politics of production" to
a "politics of consumption", by selling capitalist values oriented towards
leisure activities and an overall culture of prosperity (Ibid.).

After the first few years of amateur radio operators, large radio corporations came to dominate Western media markets as early as the 1920s and
radio receivers became a common household commodity in the 1930s.
Broadcasting industries in Europe and North America were soon subjected
to the influence of monopolistic models, which led to the formation of
public services like the British Broadcasting Corporation (BBC) in the UK
or the government-sanctioned Radio Corporation of America (RCA) in the
US. Despite the initial illusion that radio could serve as a truly democratic,
publicly funded national medium, the presence of media monopolies centralized the management of radio programming during this period. While radio
was celebrated by some for its capacity to bring together different political
and ideological groups from a variety of social backgrounds, educational
levels, economic classes, and geographical regions, others worried about
the risks of means of mass communication as dangerous tools of power
that favored the "monopolized mass production of standardized goods"
(Adorno 1945, 231). As Arnheim (1936) explains, "radio proved from the
day of its birth to be so obviously a monopoly instrument concerning the
whole community that in most countries [other than the United States] it
immediately came under the direct influence of the State."

For instance, in countries like Mexico the government took control of
radio broadcasting by applying federal regulations that limited commercial
radio stations and initially excluded any broadcast that was not in favor of
the ruling authority. In Germany, a group of regional monopolies managed
by government representatives would oversee local radio programming
schedules, which were available to the public upon payment of a fee. In
these cases, early radio was used as "an agent of cultural standardization
and political manipulation" (Scales 2016, 11). In other countries, the adoption

of a nationwide network of broadcasting infrastructures relied on the financing of private sponsors rather than on government resources. For example, in the US, many local stations opted for financing radiophonic programs via advertising. In this context, "advertising became not only a new economic force essential in the regulation of prices but also a vision of the way the culture worked: the products of the culture became advertisements of the culture itself" (Susman 1984, xxiv). In the early decades of the twentieth century, this commercial strategy fostered the institutionalization of the US media industry along with the consolidation of radio programming, ultimately contributing to the rise of broadcasting as the dominant cultural form (Hilmes and Loviglio 2002, 24). The idea of a network of infrastructures represented a fundamental change in the early history of US radio, which shifted from a set of separate local stations or groups of more powerful stations that covered entire regions to a web of interconnected broadcasting stations through which one program could be replicated in different areas of the nation (Hilmes and Loviglio 2013). Each broadcaster was composed of a network of affiliates stations, in a complex hierarchical system that Ulin (2012) defines, in relation to television, as "a grouping of local television stations that are either owned by or affiliated with the parent network company and which are all supplied the same product by the parent" (Ibid., 224) in an economy of scale. A third, rarer, industrial model for the techno-cultural transmission of radio programs allowed for the coexistence of public broadcasting and privately owned commercial radio, as in the case of France, where radio was welcomed as a democratic and neutral medium.

Whether inscribed in a public or private system, the emergence of narrative forms in radio is closely tied not only to the topological, infrastructural dimension of transmitters, but also to the institutional mechanisms that arose at the national level and entailed local networks of communication. The combination of these technological and industrial processes led to the consolidation of "archetypal broadcast forms" (Hilmes and Loviglio 2002, 27), including the anthology form. At the core of the first reconfiguration of the anthology in radio therefore lies a complex balance between economic forces and socio-political aims. In the early days of broadcasting across Western countries, radio became at once a tool for public education, information, communication, as well as for political propaganda and popular entertainment. Television was to take a similar route. As a both cultural and political strategy for the distribution of narratives, the radio anthology inherited traditional configurations in line with past literary traditions, while also developing a series of distinct features.

On the one hand, radio programming contributed to strengthening the existing link between anthologies and some literary dramas (i.e., crime, science-fiction, horror), a connection that evolved in partial continuity with the textual tradition and prefigured subsequent occurrences in television. It is no coincidence that the horror genre, with its short story tradition à la Edgar Allan Poe, would serve as a glue for holding together old, printed collections of tales with modern audiovisual content. One example is Nathaniel Hawthorne's printed anthology *Twice-Told Tales* (1837) and the later edition *The Snow-Image, and Other Twice-Told Tales* (1852). Many of these short stories were converted into radio programs, such as *Ethan Brand: A Chapter from an Abortive Romance* (originally, *The Unpardonable Sin*), which aired in 1945 as part of the radio anthology *The Weird Circle* (Syn, 1943–1945) consisting of adaptations of classic horror stories. *Twice-Told Tales* would also be partially adapted into a horror anthology film in 1963, which combined one of the stories in the original collection with two Gothic stories from other publications by Hawthorne. Other radio anthologies featuring mystery, terror, and suspense stories and often used to promote printed editions include: *Mystery House* (NBC, c.1929–1951); *Inner Sanctum Mystery* (NBC Blue Network, 1941–1952); *CBS Radio Mystery Theater* (CBS, 1974–1982), or the more recent Canadian radio anthology *The Mystery Project* (CBC, 1992–2002). On the other hand, many radio anthologies were built in close relation with the theater tradition, both in terms of the production design (e.g., cast and style) and in their way of drawing from theater plays and structuring content into a series of acts. Most of them involved professional actors reading literary classics for radio listeners, while some would source their material directly from theater plays or else rehearse original scripts and audio dramas. Sound intervals were also common, giving the sense of a fully theatrical experience.

Moreover, in some local markets, such as the US, the presence of a host came to replace the framing principle of literary anthologies, becoming a staple for many television anthologies ahead. Whereas, in literature, narrative framing is a fictional conceit to organize the text into a series of stories within the story, radio inserted the figure of the host as a real-life persona, who introduces the play and guides the audience towards interpretation. Rather than a strategy for the *mise-en-abyme* of self-reflexive embeddings, the host was adopted as a technique for the *mise-en-scène* of the medium. At a time when audiences where still used to the materiality of physical media, this narrative stratagem served as a way to metaphorically prepare the stage for the transition between the reality of media transmission and the imaginative process of storytelling. Examples of early US radiophonic anthologies with a literary influence and a theatrical production include programs hosted by screenwriters, directors, and actors (e.g., Orson Welles, Cecil B. DeMille) with a featured cast, like *The Mercury Theatre on the Air* (CBS, 1938), *The Screen Guild Theater* (CBS, 1939–48; NBC, 1948–50; ABC, 1950–51; CBS, 1951–52), and *Lux Radio Theatre* (WJZ, 1934–35; CBS WABC 1935–36; CBS, 1936–54; NBC, 1954–55). Another interesting example is the *NBC University Theatre* (NBC, 1948–1951). A format more than a form, it applied to a category of radio programming as part of a broad initiative of the National Broadcasting Co. in partnership with the University of Chicago. This category included radio series like *The World's Great Novels*, which aired classic novels mostly from Anglo-American literature and was aimed at an educational scope. Colleges and universities were invited to either collaborate with the production of radio content or include the programming schedule in their curriculum and receive college credit (Dunning 1998, 482). Printed handbooks were published as practical guides to complement this form of radio-assisted learning, such as *The Handbook of the World's Great Novels.*

Other geographic areas adopted radio as a vehicle to reinvent literary anthologies and theater plays into updated narrative and cultural forms, with few variations on the traditional anthological structure. For instance, in the UK and the commonwealth regions, radio would host full-length theater plays, operas, and stage adaptations airing directly on BBC, which became one the major producers of anglophone anthology dramas. In Argentina, following the adoption of radio as a national medium, the *radioteatro*, a narrative form with a strong anthological layout, emerged as a powerful instrument for social education and cohesiveness. As a public service, Argentinian radio adopted a "patriotic posture" (Matallana 2006, 9, my translation), which made the *radioteatro* and other early anthological radio programs part of a larger cultural experiment for social integration (Ibid., 21–22) and identitarian national quests. In Chile, *radioteatro*, with its social implications, acquired a didactic purpose, leading to the birth of programs like *El Gran Teatro de la Historia* (Radio Corporación, 1949–1959), a collection of stories and biographies around important figures in Chilean history, written by Jorge Inostrosa Cuevas and featuring theater actors (Merayo Pérez 2007, 121). Diffused also in other Spanish-speaking countries, after a period of decline between the 1970s and the late 1990s, this form has returned in updated radio programs and podcasts that give space to the social and political struggles of marginalized communities (Rodríguez Ortiz 2019). Furthermore, radio anthologies showed to be particularly effective in reframing not only theatrical, but also literary and then cinematographic narratives into broadcasting media. In the Italian market, anthological narrative forms were adapted from radio to television, resulting in a polyhedric terminology: from the *radiodramma* and the *sceneggiato radiofonico*, with a theater-oriented production to the *teleromanzo*, which was originally based on literary classics and then generated its own television narratives, and the *telefilm*, leaning towards a cinematographic esthetic and style. Moreover, in Italy as abroad, public broadcasting devoted part of the programming schedule to a series of radio lectures covering a variety of academic, scientific, and cultural subjects, "from lectures on economics (e.g., Leipzig's 1930 series *Tagesfragen der Wirtschaft* [Economic issues of the day]) to interviews with workers (e.g., Frankfurt's 1929 program *Wo uns der Schuh drückt* [Where our shoes are pressing])" (Hilmes and Loviglio 2002, 32).

Despite differences in the structure of early radio industries, which can be summed up in three models – public monopoly (e.g., UK), private-oriented corporations with a commercial intent (e.g., US), or mixed public and private systems (e.g., France) – the evolution of the anthology form was initially quite homogeneous in terms of its actual uses. In the transition of this form from printed to audiovisual media, early radio anthologies present a set of coexisting affordances: those that are intrinsic to the anthology form and those that belong to the supporting medium. The former are mainly related to content organization and distribution. When observing attempts to domesticate radio programming in local media industries, the anthology emerges as a common element for ordering what would otherwise be a sparse collection of audio content into a structured radio program. The latter vary depending on the political and industrial context. However, in most cases, the form and the medium have activated common affordances. The very action of tuning in, daily or weekly, required a framing principle to maintain an ongoing conversation between the broadcasters and their public, and to create a community of recurring listeners in a specific time slot. Among other solutions, acts of radio editorialization, based on grouping unique and self-standing short radio episodes into an anthological flow, were able to generate a "feeling of membership" in the audience (Cantril and Allport 1971, 260), necessary for tuning in. Therefore, practices of radio curation and anthologization were called to "select from existing art what is simple enough to be felt by everyone" (Arnheim 1936).

In turn, elements of cultural planning emerged as properties of the medium – from its potential to simultaneously reach multiple audiences in multiple locations – rather than exclusive features strictly connected to the radio anthology itself. This is true for both fictional and non-fictional radio anthologies. For example, radio's shared listening experiences were designed to direct collective musical interests, and were often accompanied by a printed guide that informed listeners not only about the context of the music pieces, but also about how to listen (e.g., *Everybody's Guide to Radio Music* [1926]; *L'initiation à la musique (à l'usage des amateurs de musique et de radio)*, [1935]). Halfway between educational pamphlets and curated volumes aimed at establishing an intellectual canon, "from New York to Paris, radio guides endeavored to shape taste and identity, canonizing listening practices and national composers. From these also emerged a transnational consensus, especially on the importance of jazz" (Pasler 2015, 2012). Overall, with its primary focus on content distribution and community-building, radio converted anthologies from forms of cultural preservation into educational forms of cultural adaptation. Moving away from the archival and storage of heritage records, radio anthologies made space for experimental practices that could support both the transition of classic narratives in oral media environments and the reshaping of traditional narrative structures into new storytelling strategies. While long-running, open-ended serials became one of the main innovations brought by broadcasting (e.g., soap operas), early broadcasting marked an important passage for the survival of the anthology form in spite of consequent technological developments.

In the late 1940s, radio was granted another set of affordances thanks to the introduction of portable transistor radios (Starkey 2011, 14), which rendered radio content even more versatile, adaptable to a variety of local communities, settings, and listening habits. In light of these changes, over the years, the radio industry quickly moved towards the proliferation of stations and an increasing fragmentation of content in narrowcasted specialized programming. In the US, after the establishment of the Corporation for Public Broadcasting in the late 1960s, non-commercial radio licenses began to be distributed to colleges and schools, which, along with privately owned and independent radio stations, were providing radio programming services to scattered audiences across the country. A decade later, cable services went live, adding to existing terrestrial signal reception. Moreover, during the second half of the twentieth century, cassette recorders, personal stereos, and portable audio players allowed users not only to connect to radio frequencies, but also to record, collect, and curate audio playlists that could be replayed from almost any location. By contrast, television remained for a long time a domestic medium, with a much more stationary use due to its physical constraints, at least until the 1980s when the first handheld television sets were produced. This scenario, which affected the US as well as other Western countries, makes it difficult to track the recurrence of the anthology as a consistent narrative model in radio programming from the 1950s to at least the 1990s, when internet-only radio networks brought the anthology form to the digital space. In this timeframe, television came about to attract the interest of radio producers. Many anthology dramas were converted into television anthologies, maintaining the characteristics of early radio programs.

1.4. In Television

Over the years, the infrastructural and industrial systems of broadcasting media shaped a range of policies and business models that deeply affected the production and distribution of content. Much like in the case of radio, starting from the very beginning of the history of television, we observe the presence of archetypal narrative forms, which evolved in the more or less extended serialized shows that we know today. The first three decades of television production are at the origin of a few heterogeneous trends, which eventually created two fundamental evolutionary circuits: that of the anthology series, with the episodic structure that we are analyzing here, and that of the serial, a long-running show with narrative continuity between episodes and seasons. Among different degrees of serialization and examples of polarization of narrative forms in contemporary television, we can list the following, from the least to the most serialized narratives: made-for-TV-movies; miniseries; micro-series; limited series; event series; episodic anthologies; seasonal anthologies or anthology miniseries; long-running series; serials; and telenovelas. In the wake of literary traditions, such a varied, mutating morphology of television narratives always reconnects to a pair of opposite values, one represented by effects of "hypo-serialization," and the other by effects of "hyper-serialization." Even the most recent examples of serial forms seem to be the result of these two opposite forces, one that pushes towards open-ended plots, prolonged in time and space, and the other that pushes towards narrations with a limited and pre-established duration. The question of the anthology form and its definition is a central topic in the discussion on television seriality, both if we look at its historical evolution and if we consider its local or global geographical movements.

Guillaume Soulez articulated such polarization in television seriality by stressing that anthologies are designed to "explicitly combine objects *given as distinct* around a common point, which does not determine, however, the serial matrix: the seriality is *external*, as in the collection *Alfred Hitchcock Presents*, which serves to gather around a single host-director different films that belong to the same horror genre" (Soulez 2011, online,

my translation). This external seriality, based on the container rather than
the content itself, is worth exploring through a more attentive analysis of
the television industry, so as to highlight the technological transformations
that eventually led to internet-distributed television, where the anthology
form flourished as a structural part of the platform design. The following
historical account of US television will help us reconstruct the industrial
and cultural changes in media that consolidated the anthology form as an
audiovisual form. This detailed genealogy will facilitate the understanding
of how the media configuration of over-the-top services came together in
the context of the US media ecosystem, which implemented the anthology
as one of the main design components for enhancing content distribution.
The rest of this chapter will present the distinct traits and uses acquired
by the anthological form from its initial positioning in the broadcasting
industry to its formalization in contemporary digital cultures.

Before becoming a fundamental way to arrange narrative objects on
platform environments, the anthology form underwent several fluctuations in the scenario of television seriality. Despite its intermittent falls in
production and distribution, the anthology form turned out to be a resilient
cultural and economic model. From a diachronic perspective, the form of
the television anthology in the US finds its roots in radio programs of the
1930s and 1940s, in which a host introduces and concludes each episode of
a single series acting as a framing narrative device. In television as much as
in radio, anthology series follow a serialized structure built on narratively
independent stories, and yet connected by genre, register – or tone – style,
or, in some cases, by similar themes. Similarities with radio, however,
are not limited to narrative structures. An article in *Science Illustrated*,[7]
published in January 1949, reported that, by the end of the first decade of
broadcasting television in the US, the number of networks and stations
was increasing substantially, linking different parts of the country (e.g.,
Philadelphia–Cleveland), connecting the East Coast to the Midwest, allowing people as far west as St. Louis to see programs telecasted in New York
and preparing to reach even more remote, rural areas.[8] In the timeframe
spanning from the early years of broadcast television up until the 1980s,
we witness a phase defined by media scholars as the network era (Lotz

---

7   "What Every Family Wants to Know about Television – Science Illustrated (Jan, 1949)."
Modern Mechanix (*blog*). http://blog.modernmechanix.com/what-every-family-wants-to-know
-about-television.
8   For a map of the operational (in black) and expected (in red) network of on-air stations in
the US as of 1949, see http://www.earlytelevision.org/att_network.html.

2007). In this phase, three major networks coming from the radio industry
became the main industrial players in US commercial television: American
Broadcasting Company (ABC); Columbia Broadcasting System (CBS); and
National Broadcasting Company (NBC). "From the very beginning, local
television broadcasts were represented by the networks as nodal events
within a larger national network. Even before the means for networking
television existed, the notion of networking was a key to the presentation
of early broadcasts" (Sterne 1999, 507).

The consequences of this "centralized control" can be observed in the
cultural production of content, which was influenced by a media oligopoly of
large radio corporations transitioned to television – i.e., the "big three" (Hindman and Wiegand 2008). This industrial configuration affected subsequent
evolutions of the US media landscape for a long time. "As soon as they could,
radio networks took steps to articulate and promote their vision of television
as a nationally networked medium that distributed content from a few centralized sources" (Ibid.). The outcome of this networked structure is reflected
in the homogeneity of content and narrative forms that distinguished the
first decade of US television from 1947 to 1957 (Slide 1991, 121), and the years
immediately after. Following its first large-scale infrastructural adoption in
the 1940s, broadcast television in the US witnessed a moment of gradual and
steady rise, commonly known as the first Golden Age, which was marked
by the production of content that could unify parts of the nation under a
shared sense of belonging to the same confederation of states. Relying on
a programming schedule controlled by large corporations and sponsors,
which supervised the content to be broadcasted, US television narratives
of this period were very much modulated by hegemonic standards and
modeled after specific production norms.

Shot live with a multi-camera setup from studios based in New York, US
anthology dramas of the late 1940s and early 1950s were made up of episodes
of variable length (from half an hour to an hour long), each one acting as a
sequence or textual unit in its own right and following a separate narrative
arc within a cycle of seemingly unrelated episodes and seasons. Anthology
series of this time served as catalysts for the dominant national culture and
identity, reinforcing normative ideas and addressing the wealthy households
that owned television sets. If early printed anthologies were to carry an
ideal of literary canon and artistic value, television anthologies amplified
the didactic purpose of radio adaptations and expanded their outreach
with visual means. As such, the first episodic television series had the
intent to influence society, by creating behavioral models and promoting
the concept of national unity through cultural unity. Furthermore, the

coexistence of most television productions with the Broadway scene favored multiple contaminations not only between radio and television, but also between television and theater. From the very beginning, television set out to be a medium that defines itself through other media (e.g., literary, radiophonic, theatrical, cinematographic). Similarly, through its progressive consolidation in media history, the anthology form acquired the status of cross-technological form, leveraging affordances that allowed it to easily transfer from literature to radio and television, from textual to audiovisual media. The connection of television anthologies with the literary heritage and other traditions contributed to framing some of the characteristics found in anthology series to come: strong authorial presence; a macrostructure based on recurring thematic or stylistic features; and an overall idea of canonic quality. As Jane Feuer noted, "even before a normative notion of 'everyday television' had solidified, the idea of 'quality drama' existed in the form of the live 'anthology' teleplays of the 1950s" (Feuer, in Hilmes and Jacobs 2003, 98–99).

Episodic television series of this period have indeed succeeded in rein-terpreting literary masterpieces, by packaging them in a collection of plays adapted for the small screen. However, the anthology form not only found a cross-media evolution in processes of adaptation, but it also prompted the creation of new original productions. For example, as the *UCLA Film & Television Archive* reports, "originating from New York and remaining there for the duration of the production of the series (long after most other anthology series relocated to Los Angeles), the live, bi-weekly *U.S. Steel Hour* began its impressive run with adaptations of established stage plays, before expanding into developing literary adaptations of novels and short stories, and original plays written directly for television."[9] *The United States Steel Hour* (1953–1963) represents an exceptional case. It was one of the first US television series to address controversial national issues of social relevance, by adopting the anthology form to depict a contradictory portrait of a nation, instead of using it as a way to display cultural cohesion. As Rod Serling explained in an open critique to mainstream post-war televised theater:

> In the television seasons of 1952 and 1953, almost every television play I sold to the major networks was "non-controversial." This is to say that in terms of their themes they were socially inoffensive, and dealt with no current human problem in which battle lines might be drawn. After the

9   "Live from New York: U.S. Steel Hour." *UCLA Film & Television Archive*. Last modified May 15, 2018. https://www.cinema.ucla.edu/blogs/archive-blog/2018/05/15/US-Steel-Hour.

production of *Patterns*, when my things were considerably easier to sell, in a mad and impetuous moment I had the temerity to tackle a theme that was definitely two-sided in its implications. I think this story is worth repeating. The script was called *Noon on Doomsday*. It was produced by the Theatre Guild on The United States Steel Hour in April 1956.

(Serling 1958, online)

Unlike other television markets, which mostly relied on state-owned and government-funded public channels, the US welcomed over-the-air commercial television as the main form of broadcasting to the nation, thus producing television content largely based on private financing. As an oligopolistic and centralized force, commercial television relied on a group of advertisers, most commonly large companies and corporations, who were keen on sponsoring television programs in exchange for visibility and the audience's attention. This sponsorship system favored a type of standardized, conventional television that was subjected to the sale of advertising space and therefore heavily dependent on commercial and political interests. "National planning, national advertising and a national infrastructure were to characterize the structure of American television" (Sterne 1999, 508). As Anna Everett put it in the *Encyclopedia of Television*:

> Much of the criticism of these live television dramas concerned the power sponsors often exerted over program content. Specifically, the complaints focused on the mandate by sponsors that programs adhere to a "dead-centerism." In other words, sponsored shows were to avoid completely socially and politically controversial themes. Only those dramas that supported and reflected positive middle-class values, which likewise reflected favorably the image of the advertisers, were broadcast.
>
> (Everett, in Newcomb 2014, 1003)

This is a key point to understanding the shape taken by the anthology form in this first phase, as well as the affordances acquired in its interaction with the technological, industrial, and institutional structures of US television.

Advertising-funded and introduced by a recurring host, US anthology series of the 1940s and 1950s were accurately sorted into different time slots to fit demographic targets. Their content usually maintained moral and political perspectives in line with those of the sponsor, which acted as a gatekeeper. A program like the *General Electric Theatre* (CBS, 1953–1962), funded by General Electric and hosted by Ronald Reagan, is an evident example of how the anthology form was used to convey both commercial and socio-political interests. In its almost ten-year span of broadcasting, *General Electric Theatre* laid the premises for Reagan's own future political career as the bearer of pro-capitalistic views in the guise of show host, occasional co-star, and company spokesman (Taylor 2016, 13). Chosen by Reagan himself, along with General Electric's Department of Public Relations, in between the storylines of dramas and comedies, the scripts weaved together messages in support of economic progress, free-market capitalism, individualistic achievements, and self-reliance. Other anthologies born in the Golden Age of US television reveal similar purposes. Even more than early radio anthologies, early US television anthologies abandoned the archival roots as forms of cultural preservation to fully embrace a programmatic educational and political scope and adapt to the new nature of commercially oriented product. However, a further evolution of the form came about as a consequence of changes in modes of production and industrial geo-localization.

As we observed, in its initial phase, US television infrastructures contributed to creating a centralized and oligopolistic market in the period from 1947 to 1957. This resulted in a concentration of power in three large corporations – ABC, CBS, NBC – which oversaw the content produced and distributed, and shaped the cultural identity of the nation. Given that these corporations were initially based in New York, television content was influenced by theater production and the adaptation of literary classics for the stage, thus recycling and remediating previous narratives for the televisual medium. However, starting from the 1950s, the main industrial hub for media production gradually moved from New York to Los Angeles, and by the end of the decade most television productions were based on the West Coast. At that point, television was firmly established across several Western countries, counting on a solid infrastructure and a reliable distribution network. By replacing Broadway's productions, Hollywood-based productions intervened to finance television series, changing some of their original characteristics and creating an autonomous industry with its own rules and styles. For instance, the live recording and multi-camera setup that had dominated the television scene for a decade in New York, with anthology series made of thirty- to sixty-minute-long episodes, was substituted by filmed anthology dramas that exceeded the time traditionally available for live weekly programming. The influence of this new economic and industrial landscape on television "draws on a complex web of local cultural assets that play a crucial role in imparting to the products of the industry their distinctive look and feel" (Scott 2000, 325). The transition from live, one-time-only events to pre-recorded episodes, free from the tension, time, and money constraints generated by the live event, helped reactivate some of the affordances of the anthology form. While the business models adopted still fed into an idea of commercial television driven by a sponsorship system, adhering to politicized and non-controversial entertainment, recorded television anthologies offered a more flexible solution to issues of storage and visibility. For the first time, television shows could be easily moved around time slots and scheduled for reruns.

Additionally, the change in the production location expanded the creative possibilities of the medium and favored a diversification of television genres. From their appearance on radio and then on television, anthological narratives have often been associated with dramatic genres. In the course of the late 1950s until the late 1970s, this tendency is formalized in the definition of three main strands that have shaped the evolution of television anthologies in subsequent years: crime; science fiction; and horror. Under the influence of Hollywood productions, each of these genres evolved into sub-genres like noir, police procedural, and mystery, often borrowing stories from printed media (e.g., serialized short stories, editorials and reportages in magazines or newspapers) and popular literary fiction of the era (e.g., "whodunit" detective stories; pulp fiction; hard-boiled fiction). Furthermore, the evolution of the US anthology drama was subjected to the rise of cable television, which had been accessible since 1948 upon subscription, but not yet so widespread. Following some pioneering efforts to set up cable-satellite programming, aimed at overcoming terrestrial transmission and expanding television's reach, it was only in 1975 that Home Box Office (HBO) succeeded in creating a solid distribution system of satellite-delivered television content (Parsons 2003, 1). Initially available only in the basic cable option, starting in the late 1970s, cable television began to offer premium cable paid services, by decentralizing previous hegemonic industrial powers and inaugurating the beginning of what was defined as "multi-channel transition" (Lotz 2007). Alongside multiple channels made available and a higher quantity of content, this new setting forced commercial television to abandon its predominant position and make room for new technological and industrial trends.

Basic cable television stands in hybrid territory. If, on the one hand, a subscription-based model prevents the total dependence on advertising, on the other hand parts of the financing still derive from the sale of advertising spaces. Over the years, basic cable in the US has managed to define distinctive, innovative features as parts of its programming, overcoming the limits imposed by conventional forms, formulas, and formats. In this period of techno-industrial adjustments in the history of US television, which began in the 1980s and continued until the end of the 1990s, the tendency towards the multiplication of content resulted in a further diversification of television series available to the public, and, consequently, in audience segmentation, fragmentation, and polarization (Webster 2005, 367). This expansion into niche audiences (Hilmes 2013, 266) and diversified content was in radical opposition to the numerous attempts by early worldwide television industries to unify content for limited demographic targets. New channels, content, audiences, but also new technologies and legislation, led to parallel innovations in narrative and media forms across several countries. One revolutionary change brought by cable technology in the US was the emancipation from the dependence on the sale of advertising space. While commercial television was still entirely advertiser-driven, cable television took advantage of hybrid forms of subsidy and combined revenues from both advertising and subscription, thus gaining a higher level of creative freedom and possibilities in the production of content. The subscription-driven model, which will be inherited subsequently by streaming platforms like Netflix, made pay television more reliant on audiences' demand for content than on the impositions of the sponsors. As Lotz (2007) explains, "new technologies including the remote control, video-cassette recorder, and analog cable systems expanded viewers' choice and control; producers adjusted to government regulations that forced the networks to relinquish some of their control over the terms of program creation" (Ibid., 12).

It is in this scenario that early anthology series, as they were conceived, underwent a rapid decline and almost disappeared only to be replaced by more "complex" serial products. "Pressed into the deployment of target marketing strategies by the proliferation of cable services, network TV began to introduce a new type of complex and sophisticated program- ming aimed directly at an upscale audience" (Thompson 1996, 30). Caldwell (1995) describes the stylistic complexity that distinguished television series produced in this phase using the term "televisuality," while Jason Mittell observes that "this model of television storytelling is distinct for its use of narrative complexity as an alternative to the conventional episodic and serial forms that have typified most American television since its inception" (Mittell 2006, 39). With the aim to differentiate its products from free-to-air television, the premium channels began the search for a qualitative positioning of content, looking for something unique. During the multi-channel transition, the commercial value of television started to move from the production of a homogeneous pool of similar programming material, to the production of distinct content options.

At this stage, US television started several operations of television brand- ing, intended to market specific content identities for each distribution

channel and facilitate the commercialization of televisual products. Branded
television (McCabe and Akass 2007, 88) stimulated the creation of so-called
hit series, meaning original and innovative serial content that was meant
to renovate the television scene. Vast narratives with strong running plots
were able to generate long-term marketing plans, by expanding the narrative
ecosystem radially into the various sectors of the entertainment industry.
This form naturally overcame the more scattered narrative offer of early
anthology series. Despite the surge of a media landscape that went towards
vast narratives, episodic anthology series were still thriving in both commercial networks and cable channels as niche content for nostalgic television
revivals. The need to expand the offer led, for instance, to a renewed interest
in earlier television series from the Golden Age. Although the production of
anthology dramas almost stopped, over the course of the 1980s and 1990s
US television witnessed the return of some golden programs in the shape of
re-edited television collections that granted accessibility to old anthologies.
In 1980, Irwin Sonny Fox, president of the National Academy of Television
Arts and Sciences, recovered the best anthology teleplays of the so-called
live era in a new anthology presented by PBS as *The Golden Age of Television*, a collection of the most famous episodes of the 1950s, integrated with
interviews and commentary from television professionals.

Despite the emergence of open-ended forms of narrative experimentation
in strong contrast with the episodic limits imposed by the anthological
form, anthologies survived throughout the early 2000s. On the one hand,
this has been possible thanks to television reruns or revivals of earlier
anthology dramas, as the remains of the North American post-war television
culture. These forms of re-editorialization recall a practice already found
in literary tradition: the use of the anthology as an editorial model for the
republication and update of past editions. On the other hand, the production
of US anthology dramas lasted throughout the multi-channel transition in a
few rare examples of episodic television series within the crime, sci-fi, and
horror genre. This heritage of the crime, sci-fi, horror anthology form helped
canalize later efforts to revive the anthology form in the digital era. In many
television industries in Europe and North America, these genres have played
a pivotal role in carrying on the anthological tradition in the aftermath of
the consolidation of the connection between cinema and television formats.
While crime was still attached to a strict genre formula, thus generating
semi-anthologies with repetitive patterns, such as police procedurals, sci-fi
anthologies exploited the affordances of the anthology form to experiment
with storytelling practices. Horror anthologies followed a similar path,
highlighting this use of the anthology form as a way to constantly redefine

narrative norms and standards, in synergy with parallel experiments in long-running shows.

As we have observed, taking US television as a case study, early anthology series provided socio-cultural cohesion, serving as means for generating consensus and tools for culture planning, either driven by educational purposes or promoting a system of ideologies. In a later stage, the anthology form evolved to welcome other uses. As soon as the oligopolistic industrial structure opened up to a more competitive and varied media environment, this editorial form was set aside only to find its identity through a persisting set of affordances. The pedagogical scope ceased being the main reason for the creation of anthological narratives, and even the use of the anthology as a commercially oriented product was slowly abandoned. At that time, most television series were created in a collective environment, with a group of screenwriters working on the same long-running show in the writers' room. In this context, the anthology form maintained its own screenwriting model, giving credit to authorial voices in television instead of relying on collaborative authorship. In Barnouw's (1990) words, "unlike the formula-bound episodic series, the anthology series emphasized diversity. The play was the thing. Actors were chosen to fit the play, not vice versa. The anthology series said to the writer: 'Write us a play.' There were no specifications as to mood, characters, plot, style, or locale – at least not at first" (Ibid., 154). This allowed anthologies to support a single vision (the style and aesthetics of famous directors or writers) while also stressing the necessity to differentiate each episodic chapter.

From being predominantly used as a form of preservation in ancient literature, to turning into a form of adaptation in radio, in television the anthology gained a new affordance as a polyhedric form of narrative innovation, comparable to coeval experimentations in electronic literature. In light of the US model, which influenced many broadcasting industries abroad, practices of anthologization have been adopted across different television eras and media environments as a way to structure and define certain genres and formulas, while, at the same time, subverting normative canons. Even in a phase of decline, the anthology proved to be an important resource for preserving, adapting and experimenting with cultural narratives, ultimately creating a dialogue between past and present. In digital culture, this set of affordances merges into the macro-structure of the internet: the anthology becomes the catalyzer of narratives into forms of content organization that control our very access to cultural records. Outside of fictional narratives, digital anthologies start to appear in other forms, medially located in a platform environment and yet geographically unbounded – as open-access database projects, computational archival initiatives, and born-digital repositories – in a spirit of interoperability that allowed for cross-cultural pollinations.

1.5. In Digital Culture

The issue of content organization, archiving, and distribution re-emerged as an urgent question in contemporary culture, quickly reviving the anthology form as both a technological and editorial solution to the management of ever-growing archives of analog and digital content. After all, digital culture is an anthological culture (Doueihi 2011a) by nature, both in its storage and its transmission. In the early 2000s, thanks to the introduction of the web 2.0, a new virtual environment was made available for querying and accessing digital content, prefiguring the birth of online platforms as the main hubs for content distribution. This digital mutation impacted almost all pre-existing media. The arrival of technological innovations, such as computers and other devices for the distribution of content (iPod, PSP2, mobile phones, DVD players, and digital video recorders), further diversified the cultural offer and opened up to a variety of new practices in publishing, radio, and television.

> Here, "post-network" acknowledges the break from a dominant network-era experience, in which viewers lacked much control over when and where to view and chose among a limited selection of externally determined linear viewing options – in other words, programs available at a certain time on a certain channel. Such constraints are not part of the post-network television experience in which viewers now increasingly select what, when, and where to view from abundant options.
>
> (Lotz 2007, 15)

Convenience, customization, and community-making in the post-network media experience (Ibid., 245) were conveying a seemingly higher sense of control over modes of consumption and choice. In this scenario, "the plethora of programming opportunities is meaningless without a means for viewers to find relevant shows and organize their viewing, which necessitates finding technological and distribution solution for the problem" (Ibid.).

The role of distribution systems in bridging the gap between the production and consumption of content was always a central topic in media industries since the advent of the printing press. As the historian John

Man remarked, much like the digital revolution, the Gutenberg revolution sparked an unprecedented surge in book publishing (Man 2010, 17), which grew disproportionally into the amount of printed matter that we traditionally store in libraries, bookstores, and personal collections. The introduction of digital systems and electronic publishing added another layer of complexity to the management of content, offering the promise of a hyper-connected, hyper-textual network of narrative content, yet failing to completely democratize the access to cultural production. Among others, one of the common wrong assumptions around digital and electronic media is that they dematerialize cultural industries. On the contrary, digitization is a process deeply grounded in a range of physical supports – from scanning machinery to computers, processors, and communication infrastructures. In digital culture, issues of memory and storage still pose challenges to the survival of heritage records. Nevertheless, what digital infrastructure was able to truly revolutionize was the system of transnational distribution radiating across countries. In the case of early publishing in Europe, the dissemination of books would rely on a network of agents running local and cross-border distribution (Bhaskar 2013, 35), with obvious limitations in the extent of their outreach. By contrast, industries like radio and television immediately started their expansion from local to global networks, thanks to transmitters, cables, and satellite technologies that could send signals at scale. While in publishing the digital was initially feared as a threat to the materiality of paper, and therefore to the whole industry, the transition from analog to digital signals was a natural progression for mass media like radio and television, already reliant on invisible electromagnetic waves.

Whereas the network era had consecrated television as "the cultural hearth around which a society shares media events" (Lotz 2007, 5), during the post-network (Lotz 2007) or post-channel era (Lotz 2016), from the 2000s on, the audience shattered into multiple segments, with continuous access to a variety of media content and an ever-increasing flow of information from several web-based sources outside of the television screen. This represented an epochal change in cultural production and distribution, which, up until that moment, was conceived in the material existence of separate media, transmitted either through a paper book, a radio receiver, or a television set. With new media entering cultural industries, older media were asked to redefine their very applications, in order to account for the multiplicity of displays and monitors involved in the reception of audiovisual material. The dissemination of media content across various devices for entertainment led to the creation of narrower targets in search of a personalized experience and niche products. In this opposition between mass and niche media, Lotz identified the transition towards a narrowcasting model (Lotz 2007, 199). Graeme Turner and Jinna Tay defined this phase as the "post-broadcast era," to mark a definitive separation of older media, like television, from the broadcasting model:

> It is evident that new media are re-contextualising television, changing what it is that television can do, for whom it can do it, and under what conditions. Consequently, where once broadcast television was everywhere the fundamental medium to which mass media theory had to address itself, now we need to address a much more complex mediascape where change has been vigorous but uneven, and where the local, national and regional media environments vary significantly.
>
> (Turner and Tay 2009, 72)

In light of the revolutionary change that affected all media with internet distribution, digital culture assimilated the anthology form at different levels. Here, we will list five main classificatory processes that absorbed the anthological model, either by repurposing elements from pre-existing practices of anthologization in analog media or by introducing new algorithmic practices. On the one hand, we will discuss processes related to the creation and curation of serialized content, such as hybrid forms of born-digital, online-ready, anthology-making, and podcasting. On the other hand, we will consider practices of editorialization, such as playlisting, tagging, and algorithmic filtering.

Overall, anthological content in digital culture enables streams of "finished" narratives that can be re-contextualized in a collection at any point in time. This supports the process of aggregation required to manage the great abundance of content available on online platforms.[10] Whether curatorial or editorial, narrative or data-driven, a common feature of anthology forms in digital culture is that they can transition fluidly from short to long forms

---

10 Aggregation theory notably explains the abundance generated by a multi-sided platform economy by pointing at three main causes: (1) the absence of transaction costs, which facilitates the acquisition of users/subscribers; (2) the absence of distribution costs, directly linked to a proliferation of content; and (3) the absence of marginal costs, which ensures scalability. "These three fundamentals explain how content changed from scarcity, only available through traditional media such as newspapers, magazines, books and TV, to abundance available on every person's blog, social feed and YouTube channel." – David Lifely, "Aggregation Theory: The Most Powerful Economics Theory You Didn't Learn at University," *Medium*. Last modified January 8, 2018. https://medium.com/@dlifely/aggregation-theory-the-most-powerful-economics-theory-you-didnt-learn-at-university-4dc854b8d0b.

of content organization and archiving. As we have observed in previous paragraphs, this fluidity in Western practices of narrative-based anthology-making finds its roots in the second half of the twentieth century, where literature (in book publishing, as much as in daily or weekly journals and magazines), radio and television embraced an open concept of narrative experimentation. The intuition of anthology-making practices lies precisely in the fact that they were able to anticipate the mutations of digital culture into algorithmic culture with prepackaged narrative content ready to fit online platform environments.

As we have seen in previous paragraphs, literature was one of the first narrative traditions to embrace the use of electronic devices for the production, storage, and distribution of born-digital anthology products and textual artifacts at large. Digital literary anthologies emerged as a natural evolution of short scholarly essays, works of fiction and poetry published in academic journals, newspapers, or weekly magazines as a series of separate installments organized per theme. They can be divided into two main strands: born-digital literary anthologies and digitized anthologies of analog texts. On the one hand, exclusively crafted for computational environments, electronic literature derives its aesthetics from computation and can "only exist in the space for which it was developed/written/coded – the digital space" (Price and Siemens 2013). Inherently digital, electronic anthologies originally appeared as creative works by computer scientists as early as the 1950s. In 1952, Christopher Strachey wrote a combinatory poetry program called *love letter generator* for the Manchester Mark 1 computer. This computer program would generate a series of love letters based on structural repetitions and lexical variations, in the wake of an anthological model. Among other electronic literature experiments tinkering with a choose-your-own-path, non-linear structure, electronic anthologies came into being as archival projects for the preservation of both past and present literary works, as well as for the establishment of the new literary field of electronic literature. For instance, the volumes issued as part of *Electronic Literature Collections* reinterpret traditional anthologies as collections of artifacts intended for long-term preservation and archiving, by giving them a new shape: a collage of entry points to more or less interactive electronic readings. Other publishing initiatives, like *Poems that Go*, which "explores the intersections between motion, sound, image, text, and code,"[11] have undertaken a similar task, by gathering

---

11   https://archive.the-next.eliterature.org/poemsthatgo/index.htm; https://archive.the-next.eliterature.org/poemsthatgo/statement.htm.

archives of digital essays, fiction, and poetry into curated anthologies of electronic texts.

With the arrival of the internet as a means for digital publishing, archiving and transmission, electronic anthologies took off in the form of collections of articles and lists of books for recovering past literature that had not entered mainstream distribution. In this context, not only electronic anthologies, but also digitized anthologies gained importance in their own right. Excluded from the definition "electronic literature," digitized anthologies have been fundamental for the circulation of ancient texts in the modern world. As part of archival initiatives, digitization has fostered its own anthologization practices, by re-ordering folders from physical repositories into updated digital collections. Digital archives not only transfer material media formats into machine-readable files, but they also rethink the original cataloging and classification system by providing it with a new set of labels. Once enriched with metadata, digitized textual records in archives acquire a renewed anthological structure made of keywords. Keywords serve to group fragmented archival items into web-based grids, clusters, sub-clusters, or snippets of content that are curated by machines in response to human queries. The occurrence of the anthology form in digital archives applies to textual, visual, sound, or audiovisual records alike.

While electronic anthologies can include multimedia projects, the digital-archival anthology is perhaps one of the most dynamic anthological examples. For once, it can sustain the transition of all kinds of analog media into the digital landscape. Moreover, it allows for a constant update of its documentation – by means of a collective curation of metadata by librarians, art historians, researchers, and other professionals involved in the archival process. Finally, it is able to reinterpret systems of knowledge by unveiling previously hidden connections between narratives of different kinds – e.g., literary and textual narratives in library archives; visual narratives in art and museum collections; and journalism narratives in media archives. Thanks to digitization, online repositories of archival collections became one of the main digital environments that entailed the transition of the anthology form into algorithmic culture. In literature as in radio and television, archival digitization offered a way to guarantee the survival of ancient manuscripts, radio programs, and television shows, by fostering interesting cross-media phenomena of anthologization. For instance, literary books recorded as radio content either in past or present audiobooks are now accessible via radio equipment and internet platforms. Furthermore, born-digital anthologies in radio have produced their own formatting processes, which we will discuss in the rest of this chapter as editorial design practices that emerged in the context of streaming media platforms and fitting the more specific definition of podcasting.

In television, contemporary anthologies made of separate short stories have proven to be particularly resilient. They can be canceled at any time at the end of each narrative arc, without having to drop unresolved storylines, which might remain online as unfinished editorial content. With its versatile features, the anthology form made its comeback in the context of cable television as a branding strategy for introducing alternative business models as well as new forms of creative experimentation. Limited-running anthology series appeared in a hybrid form: the seasonal anthology series or anthology miniseries. This flexible form mimics occurrences found in previous media traditions, such as literary book series or editorial collections, which collect separate long-form novels with a common framing principle, or CD box sets including several movies from the same author or actor. In this version of the anthology form, each separate story is no longer limited to the episodic structure, but it extends throughout the season, portraying separate narratives in the guise of miniseries with a beginning, a central moment of plot development, and a conclusion. Hybrid anthology-making practices like the anthology miniseries repeat some instances of older television series, while also reinventing the form. For example, in *American Horror Story* (FX, 2011–), a few actors return between one season and another, sometimes playing the same characters with different roles in the plot, through "internal crossovers" in the anthology system. In these cases, the status of anthology is defined not so much by the recurring cast, but by the set of shared themes, which, along with discursive, esthetics, and stylistic elements, drift between separate seasons and represent the organizing principle of the anthology. In addition, paratextual elements can also act as contour lines that hold different stories together. This is the case for some opening sequences, which stand as metaphors for the structure of the anthology itself, by implementing elements of repetition and variation in their design esthetic (e.g., *True Detective* [HBO, 2013–]).

Following the lead of cable television, several television productions began deploying the seasonal anthology series model. In some cases, the narrative arc can cover one season or else take up two seasons, without compromising the anthological structure. For example, some seasonal anthologies were originally designed with a narrative arc that would cover two seasons and then switched to a separate story during the third season. This is the case of *Scream* (MTV, 2015–2016; VH1, 2019), which, after two seasons, opted for a new story with a different plot and cast, announcing it as a reboot going by the title *Scream: Resurrection*. Television series with a seasonal arc present several advantages both in terms of creative flexibility and in terms of long-term content-production planning. The idea of a collection of standalone stories immediately caught the attention of online platforms, in a moment when television was transitioning towards the coexistence of linear and non-linear media apparatuses, with Netflix introducing its streaming service in 2010. Anthologies released on cable and network channels in the early years of digital television transitioned fluidly to internet-distributed television as products that can be efficiently inserted into the non-linear dynamics of online platforms. For instance, products like anthology mini-series do not need to be declared as such in the production phase, making the curatorial and editorialization processes almost interchangeable: a television series can be editorialized as a miniseries, but then curated as an anthology. Moreover, once the first season is released, it acts as a project roadmap, but the final televisual product can be produced years after. The production can be paused and reprised without the need to be undertaken on a year-to-year basis.

Mapping anthology series appeared in recent years shows interesting patterns. From a financial standpoint, seasonal anthologies have been shown to create higher engagement of famous actors, who, in turn, became executive producers of the program, proving that the anthology business model can generate a self-sustaining creative economy. In some cases, hybrid anthology series that originally appeared on network and cable channels led to distribution agreements with over-the-top platforms like Netflix, Hulu, or Amazon Video. The anthology form turned out to be a relatively good fit for internet-distributed television. In an interview at the BFI London Film Festival in 2016, Charlie Brooker, writer of the series *Black Mirror*, acquired by Netflix in 2015, explained, "I think that anthology shows like this have been waiting for a platform like Netflix or streaming services in general to come along [...] On Netflix, we can put the whole thing up and it's like a short story collection, or an album, or tickets to a film festival."[12] Since anthology series are not designed to have narrative continuity or cliffhangers, they have strived to survive on television networks that are based on audience measurement systems as indicators of a series' success. While the anthology form seems to have lost its grip on commercial television, on the contrary, it is slowly becoming a key strategy for both cable and over-the-top providers, as a way of selling branded content and intercepting niche identities (Wayne 2018). Innovative docu-series with an anthological structure have been sold to

12   See: https://www.youtube.com/watch?v=HVb2qxhDkrc.

Netflix – such as Vox's *Explained* – and Hulu distributed *The Weekly*, a series produced by *The New York Times*, which brings investigative journalism to internet-distributed television.

Close to the idea of anthology-making, as found in editorial design practices online, is podcasting. Podcasts follow an analogous process to the creation of television anthology series, as they are pre-designed and formatted in the content-production phase. Podcasting is a term brought about by the media, who first discussed online radio and the "Audible revolution"[13] as an attempt to rewrite the norms of radio broadcasting, by making downloadable radio shows periodically available on the internet. What started as an experiment, with podcasts released via a RSS feed, slowly attracted the interest of companies like Amazon or Google and of well-established music directories like Apple's iTunes. Digital podcasting was originally conceived to sustain a much older radio format, that of audiobooks, which first appeared in the US in the 1930s (Rubery 2011, 5), with audio recordings and adaptations from literary classics. Fast-forward to 1997, audiobooks reappeared in new "born-digital forms" known as podcasts (Hilmes 2013, 420). As the verb itself suggests, podcasting refers to both a practice and a form. Podcasting as a practice fully embedded in the media industry notably finds its roots in Amazon's Audible service, which, in 1997, "released the first portable audio player designed specifically for listening to audiobooks."[14]

In more recent years, podcasts became available not only as part of the content offered by major companies like Apple, Amazon, and Google, but also as a rather specific type of audio material distributed by companies entirely dedicated to the diffusion of podcast-like products. Well-known media organizations like NPR implemented the production of podcasts in their online platforms, and smaller start-ups began to offer a platform environment for uploading –*podcasted* audio-content, so to speak. Other media companies are now adopting a podcasting strategy for the diffusion of information, such as the Vox Media Podcast Network. Streaming music services like Soundcloud and Spotify also joined the podcasting movement, which is expected to grow fast: a 2019 report from the Interactive Advertising Bureau (IAB) and PwC estimated that the podcasting industry generated

13   Ben Hammersley, "Why Online Radio Is Booming," *The Guardian*. Last modified February 12, 2004. https://www.theguardian.com/media/2004/feb/12/broadcasting.digitalmedia.
14   "A Short History of the Audiobook, 20 Years after the First Portable Digital Audio Device." *PBS NewsHour*. Last modified November 22, 2017. https://www.pbs.org/newshour/arts/a-short-history-of-the-audiobook-20-years-after-the-first-portable-digital-audio-device.

a revenue of about 479.1 million US dollars in 2018 and that by 2021 it was
likely to produce more than 1 billion US dollars.[15] That said, podcasted
anthologies came not only to evolve in similar ways to television anthology series, by proposing factual or fictional narratives with an episodic or
seasonal structure, but also to actively influence anthological production
in contemporary television, by adopting the same standards and logic.

Audio podcasting, as a way of formatting culture on a production level,
is easily transferable to television anthologies. It is no coincidence therefore
that some anthology series released in recent years were either based on
podcasts, such as Amazon's *Lore*, or actively fostered the creation of fan-
based audio podcasts as new forms of fan fiction, as in the case of Hulu's
Castle Rock. The podcast-to-series strategy dates back to 2007, when the
cable channel Showtime adapted the podcast *This American Life* into a
series of the same name (Showtime, 2007–2008), and it continues to feed
the television business with podcasts like *Serial*, which was commissioned
as a series by HBO. Other interesting cases of the anthology form conflating
with the podcast form can be found online, on aggregators like PlayerFM,
which collects anthology podcasts.[16] All these classificatory processes can
be detected, with some variations on the anthological model, as practices
that establish "a conceptual grid shaped by the dynamic of the reception and by the specific knowledge related to the texts circulating on the
network and to the authorities associated with them" (Doueihi 2012, 163,
my translation).

Another classificatory process found in digital culture is that of playlisting. Drawing a parallel with music playlists on Spotify or iTunes is useful to
better understand the mechanism of anthologization in contemporary US
television, as something that is happening in close relation with platform environments. "While à la carte purchasing and the $.99 solution are examples
of economic modularity and pricing models that facilitated disaggregation,
iTunes achieved reaggregation most prominently through playlists" (Morris
2015, 159). This idea of re-aggregation is slightly different to what drives
the creation of anthology series on streaming platforms. However, it is a
symptom of the same necessity to sort digital records in a way that can guide
the viewer into repeatable consumption patterns, by organizing content
into reusable clusters, and into a shared, collective itinerary. Unlike tagging

---

15   "Full Year 2018-IAB Podcast Ad Rev Study," *IAB*. Last modified June 2019. https://www.iab.
     com/wp-content/uploads/2019/05/Full-Year-2018-IAB-Podcast-Ad-Rev-Study_5.29.19_vFinal.
     pdf.
16   https://player.fm/podcasts/Anthology.

and algorithmic filtering, which still allows for a wide variety of individual, personalized consumption paths that are constantly changing as soon as consumption happens, the practice of playlisting fosters regularity in consumption, and, when made public, can generate a collective experience through the creation of a canon. As evidence that playlists are not just artistic practices, Spotify offers a music recommender support in the form of Playlist Machinery,[17] developed by Paul Lamere, intended to help users organize, sort, and aggregate music tracks into playlists. Additional features connected to Spotify have been created by web developers to enhance the playlisting experience, such as Playlist Manager, which "merges the songs of selected playlists into one view, allowing you to easily add and remove songs from different playlists,"[18] or Magic Playlist, "an intelligent algorithm developed under Spotify's API that enables users to create a playlist based on a song."[19]

Half-way between human-driven and data-driven machine-led practices is tagging. Tagging is a type of grassroots classification that can be associated with the content either at the moment of publication or in consecutive log-in sessions. In most cases, users are asked to tag content in order to insert it in an online feed. The process of tagging creates a self-organizing cultural archive in a similar way to what happens with metadata schemes, "with an immanent classificatory system produced in the collective classificatory imagination of the users" (Beer 2013, 62). This seemingly anthological form is interesting precisely because it operates at the convergence of multiple, collective processes of classification. More specifically, tagging "systems are active creators of categories in the world as well as simulators of existing categories" (Bowker and Star 1999, 321) and "with the emergence of new information infrastructures, these classification systems are becoming even more densely interconnected" (Ibid., 326). In platform environments like Twitter or Instagram, forms of collection like hashtags additionally operate as key classifiers for running queries and for browsing content, not just for organizing it, therefore generating new ways of accessing and receiving culture. In this regard, while describing an anthological turn in digital culture, the philosopher Milad Doueihi (2011, 521) points at the fact that tagging practices redefined both processes of dissemination and selection of previously unrelated snippets of content, thus generating new forms of

---

17   http://organizeyourmusic.playlistmachinery.com/; sortyourmusic.playlistmachinery.com/; http://playlistminer.playlistmachinery.com.
18   See: http://playlist-manager.com/#/login.
19   See: https://developer.spotify.com/community/showcase/magic-playlist.

meaning. On digital platforms, manual or automated tagging of content's metadata is just one initial part of the process of classification behind content retrieval. Algorithms offer an additional system for generating collections and filtering the stream. By definition, algorithmic filtering *filters* streams of interrelated content, thus shaping consumption by following, once again, an anthological model. Streams have potentially unlimited data. Algorithmic functions found in recommender systems, such as collaborative filtering used on Netflix or pattern matching, operate on these streams to produce other streams based on a given selection.

These types of algorithmic filters in streaming platforms represent secondary processes of classification, once the primary indexing process has been defined through tagging. Even though these two classificatory processes found in digital culture do not create anthologies in the editorial sense of the term, they do create lists with an organizing principle that resembles the anthological model. These classificatory systems, which produce clusters of content that are similar to anthologies in their intent, portray examples of either grassroots classification (tagging), algorithmic-driven classification (algorithmic filtering), or a mix of both (playlisting). On online platforms, digital publication starts with data and to metadata (created via anthology-making practices such as podcasting, or via editorial curation such as playlisting and tagging). From this point, algorithms compute lists of titles. In this context, automated processes of anthological editorialization emerge to help both indexing and information retrieval on digital platforms. This anthological cycle found on digital platforms adds onto a web environment already based on classification methods. The anthology series in streaming television platforms is just one example of how the anthology form is able to contain many products in one, thus defining a classification cluster by itself. From this overview of anthological models in digital culture, interesting concepts unfold, from narratology to design and taxonomic studies. Questions arise as to how anthological models define hierarchies between records, situate points of access, or expose content in platform environments, determining the presence of points of entrance or emergence in the algorithmic stream.

1.6. Other Short Forms

As shown in previous paragraphs, throughout the history of media in the Western world, anthologies have been occasionally confined to serving a

normative aim and perpetuate a set of hegemonic beliefs as a consequence
of centralized political power and monopolistic industrial dynamics.
Nevertheless, the anthology form could never truly dismiss its connection
with the short story and its potential "of expressing the repress knowledge
of a dominant culture" (Patea 2012, 7). Stripped down to its essence, the
short story is a minimal form, portable, accessible, economical, and easily
replicable. Due to these resilient traits, it was often deployed by marginalized
communities to deliver an urgency of themes, through the passing on, telling,
and retelling of vulnerable narratives that could never gain the status of
epic, long forms in the male-dominated world of "great literature." In digital
culture, this social quality of the short narrative has become particularly
poignant, making it a form that is as brief as it is intense in terms of the
epistemological outcomes and overall discursivity it brings up. In some cases,
the short form turned into a driver for advocating justice and inclusion, such
as in the case of Twitter, which, with its fixed less-than-three-hundred-
character-length format, hosted several decentralized activist movements
grouped under collective hashtags like #MeToo or #BlackLivesMatter, used
to report gender and racial violence. As carriers of social change, short
stories are the cornerstones of most anthologies, where the main structure
of rotating or repeatedly regenerating narratives brought to the emergence
of "scattered" characters, or else "outlawed figures wandering about the
fringes of society" (O'Connor 2011, 18). After all, the short story is a form
that "never had a hero" (Ibid., 17). This very affordance of the short story
form, often inserted within anthological frameworks, influenced one of
the properties of anthologies in media cultures and their close relationship
with certain genres that were telling the stories of people existing at the
margins of the society.

   By extension, contemporary anthologies in the new media industry
became generators of narrative canons as well as spaces for alternative
models of knowledge. In a revival of the anthology form in television, for
instance, US anthology dramas returned only to adhere to the original
affordances of short story collections. With their unrestricted range of
subjects, fragmentary nature, and brevity, they helped subvert the idea
of "least objectionable programming" (Thompson 1997, 39) in the context
of a broader "turn toward 'relevance'" (Gitlin 2000, 168). But how does this
relevance manifest itself in the short form in opposition to longer forms? One
notion worth considering to distinguish between short and vast narratives
and their impact on cultural practices is that of "narrative extent" (Wardrip-
Fruin and Harrigan 2009). Based on this concept, vast narrative forms
can be identified by their attribute of exceeding the traditional narrative

boundaries, whether a chapter or an episode. In contrast, the short story form is a narrative existing within textual and material limits. Short narratives contained in anthologies are often considered non-extended narratives, in that they include restraining mechanisms in the evolution of the storytelling and overall a tendency towards closure. However, simply reasoning in terms of the material or structural patterns of a narrative is not sufficient to account for a mediascape where narrative forms are fluid, adaptable, and ever-changing. Defining short forms in digital culture requires further analysis of their spatial and temporal extension.

Rather than focusing on arbitrary physical boundaries, it is more accurate to state that, by nature, short narratives tend to limit the options for the expansion of the narrative ecosystem. These constraints can have positive trade-offs, since they minimize the external pressure that might affect the lifespan of the narrative. For example, long stories serial products in linear television are always subject to external dynamics. Audience ratings, industrial and technological shifts, and commercial and financial decisions all contribute to storytelling choices. In a business model where production and distribution of content is dilated through time, confined in specific weekly slots and dominated by the seasonality of television, even individual decisions made by actors or screenwriters to abandon the series can affect the narrative architecture. The multiplication of digital platforms amplified the potential of a story to evolve into multiple strands and generate broader narrative universes where unlimited storylines can exist within them. If, in online media, vast narratives are particularly inclined to generate trans-media extensions and can therefore be easily affected by contextual forces, short narratives are safeguarded by their own self-imposed structural, temporal, and spatial limits. For this reason, even in situations of extreme platform openness, they are able to maintain a certain level of authorial control over the evolution of the story.

"Transmedia storytelling" (Jenkins 2006) and processes of narrative expansion at the convergence of different platforms and devices have led several scholars to think that "deep media" (Rose 2012) are strictly related to vast narratives. "This is 'deep media': stories that take you deeper than an hour-long TV drama or a two-hour movie or a 30-second spot will permit" (Ibid., 3). Yet, in recent years, we have seen short narratives arise in digital culture as forms that can be collected, expanded, or shortened to convey a modular sense of depth. Precisely through their way of repeatedly immersing the audience in small narrative bits, they have easily adapted across media. When it comes to algorithmic media, which are still in a process of making and experimentation, the distinction between vast narratives and short narratives is hard to pinpoint. At first glance, the computational possibilities brought by emerging media technologies show two distinct evolutions of vast versus short narratives. On the one hand, digital and algorithmic technologies offer new paths for expanding vast narratives through participatory practices and augmented experiences. On the other hand, they transformed short narratives by making them more susceptible to undergo processes of anthologization.

The linkage between short story forms and anthologies is useful for understanding cultural and technological influences of non-linear medias- capes on the creation of hybrid serial content. For example, the season-long anthology form in television not only inherited an anthological form, but it was also the outcome of parallel evolutions of other short-narrative forms in television, like miniseries, which were repurposed in digital environments. Miniseries represent some of the shortest narrative forms in television, so much so that they are sometimes considered "made-for-TV movies" broken down into several parts, as in the case of multiple-episode television films. Among others, in Italian television, films made for broadcast have, until recently, been used as a format that could be divided into separate episodes or installments in order to recount historical narratives, portray religious figures related to the Catholic tradition (e.g., *Gesù di Nazareth* [1977], a British–Italian co-produced movie written by Franco Zeffirelli, Anthony Burgess, and Suso Cecchi d'Amico, featuring an ensemble cast of actors like Laurence Olivier, Anne Bancroft, Anthony Quinn), or adapt famous operas and theater plays for the television screen, which were shot like movies instead of being recorded live (e.g., *Cavalleria rusticana* [RAI, 1982], directed by Franco Zeffirelli and starring Plácido Domingo). In Italy, like in other countries, short stories were used to educate the masses to a certain type of entertainment aimed at celebrating historical events, religious culture, literary and theater tradition. In parallel, the horror genre emerged as a subversive influence in commercial television programming, with short- story collections like the anthology miniseries *Brivido giallo* (1987–1989), directed by Lamberto Bava and including several made-for-TV-movies, or *Le case maledette* (1989), which was never broadcast due to its violent scenes, though it was released as a VHS anthology.

Whether in the form of anthologies or made-for-TV-movies, miniseries became a short form in their own right across many media markets. Even though it is still not clear within which limit this terminology is valid, we can say that, on average, miniseries develop in a range between two to fifteen episodes, and their production usually involves narrative arcs with a predetermined limit. Quoting the *Encyclopedia of Television*, "a miniseries is a narrative drama designed to be broadcasted in a limited number of episodes. If the distinction is maintained between 'series' (describing a group of self-contained episodes) and 'serial' (a group of interconnected episodes), the term 'miniseries' is an acknowledged misnomer, for the majority of broadcast material presented in the genre is in fact produced in serial form" (Newcomb 2014, 1499). Before the adoption of an anthology format for television miniseries, short narrative structures were already showing a tendency to intersect and hybridize in various forms of micro-storytelling (in literature) or micro-programming (in television). Micro-programming, in particular, became common in television markets all over the world because of its convenience, assuming manifold shapes and lengths. Italian television, for instance, had a lower budget for serial productions relative to the US market, and was rarely able to sustain long-running shows as the predominant offer of content. For this reason, television productions in Italy have often opted for a "weak or short seriality," spanning between two to six episodic installments (Buonanno 2002) and fitting in the miniseries category as the authentic national formula (Ibid.).

Nevertheless, the echoes of this form are found even in media industries that have traditionally shown a preference for long-running shows, such as that of Brazil, where so-called miniseries can consist of up to sixty chapters. In the 1980s, the Brazilian network Rede Globo, along with other television channels in Latin America, started inserting mini- and micro-series in its television offer alongside *teleteatro* (Carter 2018). In Japan and South Korea, the *dorama* created its own genre, where the story can run for twenty-five or more episodes, and yet still have a fixed length with a predefined ending (Clements and Tamamuro 2003). In the US, television miniseries appeared during the 1970s, when multi-episode stories based on literary adaptations (Wheen 1985) started to be produced in the wake of British "novel-to-television programs" with similar stylistic features (Edgerton 2009, 295). Even though they are now evolving into a more varied array of narratives, miniseries initially offered a type of content revolving around literary classics, historical settings, and bestseller novels. More recently, digital cable technologies and new forms of television based on subscription have adopted the miniseries form as a synonym of quality production and channel branding, reinventing it in a new format. In 2013, Alan Sepinwall announced "the rise of this era's other big new scripted format: the anthology miniseries" (Sepinwall 2013, 437), stressing the appeal for many creators of opting for a thirteen-episode series for cable or streaming instead of going for twenty-two episodes in commercial television (Ibid., 438). Under the umbrella term of "limited-run television series," miniseries have been officially listed in the rules and procedures for the Primetime Emmy Awards with reference to programs "with two or more episodes with a total running time of at least 150 program minutes that tells a complete, non-recurring story, and does not have an on-going storyline and/or main characters in subsequent seasons."[20]

Short and limited-story forms present specific affordances in collision with new media technologies. Given the context of non-linear media and streaming platforms, this flexible idea of standalone episodes or seasons that can easily be anthologized caught the attention of major players. While anthology miniseries were produced by cable channels before the Netflix business model became a trend in the US television industry, they are still symptoms of a moment of redefinition in the mediascape, where over-the-top platforms are presenting new plans of vertical integration, alternative strategies for television production, and innovative subscription-based models for non-linear distribution (Lotz 2017). Discussing short narratives in their interplay with anthologies in digital environments thus necessitates a closer observation of media and economic dynamics, other than narratological or cultural ones. The return of short- to medium-length forms of anthology in digital cultures as a mix of various narrative forms and genres – an interbreeding between the anthology form and miniseries – was made possible by a media, technological context that favored its return. With their limited form, straight-to-season anthology miniseries are able to reduce the financial risks of producing less controllable long-running shows, while still offering more programming time than the episodic format for the evolution of the narrative arc throughout the season.

This implies new creative processes, new consumption models, and a completely different risk/reward management, which relies on a variety of storytelling forms – old and new – that are asked to reinvent themselves in the context of the online platforms. The resilience of short forms of storytelling in contemporary non-linear media is such that it allows it to claim the status of anthology after being distributed, based on the success of the first season, without necessarily announcing an adherence to the anthology form from the very beginning of the show. In a platform economy (Kenney and Zysman 2016), the potentially unlimited opportunities for content

---

20   Michael Schneider. "Emmys: 'American Horror Story,' 'The Sinner,' 'American Vandal' are Out of the Running for Limited Series," *Variety*. Last modified April 9, 2019. https://variety.com/2019/tv/news/american-horror-story-the-sinner-american-vandal-emmys-limited-series-1203184952.

aggregation and a vertically bundled experience[21] make the amount of media content sometimes difficult to handle, both for producers and consumers. Shorter forms of programming have drawn the interest of platform services[22] as a possible solution to the problem. Limited-narrative forms contained in the anthology miniseries fit the idea of creating a collection of bite-size stories, easy to manage. Even outside of the anthology form, it is increasingly evident that much shorter seasons are being produced for television compared to older series comprising twenty-episode seasons. This might be the result of a digital value and supply chain that makes available large quantities of content, leveraging the anytime-anywhere logic, where viewers simply tend to prefer shorter forms in the vast shelves of digital libraries. The following chapters provide a general taxonomy that encompasses different occurrences of the anthology form in connection with limited forms. By outlining some of the main concepts mobilized by the anthology form, we will try to understand its transition into contemporary infrastructural, platform, and algorithmic systems.

List of works cited

Apprich, Clemens. 2017. *Technotopia: A Media Genealogy of Net Cultures*. Lanham, MD: Rowman & Littlefield.

Apprich, Clemens, and Götz Bachmann. 2019. "Media Genealogy: Back to the Present of Digital Cultures." In *Digitisation*, edited by Gertraud Koch, 293–306. New York: Routledge. https://doi.org/10.4324/9781315627731-16.

Bardolph, Jacqueline, Viola, André, and Jean-Pierre Durix. 2001. *Telling Stories: Postcolonial Short Fiction in English*. Amsterdam: Rodopi.

Barnouw, Erik. 1970. *The Image Empire: A History of Broadcasting in the United States, Volume III–From 1953*. Oxford: Oxford University Press.

Bhaskar, Michael. 2013. *The Content Machine: Towards a Theory of Publishing from the Printing Press to the Digital Network*. London: Anthem Press.

Bloom, Harold. 1994. *The Western Canon: The Books and School of the Ages*. San Diego, CA: Harcourt Brace.

---

21   Simone Cicero. "Market Networks, Innovation & Digital Value Chains," *Medium*. Last modified September 29, 2018. https://stories.platformdesigntoolkit.com/market-networks-innovation-digital-value-chains-60e676ca7d2.

22   Sahil Patel. "Why Netflix and Amazon are Experimenting with Short-Form Programming," *Digiday*. Last modified April 27, 2018. https://digiday.com/media/the-streaming-giants-are-experimenting-with-short-form-but-dont-call-it-a-gold-rush.

Caldwell, John Thornton. 1995. *Televisuality: Style, Crisis, and Authority in American Television*. New Brunswick, NJ: Rutgers University Press.

Cantril, Hadley, and Gordon Willard Allport. 1971. *The Psychology of Radio*. New York: Arno Press.

Carter, Eli Lee. 2018. *Reimagining Brazilian Television: Luiz Fernando Carvalho's Contemporary Vision*. Pittsburgh, PA: University of Pittsburgh Press.

Eco, Umberto. 1976. *A Theory of Semiotics*. Bloomington, IN: Indiana University Press.

Eco, Umberto. 1984. *The Role of the Reader: Explorations in the Semiotics of Texts*. Bloomington, IN: Indiana University Press.

Eco, Umberto. 1985. "Innovation and Repetition: Between Modern and Post-Modern Aesthetics." *Daedalus* 114 (4): 161–84.

Eco, Umberto. 1990. *The Limits of Interpretation*. Bloomington, IN: Indiana University Press.

Eco, Umberto. 2005. *On Literature*. Boston, MA: Houghton Mifflin Harcourt.

Edgerton, Gary Richard. 2007. *The Columbia History of American Television*. New York: Columbia University Press.

Gitelman, Lisa. 2008. *Always Already New: Media, History, and the Data of Culture*. Cambridge, MA: MIT Press.

Gitlin, Todd. 1979. "Prime Time Ideology: The Hegemonic Process in Television Entertainment." *Social Problems* 26 (3): 251–66. https://doi.org/10.2307/800451.

Gitlin, Todd. 1982. "Television's Screens: Hegemony in Transition." In *Cultural and Economic Reproduction in Education*. New York: Routledge.

Gitlin, Todd. 2000. *Inside Prime Time: With a New Introduction*. Berkeley, CA: University of California Press.

Hanson, Clare. 1989. *Re-Reading the Short Story*. London: Palgrave Macmillan.

Harrigan, Pat, and Noah Wardrip-Fruin. 2009. *Third Person: Authoring and Exploring Vast Narratives*. Cambridge, MA: MIT Press.

Hilmes, Michele. 2012. *Network Nations: A Transnational History of British and American Broadcasting*. New York: Routledge.

Hilmes, Michele. 2013. *Only Connect: A Cultural History of Broadcasting in the United States*. Boston, MA: Cengage Learning.

Hilmes, Michele, and Jason Jacobs. 2003. *The Television History Book*. London: British Film Institute.

Hilmes, Michele, and Jason Loviglio. 2002. *Radio Reader: Essays in the Cultural History of Radio*. London: Psychology Press.

Hindman, Douglas Blanks, and Kenneth Wiegand. 2008. "The Big Three's Prime-Time Decline: A Technological and Social Context." *Journal of Broadcasting & Electronic Media* 52 (1): 119–35. https://doi.org/10.1080/08838150701820924.

Hinds, Harold E., Ferris Motz, Marilyn, and Angela M.S. Nelson. 2006. *Popular Culture Theory and Methodology: A Basic Introduction*. Madison, WI: Popular Press.

Innis, Harold Adams. 1950. *Empire and Communications*. Oxford: Clarendon Press.

Iriye, A., and P. Saunier. 2009. *The Palgrave Dictionary of Transnational History: From the Mid-19th Century to the Present Day*. London: Palgrave Macmillan.

Jänicke, Stefan, Franzini, Greta, Cheema, Muhammad Faisal, and Gerik Scheuermann. 2015. "On Close and Distant Reading in Digital Humanities: A Survey and Future Challenges." https://doi.org/10.2312/eurovisstar.20151113.

Kenney, Martin, and John Zysman. 2016. "The Rise of the Platform Economy." *Issues in Science and Technology* (blog). March 29, 2016. https://issues.org/rise-platform-economy-big-data-work/.

Levine, Caroline. 2006. "Strategic Formalism: Toward a New Method in Cultural Studies." *Victorian Studies* 48 (4): 625–57.

Levine, Caroline. 2015a. *Forms: Whole, Rhythm, Hierarchy, Network*. Princeton, NJ: Princeton University Press.

Levine, Caroline. 2015b. "Forms, Literary and Social." *Dibur Literary Journal*, no. Form, ISSUE 2, Spring 2016, Dedicated to Benjamin Harshav (Vilnius, 1928–New Haven, 2015) (May). https://arcade.stanford.edu/dibur/forms-literary-and-social.

Lorusso, Anna Maria. 2015. *Cultural Semiotics: For a Cultural Perspective in Semiotics*. New York: Palgrave Macmillan.

Lotman, Jurij M. 1990. *Universe of the Mind: A Semiotic Theory of Culture*. Bloomington, IN: Indiana University Press.

Lotz, Amanda D. 2007. *The Television Will Be Revolutionized*. New York, NY: NYU Press.

Lotz, Amanda D. 2017. *Portals: A Treatise on Internet-Distributed Television*. Michigan Publishing.

Lotz, Amanda D.. 2018. *We Now Disrupt This Broadcast: How Cable Transformed Television and the Internet Revolutionized It All*. Cambridge, MA: MIT Press.

Loviglio, Jason, and Michele Hilmes. 2013. *Radio's New Wave: Global Sound in the Digital Era*. New York: Routledge.

Man, John. 2010. *The Gutenberg Revolution*. New York: Random House.

Mandler, J.M. 2014. *Stories, Scripts, and Scenes: Aspects of Schema Theory*. London: Psychology Press.

Manovich, Lev. 1999. "Database as Symbolic Form." *Convergence* 5 (2): 80–99. https://doi.org/10.1177/135485659900500206.

Manovich, Lev. 2001. *The Language of New Media*. Cambridge, MA: MIT Press.

Morris, Jeremy Wade. 2015. *Selling Digital Music, Formatting Culture*. Berkeley, CA: University of California Press.

O'Connor, Frank. 2011. *The Lonely Voice: A Study of the Short Story*. New York: Melville House.

Price, Kenneth M., and Ray Siemens, eds. 2013. *Literary Studies in the Digital Age: An Evolving Anthology*. New York: MLA Commons.

Rose, Frank. 2012. *The Art of Immersion: How the Digital Generation Is Remaking Hollywood, Madison Avenue, and the Way We Tell Stories*. New York: W.W. Norton & Company.

Rubery, Matthew. 2011. *Audiobooks, Literature, and Sound Studies*. New York: Routledge.

Rubery, Matthew. 2016. *The Untold Story of the Talking Book*. Cambridge, MA: Harvard University Press.

Ryan, Lindy. 2016. *The Visual Imperative: Creating a Visual Culture of Data Discovery*. Burlington, MA: Morgan Kaufmann.

Ryan, Marie-Laure. 2004. *Narrative Across Media: The Languages of Storytelling*. Lincoln, NE: University of Nebraska Press.

Sabin, Roger, Wilson, Ronald, and Linda Speidel. 2015. *Cop Shows: A Critical History of Police Dramas on Television*. Jefferson, NC: McFarland.

Sayers, Jentery. 2018. *The Routledge Companion to Media Studies and Digital Humanities*. New York: Routledge.

Sepinwall, Alan. 2013. *The Revolution Was Televised: How The Sopranos, Mad Men, Breaking Bad, Lost, and Other Groundbreaking Dramas Changed TV Forever*. New York: Simon and Schuster.

Serling, Rod. 1958. *Patterns: Four Television Plays*. New York: Bantam.

Seruya, Teresa, D'hulst, Lieven, Assis, Rosa, Alexandra, and Maria Lin Moniz. 2013. *Translation in Anthologies and Collections (19th and 20th Centuries)*. Amsterdam: John Benjamins Publishing Company.

Shiller, Robert J. 2017. "Narrative Economics." *American Economic Review* 107 (4): 967–1004. https://doi.org/10.1257/aer.107.4.967.

Slide, Anthony. 1991. *The Television Industry: A Historical Dictionary*. Westport, CT: Greenwood Press.

Simpson, John Andrew. 1989. *The Oxford English Dictionary*. Oxford: Clarendon Press.

Starkey, Guy. 2011. *Local Radio, Going Global*. New York: Springer.

Sterne, Jonathan. 1999. "Television under Construction: American Television and the Problem of Distribution, 1926–62." *Media, Culture & Society* 21 (4): 503–30. https://doi.org/10.1177/016344399021004004.

Turner, Graeme, and Jinna Tay. 2009. *Television Studies After TV: Understanding Television in the Post-Broadcast Era*. New York: Routledge.

Ulin, Jeff. 2012. *The Business of Media Distribution: Monetizing Film, TV and Video Content in an Online World*. New York: Routledge.

2. Design

Abstract

Drawing upon the historic-genealogical research presented in Chapter 1, this chapter takes a design-oriented approach to the definition of the anthology form. It starts by providing an overview of narrative theory, as applied to the study of culture through the notions of form and structure, content, and context. It then looks at the definitions of format, as one of the structural components affecting the distribution of media content, along with other concepts related to the field of media studies. The chapter moves forward to explore the notions of forms and affordances in the field of design, in order to observe generative processes of anthological content organization in mediated environments. Based on a formal framework for the study of digital culture, it finally proposes a taxonomy of the anthology form in its contemporary occurrences.

Keywords: Anthology; Design; Narratology; Forms and Affordances; Digital Culture

2.1. Narratives

Initially appearing in literary contexts, from its very origin the anthology form came to define a collection of separate, standalone narratives. The concept of narrative is therefore at the core of the anthology, which is primarily a form built on the assemblage of multiple stories. As instruments of knowledge transmission, at first glance anthologies and narratives can be said to operate on two levels: one that is predominantly super-textual and structural, and one that is most often intra- and inter-textual. Both rely on a process of narrative design that influences cultural identities, personal experiences, and a community's sense of belonging. Much like anthologies are greater than each narrative they contain, narratives are greater than the text. They are found beyond the realm of literary studies, in fields as varied as history, anthropology, sociology, and political science. Even economics, a discipline that marginally reasons in terms of storytelling dynamics

Taurino, Giulia. *The Anthology in Digital Culture*. Amsterdam: Amsterdam University Press, 2023.
DOI: 10.5117/9789463724265_CH02

as driving forces of quantitative fluctuations, is now opening up to this narrative turn. While considering the power of narratives in influencing economic behaviors, the economist Robert J. Shiller proposed the notion of "narrative economics" (Shiller 2017), insisting on the fact that narratives drive the world that we live in, sparking major economic events (Shiller 2019). The study of narratives requires academic toolkits. While humanists have access to narrative theory, scholars in other disciplines might not be accustomed to the qualitative evaluations offered by narratology frameworks. As Shiller argues, the database, itself modeled on the anthology form as an organized collection of records and structured information, might be just the right tool for economists to be able to study perennial economic narratives (Ibid.) that tend to repeat at different stages in history.

The present chapter is not intended to propose a narratological approach, rather it aims at placing narratives – and anthologies – in a broader cultural, social, economic, and political complexity, as they demonstrated being ubiquitous entities in individual and collective human life. We will notably discuss notions that have transitioned from narrative theory and cultural studies to design, and vice versa. The aim is to clarify what is meant by anthology as a narrative and cultural form, as well as to offer a contextual framework for the language and methodology contained in this book. Databases of the written word have been pivotal for this research. So, too, have been databases of sound and audiovisual records that helped us reconstruct the evolutionary changes of this cultural form through distant and close reading. Even though narratives have spread in all domains, and socio-cultural datasets are now essential resources in fields like digital humanities or computational sociology, the study of narratives is most commonly associated with narratology. Building on previous normative and formal paradigms, this discipline was the first to propose a programmatic theory, a method (Kindt and Müller 2003) for understanding storytelling and its occurrences in human societies under certain structural conditions and logical constructs. However, since the initial attempts to define a "science of narrative" (Todorov 1969), the very notion of narrative itself emerged as problematic.

In his seminal work on *Narrative Discourse*, the French scholar Gérard Genette (1983) addressed the issues of defining this term, considering not only its ambiguous and multifaceted meaning, but also its multiple functions and properties. He notably distinguished three possible definitions of the word "narrative." The first definition indicates the actual textual or verbal statement, the expression and *mise-en-discours* of the narrated events. The second meaning refers to the subjects of the discourse and their relations. Finally, a third meaning can be used to define the moment of narration, that is to say, the very act of telling, narrating a story. In his work, Genette focused mainly on the first case, where a narrative text can be read as a set of temporal, spatial, functional (logic, causal) links, similarly to Todorov's (1969) classification into different categories of correlation – namely, tense, aspect, mood. Such relationships can exist between narrative discourse and story, between narrative discourse and narrating act, or between narrating act and story. The second meaning appears as the most abstract and perhaps challenging one. We can picture narratives as *form*-less content, the fluid material that will eventually assume a shape by means of a narrative structure. "'Analysis of narrative' in this sense means the study of a totality of actions and situations taken in themselves, without regard to the medium, linguistic or other, through which knowledge of that totality comes to us" (Genette 1983, 25).

From a media studies perspective, the third meaning is to be intended when using the term narrative, i.e., a performative action that involves several entities and aspects outside of the text itself. In this regard, considering the design of narratives in their existence as part of actualized forms of storytelling can lead to a more insightful analysis of the anthology form and open up several possibilities for reflecting upon the interplay between text design and media context. To investigate the notion of narrative form, I will dedicate a few paragraphs to exploring some of the concepts that originally emerged in narrative theory – i.e., form, content, structure – and were later applied to media and design, with interesting research directions. Narratology moved its early steps from the idea of a form (Propp 2010 [1928]) or structure (Levi-Strauss 1955; Barthes 1975) on which stories are built. These notions respectively evolved into the currents of Russian formalism and French structuralism. When Vladimir Propp published his *Morphology of the Folktale* in 1928, he was proposing a grammar for the analysis of narratives, by borrowing a botanical term used for addressing the *structure* of a plant. As he stated in the foreword of his book, "the word 'morphology' means the study of forms. In botany, the term 'morphology' means the study of the component parts of a plant, of their relationship to each other and to the whole – in other words, the study of a plant's structure" (Propp 2010, xxv). Despite the early stage of his work on narrative forms, Propp was inaugurating a groundbreaking approach to story grammars, which would later be adopted in applications like quantitative narrative analysis, with the idea of coding narrative sequences, functions, categories, and other data from textual sources (Franzosi 2010).

This formalist approach was criticized by Claude Levi-Strauss, who supported a structuralist perspective in favor of less abstract models and formulas, as part of his theorization of a "structural anthropology" (Levi-Strauss 2008). As he wrote, "*form* is defined by opposition to content, an entity in its own right, but *structure* has no distinct content: it is content itself, and the logical organization in which it is arrested is conceived as property of the real" (Ibid., 168). The relation between these three key concepts – form, content, structure – lies at the foundation of several debates in narrative theory and clarifies the nature of anthological entities as *forms* that give a *structure* to a *content*. In short, on the one hand, Propp classifies two entities as part of each narrative: the form, which leads to a morphological study, and the content, which remains inconsistent and unintelligible without the former. On the other hand, Levi-Strauss stresses the difference between formalism and structuralism by pointing precisely at the fact that "this opposition does not exist; structuralism does not treat one as abstract and the other as concrete. Form and content are of the same nature, amenable to the same type of analysis. Content receives its reality from its structure, and what is called form is a way of organizing the local structures that make up this content" (Ibid., 179).

Following the structuralist movement, in 1969, Todorov initiated what he called "structural analysis of narrative," which was outlined in one of his essays as a theoretical framework having a "logical rather than spatial significance" (Todorov 1969, 70). His aim was "to propose a theory of the structure and operation of the literary discourse, to present a spectrum of literary possibilities, in such a manner that the existing works of literature appear as particular instances that have been realized" (Ibid., 71). Such a structuralist approach encountered several challenges over the years, ending up in the reformulation of scholarly research in the field of narratology in favor of post-structuralist theories. Post-structuralism recognizes the narrative text as intertwined with a process of signification that is placed within a social and cultural space, thus acknowledging the unescapable relationship between the text and its contextual meaning. In turn, this poses the premises for postclassical narratology, by welcoming methodological approaches that examine textual narratives as "context-sensitive" (Alber and Fludernik 2010, 22). Similarly, formalism encountered a new wave of renovation in neo-formalist theories. An interesting variation on the idea of form is proposed by Caroline Levine, who re-elaborated this concept by suggesting a broader definition based on design studies, to include cultural and social practices that surround the narrative text. Overall, it seems that, at the turn of the twenty-first century, the debate on the triad form/content/structure opened up to a common dialogue on the circumstantial and environmental factors that affect the production and circulation of textual records.

What most narratologists are now concerned with is the relationship between the internal components of the text and the external context. From a post-structural and neo-formalist perspective, anthologies can be defined as ways to *structure* narratives and deliver knowledge. In this knowledge-transfer process that they activate, they also produce meanings, stem conversations, and offer conceptual frameworks to interpret human societies, cultures, and institutions. In some cases, they are used to give visibility to individual cultural actors and generate narrative canons. In this sense, the anthology can be defined as a *form* that gives a *structure* to narrative *content* in relation to a *context* – be it cultural, social, industrial, or others. As a form made of multiple narrative accounts, the anthology connects the stories it contains to a broader exchange with other cultural forms of knowledge organization and classification systems. This post-modern, post-structuralist approach is essential to evaluate the epistemological dimension of anthological narratives, as reflective mechanisms triggered by experiences and triggering interpretations. Narrative itself is "a mode of knowledge [...]. Knowledge is articulated and communicated in society in the form of narratives" (McQuillan 2000, 323). Understanding narratives and anthologies as *forms* and "modes of knowledge" allows us to observe them not as mere self-existent structures, recalling an archaic narratological perspective, but as artificial constructs entangled with formal rules, cultural systems, as well as cognitive functions.

As a subfield of postclassical narratology that investigates the nexus between narratives, knowledge representation, and human mind, cognitive narratology adds an interesting take, especially in application to algorithmic-driven forms of anthologization and their ability to reproduce semiotic structures typical of the human mind. For instance, if we compare how humans and computing machines "cognitively" process stories into scripts and parse them into units or sequences, we can find similarities between the way algorithmic recommendation systems work and analog practices of editorial content organization, in that they both respond to an acquired cognitive capacity to curate a list of records. Bearing in mind cognitivist approaches in connection with a design perspective, in this section we will discuss the anthology form as a type of "mental structure, including categorical, matrix, serial, schematic, and story structure" (Mandler 2014 [1984]), which, in post-digital culture, becomes increasingly interwoven with AI-generated structures. In combination with algorithmic practices, the anthology as a narrative form has acquired a mnemonic value and actively "altered the practices and possibilities of collective remembering" (Linke 2015, 181). In the previous chapter, when addressing various types of anthology as culturally and technologically embedded narrative forms, we have shown how they often acted as structured manifestations of a "collective memory" (Halbwachs 1980) and shared human knowledge. We have observed them as cultural forms that provide solutions for the editorialization, organization, storage, and circulation of content. In the following paragraphs, we will distinguish between different notions associated with the analysis of narratives. Having outlined a few definition of terms like format, formula, and form, we will adopt a neo-formalist theoretical perspective that combines elements of cultural theory and design studies to ultimately propose an updated definition of anthology as a form that embraces certain sets of affordances. As we move forward throughout the chapter, we will approach the study of the anthology in algorithmic culture, by observing how this form connects the narratives it contains to a broader exchange with other cultural forms of content organization and classification systems.

2.2. Formats

In Chapter 1, we considered how the functions of a media object can influence its form, as much as its form and materiality can create constraints to its actualized uses and potential functions. Form is a compelling concept. It appeals to an interdisciplinary perspective and allows us to consider objects like anthologies as formal entities, with narratological, cultural, social, transhistorical, and economic implications. However, its level of abstraction forces us to integrate other concepts in the discussion on the anthology form in addition to previously mentioned terms like canon or genre. While formal design patterns entail a set of affordances, these can result in more or less functional, more or less programmatic, more or less arbitrary and abstract practices. Before going in-depth into a detailed taxonomy of the anthology form in digital and post-digital culture, we will therefore provide a definition for three key terms, which will serve us to better understand the relation between media content and its functionality: namely, format, formula and form. Firstly, issues related not only to formats, but also to narrative formulas and genres will be examined through the work of several scholars (Chalaby 2016; Ellis et al. 2016; Aveyard et al. 2016). In doing so, we will approach various subject areas: from cultural studies (Cawelti 1969) to sociology (Gitlin 1979); from narrative theory, with the concept of "form" proposed by Caroline Levine (2015), to media studies (Moran 1998; Moran and Malbon 2006) and transnational studies that observe global patterns of content distribution (Shahaf and Oren 2013). In the following paragraphs, we will look at each term more closely and explain how anthologies articulate into formats, formulas, and forms. With a cross-historical, cross-cultural, cross-media perspective, this operation will help us not only clarify the terminology generally adopted when addressing anthological occurrences, but also isolate a relevant taxonomy and set of concepts as part of a morphology of the anthology form.

Scholarly traditions do not always agree on a shared definition and use of the words form, format, and formula as applied to narratives and media. These terms change their meaning not only across disciplines, but also across different countries and linguistic areas. In this section, we will propose a common vocabulary that can be used as a reference point for further discussions and analysis found in this book. Much like in the realm of linguistics and semantics, the idea is to avoid localized definitions, which would risk generating a scattered conversation on different meanings of the same term. Rather, we will agree on a terminology that can sustain an effective communication exchange around labels assigned to the afore-mentioned concepts, while also admitting the presence of specificities in single markets leading to variations and exceptions. For instance, within a certain level of generalization, we can state that, across different media, the format traditionally acts with a double value: on the one hand, as a production and commercial unit to be sold and reproduced in various venues; on the other hand, as a model on which the narration is developed. In the shaping of media formats, economic norms merge with the languages and codes of storytelling, thus generating semiotic universes that interact with surrounding cultural systems and social contexts. Moran (1998), one of the first scholars who considered the notion of format as a subject of study, traces the origin of the terms back to the printing industry and identifies dictionary synonyms like pattern, model, and shape. While in the domain of publishing, formats are mostly associated with visual qualities, occasionally assimilated with processes of anthologization, in television studies, formats carry "a particular industrial set of implications" (Ibid., 13), as they can be "generative" or "organisational" (Ibid.).

Using an effective metaphor borrowed from a television producer, Moran describes the television format as a pie-and-crust model, in which the outer layer always remains the same, while the filling changes and regenerates from week to week (Moran 1998, 13). For these reasons, the anthology is often described in the public discourse as a format, with reference to the way it acts as a "crust" or container for the production of narrative content. In his attempt to summarize a comprehensive research on the concept and practice of format, Moran introduces the idea of variable versus invariable elements in a program, which closely relates to the anthology, since it follows patterns of divergence and convergence in its main structure. He notably defined format as "a set of invariable elements in a serial program out of which the variable elements of individual episodes are produced" (Ibid.). Yet, while all anthology series might fit a meaning of the term inherited from the printing industry or a very vague formulation of television format, they certainly do not fit Moran's latest definition.

More recently, together with Malbon, he defines format as "the total body of knowledge systematically and consciously assembled to facilitate the future adaptation under license of the program" (Moran and Malbon 2006: 7), rather than it being a single fixed, recurrent, reproducible element within a serial product. This additional pragmatic dimension of licensing refers to the adaptation and reuse of televisual material, which can include cases of revived anthology series. This also explains why the anthological structure is sometimes considered as a format ready to be marketed and commercialized, as reflected by the widespread terminology of "anthology format". Just like anthology shows, television formats date as far back as the birth of television as a medium. However, while some anthological occurrences in television can be said to respond to format logics, not all anthology series are formats. It is therefore necessary to clarify this distinction by outlining a brief history of format research and giving a more precise outline of what formatted anthology series look like. Format is, in fact, a construct of the media industry, and only later did it become a concept used in scholarships for the analysis of audiovisual content and its production or distribution strategies.

Two histories of format thus exist, one that deals with the actual practice of television formatting and the other that considers theoretical evolutions in format studies. An additional definition of format in the television industry is given by Chalaby (2016, 8–13), who emphasizes the presence of four dimensions implied in this notion: (1) a legal dimension, which includes matters of copyright; (2) a cultural dimension, built in the adaptive interaction between the local and the global; (3) an economic and financial dimension, relating to capital budgeting, investment appraisal, and related risks; and (4) a productive dimension, concerned with industrial norms. While tracing his history of television formats, Chalaby suggests that the format business, meaning the production, trade, and adaptation of reproducible television programs, came to life as an Anglo-American invention (Chalaby 2012). As one of his articles points out, the format trade in the broadcasting industry started even before television, during the early days of radio, when cross-border adaptations were produced under licensing agreements between several anglophone countries, including the US, the UK, Australia, and Canada (Ibid., 37–38). As previous research on the historical and legal foundations of the concept make clear, from the outset, the word "format" meant at least three things: border-crossing; commercial agreements; and monetary exchange (Chalaby 2012, 2016). These elements were summed up in a script, a packaged document containing the core idea for the program, along with directions for the production process and other contextual requirements, according to copyright standards and intellectual property.

Elsewhere, licensed content with an enclosed script was much rarer, resulting in a diffused practice of pirating or simply non-trackable borrowing and an overall lack of copyright protection (Chalaby 2016). With new players entering the market thanks to the arrival of cable television in the 1980s, formatted content assumed a strategic value in both local industries and the global value chain. By offering the option to replicate foreign content in local programming schedule, or vice versa, formats minimized the financial risks of producing new programs and, at the same time, served as "proofs of concept" (Chalaby 2011, 305). "The entire premise of the TV format trade hinges on two benefits: cost effectiveness and risk management" (Chalaby 2016, 170). This premise stands at the origins of the contemporary format industry system, where formats in both factual and fictional entertainment secure the programming schedule of most linear television channels worldwide. Throughout its evolutions in different eras, geographical areas, and markets, the term format in the television industry ultimately came to refer to "a show that can generate a distinctive narrative and is licensed outside its country of origin in order to be adapted to local audiences" (Chalaby 2011, 296). While exporting a format requires drafting a legal agreement or contract, it also means adapting the content to a different cultural environment. Even though the practice of formatting involves a process of localization and adaptation, some elements must remain stable for a product to obtain the status of format. The ensemble of characteristics that make television formats, via dynamics of acquisition, adaptation, and transfer, determine the impossibility of fitting all television anthologies under the umbrella term of anthology format.

While formats acquire their status in the process of replication beyond national or local boundaries, under certain legal, economic, and productive circumstances, an anthology is an anthology even when there is no transnational movement involved. In the consolidated and widespread fashion of transnational television formatting, global anthology formats came into existence only recently as a marginal tendency within the larger trend to reproduce scripted television series outside national borders. Few anthology series actually joined the global format trade as a commercial product. Scripted TV formats had a late rise in the global market (Chalaby 2016, 168). The format revolution of the 1990s did not really take into account scripted fictional entertainment (Ibid.). Nevertheless, from the 2000s on, some scripted anthologies began joining the global format trade and anthology formats are now acquired by both anglophone and non-anglophone markets. One example is the Argentinian procedural series *Mujeres Asesinas* (Canal 13, 2005–2008), which was exported to the US market with the title of *Killer Women* (ABC, 2014). The series can be described as an episodic anthology, or semi-anthology, with each episode containing a different story on a different character. While it was canceled in the US after only one season, it had a higher success in Mexico, where the format was acquired by Canal 5 and aired for four seasons as of 2019.

Serial narratives such as police procedurals, where the long-running plot is not predominant, are interesting examples of an anthology structure that can be easily replicated into a format. A procedural format that was exported with relative success is the Danish series *Forbrydelsen* (DR1, 2007–2012), which was sold to Fox Television Studios and Fuse Entertainment in 2011. The US version was distributed with the title *The Killing* (AMC, 2011–2013; Netflix, 2014), by moving the setting from Copenhagen to Seattle. Restyled for a US audience, this format brought the European genre of Nordic noir to North American television. The same legacy continued with the acquisition of the Danish–Swedish coproduction *Bron/Broen* (SVT1/DR1, 2011–2018) by Shine America and FX, resulting in the show *The Bridge* (FX, 2013–). With its international setting, which places the series at the border between two countries (Denmark and Sweden in the original series, the US and Mexico in the North American adaptation), *Bron/Broen* is an interesting experiment in the cross-cultural adaptation of a scripted format. It was later remade in the UK and France, taking the name of *The Tunnel* (Sky Atlantic/Canal Plus, 2013), in Estonia and Russia (*Most/Sild*, [NTV, 2018–]), in Malaysia and Singapore (*The Bridge* [HBO Asia/NTV7/viu, 2018–]), and in Germany and Austria (*Der Pass* [Sky Deutschland, 2019–]). While *Forbrydelsen* and *Bron/Broen* are not anthology forms in the strict sense of the term, they can still be considered as semi-anthological formats. In both of these examples, each seasonal or bi-seasonal narrative arc deals with a separate case. In this sense, a product like the crime series *Law & Order* also generated formatted adaptations of an anthology-like product, with adaptations in Russia (NTV, 2007–2011), France (TF1, 2007–2008), UK (ITV, 2009– 2014) and South Africa (2012).

The fact that we need to include these hybrid examples – halfway between long-running shows and the anthology model – is representative of the scarcity of more traditional anthology series that actually went to formatting. Scripted television formats that can be labeled as anthology series are: *The Syndicate* (BBC 1, 2012–), a British show that was turned into the US remake *Lucky 7* (ABC, 2013); the Australian drama *Secrets and Lies* (Network Ten, 2014–) adapted for ABC (2015–2016); *Accused* (BBC, 2010–2012), which was ordered for adaptation as a co-production between Fox Entertainment, Sony Picture Television, and All3Media America and premiered in 2023. Another anthology product acquired by the US market is *Black Mirror* (Channel 4, 2011–2014; Netflix, 2016–). Whether *Black Mirror* was licensed and sold as a format is not clear. The series was released in the UK television market as a production by Endemol Shine for Channel 4. As reported by *The Guardian*, a dispute between the series' creators, Charlie Brooker and Annabel Jones, and Channel 4, during the negotiations for commissioning the third season, led to Channel 4 losing the right to screen the sci-fi series. Netflix then acquired the screening rights, and *Black Mirror* became part of the platform's library as a Netflix Original in 2016.[1] This transatlantic displacement and "trans-televisual move" (Hills et al. 2019, 235) reflect some features typical of the format trade: border-crossing; licensing agreement; monetary exchange; and adaptation for a different market. In this process, *Black Mirror* was repositioned for a broader audience, undergoing a format-like restyling in both financial and cultural terms.

Overall, what emerges from these examples is that anthology series rarely adhere to formatting practices. This might be due to the higher risks involved in reproducing scripted television formats in general, as opposed to more diffused practices of unscripted formatting (Chalaby 2016, 170). Even when we are able to identify scripted anthology format, there is often some peculiarity involved, which makes most cases an exception. An overview of practices of formatting as applied to anthologies in Western media markets demonstrates that, beyond specific commercial agreements, the anthology format has not generated any visible trend to date. Even the word format, as a concept borrowed from literary studies, with its materialistic connotation of an analog device or physical support, does not completely apply to an idea

---

1   John Plunkett. "Netflix Deals Channel 4 Knockout Blow over Charlie Brooker's Black Mirror." *The Guardian*. Last modified March 29, 2016. https://www.theguardian.com/media/2016/mar/29/netflixchannel-4-charlie-brooker-black-mirror.

of anthology that is transferable to digital culture. Perhaps more pragmatic uses of the term format can be adopted to define the practice of re-formatting in relation to anthology series, as the technological/computational operation to make an existing textual or audiovisual record machine-readable and transferrable into a platform environment. Still, using the concept of format or formatting to describe the nature of all anthology series might be misleading. In order to avoid confusion, we have to consider other, more relevant terms, with less of a focus on questions of copyright or the mechanical, electronic, and computational configurations of media supports. While formats can still be considered as places of cultural negotiation, or, to use Heidi Keinonen's words, as circuits of both "economic and cultural exchange" (Keinonen 2017, 996), it is necessary to explore more in-depth concepts like formula and form, which will allow us to look at practices of anthologization as frameworks for content organization.

2.3. Formulas

A term that should be considered when discussing the design and morphology of the anthology form is that of formula. In ancient Greek studies, this term has been used to define the linguistic repetition found in Homeric poems of "a group of words which is regularly employed under the same metrical conditions to express a given idea" (Parry 1930, 84). In modern media, the concept of formula broadly refers to a process of absorption of cultural practices or norms that can be associated with the formation of a genre precisely through processes of formulaic repetition. Formulas and genres commonly share the presence of a series of tropes, patterns, and cues that recur across similar texts in the history of storytelling. The notion of formula was introduced in the study of popular literature by John G. Cawelti. In defining this term, Cawelti explains that word formula refers to:

> a conventional system for structuring cultural products. It can be distinguished from form which is an invented system of organization. Like the distinction between convention and invention, the distinction between formula and form can be best envisaged as a continuum between two poles; one pole is that of a completely conventional structure of conventions – an episode of the Lone Ranger or one of the Tarzan books comes close to this pole; the other end of the continuum is a completely original structure which orders inventions.
>
> (Cawelti, in Hinds et al. 2006, 187)

On the one hand, Cawelti's definition of formula offers a parameter for assessing the extent to which a narrative product was intentionally designed as anthological by means of formulaic storytelling structures. On the other hand, the term formula gives origin to concepts like "deformulation" (Lifschutz 2015, 36) or reformulation, meaning the ability of a series to detach from the initial formula only to recompose its formula anew, which makes this terminology suitable for studying more recent processes of anthologization.

This idea of a concrete "conventional structure," as opposed to the more abstract ordering instance of a form, moves away from the strictly commercial or legal value of format. In a way, it is adjacent to the notion of genre. Cawelti clarifies the relation between the formula and genre, by specifying that these two terms, rather than denoting two completely different things, reflect instead "two phases or aspects of a complex process of literary analysis. This way of looking at the relation between formula and genre reflects the way in which popular genres develop. In most cases, a formulaic pattern will be in existence for a considerable period of time before it is conceived of by its creators and audience as a genre" (Cawelti 1976, 24). In other words, once the formula is born as a cultural product, it can evolve into a genre. For example, adhering to the anthology form, a series like *True Detective* originated its own seasonal formula, starting from the first season, through a set of recurring stylistic strategies and repetitions. It created a convention, which, in turn, replicates the features of true crime, a distinctly American genre that builds upon a long tradition of true crime detective magazines initiated in the 1920s at the time of the Prohibition and Great Depression. In general, crime stories are traditionally very formulaic. "The formula of the classical detective story can be described as a conventional way of defining and developing a particular kind of situation or situations, a pattern of action or development of this situation, a certain group of characters and the relations between them, and a setting or type of setting appropriate to the characters and action" (Cawelti 1976, 80) It is perhaps not coincidence that the anthology form developed in close connection with this and other highly formulaic genres (like horror), which can be easily reproduced into a homogeneous collection of episodes or seasons.

This archetypal function of literary formulas with regard to genres led some scholars to rethink the concept of formula as representative of a standardization process, rather than a purely formal patterning process. For instance, focusing on television, Gitlin associates the word formula with the tendency to standardize television programs that dominated the media landscape until the 1980s. As he puts it, with reference to one of the most famous US legal dramas of the late 1950s and 1960s, "Perry Mason was Perry Mason once and for all; watching the reruns only devotes could know from character or set whether they were watching the first or the last in the series. For commercial and production reasons which are in practice inseparable [...] the regular schedule prefers the repeatable formula" (Gitlin 1982, 245). In some cases, Gitlin uses the terms formula and format almost interchangeably, defining the docudrama as a format rather than a formula. This confusion is present even in more recent contexts. Media outlets commonly adopt the term "format" to define formula-like features, when referring to "a collection of (or the sum of) the key elements and characteristics that make up the concept of a programme, giving it a unique look and feel and its broadcasting identity. It is the style, plan or arrangement of a particular show" (Gough 2002, 26). Another blurred definition of formula as "genre formula," closer to the market-oriented definition of format, is found in Bennett et al., who explain: "Genre formulas provide a recipe for proven success which producers hope will guarantee future popularity in the market place" (Bennett et al. 2005, 44—45).

To avoid further confusion, we propose to adopt the definition suggested by Esquenazi (2014), who uses the term formula as a meta-description for designating, "not the script, but the machine that generates scripts, not the group of characters but the stock of models of characters, not the *mise-en-scène* but the definition of a framework for the *mise-en-scène*" (Ibid., 91, my translation). This notion accurately describes the entanglement between formula and genre and pairs with Cawelti's previous definitions. To this point, it is important to stress that the concept of formula differs, both theoretically and methodologically, not only from recent definitions of format and form, but also from older theorizations of genre and myth. If, on the one hand, formula refers to problems of cultural specificity, genre is perceived as being more of a universal pattern emerging across cultures (Cawelti 1969, 188), similar to the myth (Frye 1957). Going beyond the conceptual triad of format/formula/form, the notion of genre is to be observed as a social construct and mode of categorization that appears in literature and is later adopted for content classification in digital distribution. Over the twentieth century, the relevance of this term has been questioned and reframed by several scholars. For instance, in an article published in 1976, Todorov expressed doubts about the use of an anachronistic term like genre for discussing contemporary literature.

Only a few years after Todorov's article, the British philosopher Steve Neale tried to redefine this concept by applying it to the cinematographic industry. In his book *Genre*, he writes:

Genres institutionalise, guarantee coherence by institutionalising conventions, i.e. Sets of expectations with respect to narrative process and
narrative closure which may be subject of variation, but which are never
exceeded or broken. The existence of genres means that the spectator,
precisely, will always know that everything will be 'made right in the
end', that everything will cohere, that any threat or any danger in the
narrative process itself will always be contained.

(Neale 1980, 28)

This definition is correct if we think of cinema productions that are inscribed
within a predefined commercial scheme and that obey well-established
narrative norms. It might also be applied to early US. television, when the
television industry was governed by an oligopolistic structure, but it does not
quite fit the current scenario where genres tend to diversify. Nevertheless,
Neale underlines a valid concept that can be retained in a study of how
genres influenced some evolutionary aspects of narrative forms until today.
He notably proposes to observe genres not as systems per se, but rather as
"processes of systematization" (Ibid., 51), thus grouping formula and genre
in a similar type of media intervention. Reasoning on this idea of genre as a
process, David Buckingham additionally noted, with reference to television
programs, that genre is not simply "given by the culture: rather, it is in a
constant process of negotiation and change" (Buckingham 1993, 137).

In the constant process of systematization, negotiation, and change that
makes genres transhistorical and transcultural, recurring genres across
media mutated with a diversity of outcomes. To give an example, early US
television produced very formulaic programs, subjected to rigid production
norms and fitting into precise genres under the influence of the Hollywood
studio system. These programs adhered to conventions and aimed to meet
the expectations of the audience. Furthermore, other than being a formal and
formulaic frame for grouping narratives into categories based on semantic
and syntactic elements, as the scholar Rick Altman (1999: 162) put it, genres
act as labels that influence not only the production of media content, but
also its reception. Perhaps, "genres do not exist until they become necessary
to a lateral communication process, that is until they serve a constellated
community" (Ibid.). Modes of consumption, along with modes of production
and distribution, are, indeed, fundamental in the genesis of media content
and its typologies, be they genres, formats, formulas, or forms. In this mutual
exchange between production and reception, genres and formats or genres
and forms do sometime overlap. As Moran and Malbon point out, "the
distinction between a genre (which cannot gain copyright) and an original

work (which has copyright) is fairly obvious at the extreme ends of the scale, but becomes increasingly uncertain and blurred as we move towards the centre point of these extremes" (Moran and Malbon 2006, 113). And when it comes to a differentiation between format and genre, they simply conclude, "[s]omewhere between writing what might generically be called a boy meets girl [a girl meets girl] comedy and the script for Punch-Drunk Love lays the grey area of copyright" (Ibid.).

Over the years, narrative contaminations that challenged audience expectations became increasingly common across media, making the boundaries between genres more and more permeable (Abercrombie 1996: 45), in favor of a fluid transition between different formulas, modes of storytelling and narrative categories. This position was notably taken by Nicholas Abercrombie, who suggested that the fact that a medium like "television comes at the audience as a flow of programmes, all with different generic conventions, means that it is more difficult to sustain the purity of the genre in the *viewing* experience" (Ibid., his emphasis). Nowadays, in the context of an increasing hybridization of genres, where the separation between different radio or television genres is no longer so rigid, this concern seems to find solid ground. In fact, contemporary media, while retaining certain formulas, challenged the concept of genre in many ways, by opening up to cross-genre but also cross-cultural contaminations. The specificities of a television show might, in some cases, emerge precisely from the way it adopts or disregards the norms of a given genre. In 2001, Jason Mittell proposed to study television genres as both structured and fluid cultural schemata, standing between textual specificities and mechanisms of hybridization. In his theoretical perspective, television genres emerge as cultural categories in their full complexity, thus requiring an observation based on "interrelated sites of audience, industrial and cultural practices" (Mittell 2001, 18). This also suggests that genres are ultimately part of larger cultural systems, where hierarchies of power and networks of relations interfere with the affordances of the medium.

While not trying to define a systematic television-specific genre theory, I argue that it is still possible to use an observation of television genres as a method for tracking resemblances between televisual products, as they adhere to a recurring set of cultural practices. A cultural approach to television genres (Ibid.) also supports a classification where additional taxonomies can be traced at the intersection of formulas, forms, and cultural practices (i.e., horror anthologies). Over the years and throughout several transformations, genres endured and proved to be still relevant in the study of both early and contemporary television.

For instance, a genre-oriented indexing, along with other categorizations, is what turned the Netflix platform into a recommendation system.[2] Over thirty-thousand sub-genres can be unlocked on Netflix by simply typing the relative number or code assigned.[3] In their interaction with industrial dynamics of production, distribution, and reception, these notions – format, formula, and genre – allow the examination of television series both in commercial terms, as reproducible models in the media marketplace on a local or global scale, and in terms of an economy of narrative, by imposing normative, temporal, or stylistic limits to the development of storytelling.

According to the market's demand, which must be considered when it comes to production choices, cultural norms influence the creation of a first *schema* to build the narration – the scheme being a format, a formula, or a genre. These terms are useful for understanding the importance of repetitions, regularities, reoccurrences in the history of the anthology form, as well as for describing processes of absorption of cultural practices and norms. Such concepts are therefore equally indispensable for establishing the path of analysis, since they contribute to defining anthologies in their conceptual, industrial, and cultural complexity. Yet they lack a more structural, design-oriented meaning, which we find in the notion of form. If, on the one hand, format can be summed up in the primarily practical act of licensing and regulating the trade of media content, the notion of form, on the other hand, stands on the opposite side. A form is first and foremost an abstract model of systemic self-organization and patterning relying on programmatic choices. While the concept of format frequently leads to a market analysis, the concept of form embraces a techno-cultural analytical perspective on media industries. In between lie the definitions of narrative formula and genre, which account for a middle ground where both industrial and cultural dynamics intervene.

2.4. Forms and Affordances

"There are countless forms of narrative in the world" (Barthes 1975, 237). With this phrase, the French semiotician Roland Barthes introduces a

---

2   "How Netflix's Recommendations System Works." *Netflix Help Center.* https://help.netflix.com/en/node/100639.

3   "List of Netflix Categories." *What's on Netflix.* Last modified January 24, 2018. https://www.whats-on-netflix.com/library/categories.

structural analysis of narrative, proving that, even though structuralism detaches itself from formalism, it still conveniently employs the term "form" interchangeably with the term "structure." Found in both formalist and structuralist theories, the concept of narrative form tackles several aspects related to narratives as texts – where "texts" is intended in its comprehensive sense. Starting with an extremely simple definition, a narrative form can be intended as the shape and length of a narrative text. In her theoretical overview on narrative forms, Suzanne Keen enriches this definition by arguing that "the historical, material, and cultural conditions surrounding the production of a narrative often have a profound effect on its presentation: the form in which it comes to a reader" (Keen 2015, 21). Similarly, "this form in turn may have an impact on its immediate success in the marketplace, on its chances for surviving its immediate moment or short-term 'shelflife,' and the statistically unlikely event that it will be studied [...]" (Ibid.). As simple as it seems, the idea of form as shape or length has an important place in anthropological research. Short and long forms convey different narratives in different cultures. Short stories like ballads or brief tales often have a different function from novels or epic works. From classical epic to contemporary television series, each narrative may contain shorter "formal arrangements" (Ibid., 22), be they chapters, episodes, sequences, or verses. These sections give rhythm, create a pause or an interval, guiding the readers/viewers and their interpretation.

A similar account of narrative form as something that is dependent on – and, at the same time, actively influences – historical, material, and cultural conditions can be found in several theories loosely based on early formalism. For instance, among the offsprings of early formalism, New Historicism, originating from the works of Michel Foucault, Clifford Geertz, and Raymond Williams and theorized by the scholars Stephen Greenblatt and Catherine Gallagher, offered an interesting take on the notion of form. A reflection on the nexus between history, literary forms, and social formations had already been initiated by Marxists like Georg Lukacs, Pierre Macherey, and Fredric Jameson, who "have been inclined to understand literary forms as expressions of social and economic realities" (Levine 2006, 625). More specifically, "literary forms, read in their rich complexity as struggles among conflicting sign systems, [...] bear witness to a dialectical social agon, offering us our best access to both existent and emergent systems of social relations. Foucauldian and New Historicist critics, too, have argued that literary forms do not merely reflect social relationships but may help bring them into being" (Ibid.). Returning to narrative theory, but also incorporating design, cultural studies, and media theory, the versatile notion of form moves the focus beyond strictly legal, economic, and productive dimensions, outside of the process of negotiation between two commercial entities (production-distribution companies and those who buy the finished cultural product). A form is detached from rigid dynamics of institutional bargaining typical of the format. Instead, it takes shape in non-institutionalized practices built upon traditional uses, materiality, design functionality, and "textual co-operation" (Eco 1984).

To account for this cultural, design-oriented, narratological aspect, I will adopt the more comprehensive notion of "form" as theorized by Caroline Levine in her book *Forms: Whole, Rhythm, Hierarchy, Network*. Together with Levine, I use the term form to define "an arrangement of elements – an ordering, patterning, or shaping" (Levine 2015, 3). Such a polyhedric notion does not simply refer to processes of *form*-ation, but it embraces within itself four distinct, overlapping elements. The first three are addressed using the following terms: (1) "whole," as the totality of a form; (2) "rhythm," as its temporality; (3) "hierarchy," as an ordering, a gradation between forms. The fourth term introduced by Levine to discuss the notion of form is "network" (Levine 2015). As she notes: "Sprawling and spreading, networks might seem precisely formless. But studies of networks in mathematics, physics, and sociology have shown how networks follow knowable patterns, surprisingly systematic ordering principles" (Levine 2016, 78). Drawing upon Marxist and New Historicist theories, along with a formalist vision, Levine thus introduces a new framework for the study of narrative forms, that of "strategic formalism," or "post-post-structuralist formalism," as she defines it.[4] As she explains, on the one hand, this paradigm "relies on historicist work in the field to understand the ways that literary forms have force in the social world and are capable of shaping political arrangements. On the other hand, it extends formalist insights to make the case that social hierarchies and institutions can themselves be understood as forms" (Ibid., 626).

This is a fundamental premise for understanding Levine's later work, which inserts itself within a neo-formalist movement, to ultimately propose a new approach for analyzing not only the cultural value of narrative forms, but also their interplay with social formations. In her vision, forms can be literary, social, political, transhistorical, and even economic. By adopting

4   "Deliberately echoing Gayatri Chakravorty Spivak, here, I am proposing something of a post-post-structuralist formalism. It is deconstructive in that it acknowledges the political perils of abstractions, of binaries, of apparently transhistorical forms, while also presuming that we cannot do without them. [...] The point is not to do away with simplifying, iterable forms, then, but to follow them as they cross paths with other forms" (Levine 2006, 632-633).

a similar approach, I acknowledge that forms are always cultural and that the overlapping of forms generates an intricate structure, where complex systemic processes of ordering and patterning are not so easy to discern. At this level of abstraction, a formalist vocabulary, is needed to investigate temporal and spatial, but also relational mechanisms in human cultures ad societies. "If cultural studies has taught us to see power relations as systemic and patterned – as formalized – then it is time to think about culture in terms of its forms" (Ibid., 631). And if forms are "ways of imposing order, of shaping and structuring experience" (Ibid., 635), then cultures should be read "as dense networks of different kinds of interacting forms" (Ibid.). Perhaps one of the most important points in Levine's strategic formalism is her attention not only for what forms are, but also for what forms *do*. A practical evaluation of the notion of forms leads us to observe their functions, utterances or, as she refers to them, *affordances*. Drawing analogies with the affordances of specific materials – diamond, wood, glass – Levine borrows "the term 'affordance' from design studies. The affordances of materials are the kinds of uses or actions that are latent in them – their capabilities. [...] Specific designs, which organize these materials and others, then lay claim to their own range of affordances" (Ibid., 76).

Much like "a wooden chair affords sitting, as well as sociability when placed around a dinner table" (Ibid.), the anthology form *affords* specific uses, or else offers the possibility to actualize certain *affordances*. With respect to this matter, Jonathan Kramnick and Anahid Nersessian also ask what do forms *explain*, arguing that one of the weaknesses of this concept might be precisely that it explains everything. Seemingly ubiquitous, the concept of form has indeed been "applied to circumstances widely disparate in scale, character, and significance" (Kramnick and Nersessian 2017, 650). Pairing the concept of form with that of affordances can help clarify the relevance of neo-formalism, which recalls David Bordwell and Noël Carroll's definition of post-theory (1996). Through this framework, Bordwell and Carroll challenged film scholars to embrace a cognitive stance, instead of adopting a universal, unified theory, and to consider the factitive action of audiovisual media on audiences, which ultimately leads to a variety of practices. Still, the concept of affordance doesn't resolve the issue with a notion as broad as that of form. Marjorie Levinson (2007) expressed her skepticism for the lack of a shared commitment and agreement on what form actually is. In this debate, Kramnick and Nersessian conclude that the fact "that form appears sometimes as shape, sometimes as pattern, sometimes as habit, line, structure, model, design, trope, and so on suggests not that formalism is incoherent but that form [...] is not a word without content but a notion bound pragmatically to its instances" (Kramnick and Nersessian 2017, 661). By instances they mean versions of forms. This is how Levine came to a categorization of the concept in her book on forms (Levine 2015).

Through a series of instances, not only does Levine tell us what forms are, but she also tells us what they are *not*: ruptures; gaps; interruptions; subversions; collapsing binaries; impulses of force, affect, and desire (Ibid., 77). By clarifying what they are and what they are not, but also what they do, she finally recognizes four typologies of forms that emerge across several disciplines: whole; rhythm; hierarchy; and network. When Levine outlines these four major forms, she does not refer specifically to the anthology. And yet, these elements prove to be particularly pertinent for the analysis of contemporary anthologies. The first concept she describes is that of whole. Whole is a containing, totalizing, organic form (Ibid., 24), a model traditionally used in literary studies for defining narrative closure and formal unity. However, when she talks about "whole" as a unifying force focusing on its role of container, she does not imply an overall, absolute homogeneity. Nor does she advocate for narrative closure, as even enclosed forms can be portals to other forms, thus never really achieving full closure. What she focuses her attention on is rather the problem of wholeness as bounded, restricted space, meaning a space with boundaries and enclosures, be they spatial, temporal, narrative, or of another nature. Whole, she explains, affords both inclusiveness and exclusion. In this dialectic closure/enclosure lies the meaning of this form and its inner relevance. As Levine puts it: "This analysis will push us beyond the model of literary form as containment, and invite us to reconsider the relation between literary forms and social containers as something other than reflective homologies" (Ibid., 40).

Taking the anthology form as a case study, the anthology principle indeed functions as a whole. The very act of anthologization creates a formal unity, through both constraining and enabling processes. On the one hand, it constrains, in the sense that it imposes boundaries and a containing mechanism: the anthology always implies a principle of organization that tells us what can go inside and what cannot (inclusion/exclusion). On the other hand, the anthology form enables variations, be they esthetic, stylistic, thematic, narrative variations (e.g., different characters or plot) . The power of variations is such that it entails a friction between unities and disunities, and, ultimately, between different, interacting forms. This opposition between unity and multiplicity is intrinsic to the idea of a whole, which exists in the binomial relation homogeneity/dishomogeneity. Or, as the philosophers Gilles Deleuze and Félix Guattari put it: "You will never find a homogeneous system that is not still or already affected by a regulated, continuous, immanent process of variation" (Deleuze and Guattari 1987, 103). Agreeing with them, Levine adds that "[h]omogeneity always depends on variation; but there is no variation without the shaping power of homogeneity" (Levine 2006, 653). In the analysis of the anthology form and its clash with other forms, I will therefore account for the interactions that it creates as a structuring and ordering whole.

Another scholar who approached these formal entities defined as "wholes" is Franco Moretti. In his theoretical approach to the term, he does not go as far as Levine; and yet, he suggests a very similar perspective to the one just outlined. In his book *Graphs, Maps, Trees: Abstract Models for a Literary History*, published in 2005, he reports the necessity to approach literature as a whole, instead of a fragmented ensemble of single, discrete texts. "A field this large cannot be understood by stitching together separate bits of knowledge about individual cases, because it isn't a sum of individual cases: it's a collective system, that should be grasped as such, as a whole" (Moretti 2005a, 4). The connection between forms and systems will be discussed in more detail in the third and fourth chapters on infrastructures and platforms.

As a second example of form, Levine introduces "rhythm," stressing its temporal dimension. It would perhaps be more appropriate to define this form as temporal rhythm, since it implies repetitions and enduring patterns over time (Levine 2015, 21). While some cultures perceive rhythm as a recurrent, symmetrical motion, recalling the etymological root of the term, scholarly studies based on the perceptual observation of musical meters see rhythm as a flow, instead of a series of discrete units, unfolding over time (Cooper and Meyer 1963, 2). In short, the core meaning of the term rhythm, encompassing different definitions and embracing the constants commonly found across them, can be summed up in two main components: a time component (a durational aspect, frequency, tempo, or others) and a geometrical component (a pattern, alternation, repetition). In Levine's perspective, temporal rhythms "must be seen to function together and differently, overlapping and colliding, to produce a diachronic complexity [...]" (Levine 2015, 67).

The diachronic periodicity of rhythm, its ability to generate cycles, is what ultimately makes it a form. "While its meanings and values may change, the pattern or shape itself can remain surprisingly stable across contexts. [...] No matter how different their historical and cultural circumstances, that is, bounded enclosures will always exclude, and rhyme will always repeat" (Ibid., 7). Regular or irregular, contrastive or uniform, repetitions over time define rhythm as a form. By mentioning several examples, Levine additionally suggests that "[a] rhythm can impose its powerful order on laboring bodies as well as odes. Binary oppositions can structure gendered workspaces as well as creation myths" (Ibid.). Much like wholes, within this perspective, socio-political rhythms are therefore considered in terms of their relations with narrative or esthetic rhythms. Without looking at these connections as merely causal, Levine invites us once again to look at the ways these forms "meet, reroute, and disrupt one another" (Ibid., 23). In anthology series, if the whole achieves a closure through exclusion and inclusion, rhythms set the actual patterning of the narrative structure. This can be found on a small or large scale either by observing how a single anthology is constructed in terms of narrative form, or by reasoning on a larger corpus in terms of a cultural form. Finding rhythms and patterns is fundamental for a research that aims to adopt a "distant reading" (Moretti 2013) of serialized cultural objects with the intent of finding regularities and disruptions across them, as they are themselves inclined to follow a rhythmic movement of repetitions and variations.

Considering a distant reading as a framework, other interesting questions might arise from this brief reflection on formal rhythms: if rhythm is a time-related concept, how can we measure it? Disciplines like "quantitative formalism" (Allison et al. 2011; Algee-Hewitt 2017) have attempted to count recurring patterns across texts, by isolating clusters or aggregating texts. In the digital humanities, a rhythm-sensitive research can be deployed to understand movement over time, but also to account for computational, digital, or algorithmic turns in media. In this regard, Shintaro Miyazaki further explores the concept of "algorhythmics", which turns out to be particularly useful for understanding non-linear television and digital culture at large. As he explains, "rhythm [...] is an effect of ordering and meas-urement. 'Algorhythmics,' then is a research field, that inquires time-based, technological processes, which occur when matter is modulated by symbolic and logical structures, such as instructions written as code" (Miyazaki 2016, online). Finally, "understanding the efficiency and performance of algorithms is crucial to also understanding the sociopolitical and economic aspects of digital cultures, because algorithms are now common components of most infrastructures" (Miyazaki, in Sayers 2018, 244). Algorithmic-driven infrastructures are included in over-the-top television platforms. Being algorithmic-driven or simply based on cultural or narrative-shaping forces, rhythms will be therefore considered here as pivotal forms that interact with wholes, but also with hierarchies and networks. Applied to audiovisual anthologies, rhythms can help us identify temporal divisions (i.e., seasonal, episodic).

With his analysis of cultural patterns and processes of codifications or parsing in world literature, Moretti introduced his own personal vision of a "sociology of symbolic forms," by stating that "it is impossible to deny that human society is a multifarious, complex, overdetermined whole; but the theoretical difficulty obviously lies in trying to establish the hierarchy of different historical factors" (2005b, 19). Levine (2015, 87), in dialogue with Moretti's theories, adopts the concept of *hierarchy* to discuss hegemonic systems, political spaces, and even relational binaries (in identity, gender, race, class, and so forth). Hierarchies are present almost everywhere in the social sphere. While I will use the formal concepts of whole and rhythm mostly in application to narrative forms, recurring within a single text or across multiple texts, I will adopt the notion of hierarchy in its political dimension and interaction with sociocultural factors. Levine describes hierarchies as organizational dynamics in literary texts, which concern "investments in certain values and characters over others" (Ibid., 21), opting for a close reading approach. However, she includes this perspective in a socially and "politically aware historicism" (Ibid.). Her theory covers more than single narrative forms, to consider the way they "have force in the social world and are capable of shaping political arrangements" (Levine 2006, 626). It "extends formalist insights to make the case that social hierarchies and institutions can themselves be understood as *forms*" (Ibid., her emphasis).

Without focusing too much on procedural hierarchies in anthological narratives, I will apply this category to the overall institutional and industrial network that the production and distribution of serial narratives in television always imply. Far from tracing a simplistic, rigid separation between whole and rhythm, on the one hand, and hierarchies and networks, on the other hand – they all overlap to some extent –, I will nevertheless consider the privileged way in which networks and hierarchies tend to influence each other. Instead of assessing a hierarchy of values, the intent is to discuss hierarchies emerging from historical and industrial factors, in their interplay with networked mechanisms. Finally, taking a more critical perspective, I will ask whether networks of production and distribution of television content maintained the same degree of hierarchy over time or are perhaps shifting towards a non-hierarchical clustering model of content's circulation. In oligopolistic markets, the presence of inequalities due to hierarchical conformations are quite obvious. However, when forces from multiple sources come into play in both linear and non-linear television environments, the topology of the institutional network might not respond to a hierarchical geometry. Before moving forward to observe the hierarchical form of a non-linear network, we need to define the concept of network itself.

Forms and the links between them, which together contribute to the creation of networks, are the key to understanding the return of anthology series in contemporary media landscapes. The concept of network opens up a far wider discussion compared to other formal categories, and introduces the topic of interdisciplinarity. The concept of network is an essential part of larger theoretical frameworks in narrative theory and cultural studies. In particular, Levine was one of the first scholars to have fully theorized the presence of a close relationship between narrative forms and networks.[5] Before publishing her extensive neo-formalist work *Forms: Whole, Rhythm, Hierarchy, Network* in 2016, she outlined the following definition of form:

> Form [...] refers to shaping patterns, to identifiable interlacing of repetitions and differences, to dense networks of structuring principles and categories. It is conceptual and abstract, generalizing and transhistorical. [...] It does involve a kind of close reading, a careful attention to the ways that historical texts, bodies, and institutions are organized-what shapes they take, what models they follow and rework. But it is all about the social: it involves reading particular, historically specific collisions among generalizing political, cultural, and social forms.
>
> (Levine 2006, 632).

In this citation, extrapolated from the essay "Strategic Formalism: Toward a New Method in Cultural Studies," the term network is associated with the meaning of form as one of its possible occurrences. In her latest monograph, Levine (2015) spends an entire chapter discussing this peculiar association between networks and forms, by considering the network as a form itself. As she points out, in a certain academic tradition, networks are usually described as being formless, ever-spreading, or generically containing some degree of connectivity. However, a more attentive observation of networks carried out across a wide range of fields, from mathematics and physics to sociology, showed that they have a tendency to generate recurring patterns and shapes. Levine also notes that, "while it is certainly true that networks do not fit formal models of unified shape or wholeness, even apparently chaotic networks depend on surprisingly systematic ordering principles"

---

5   Moretti's view will be marginally considered in this section of the book, only to be further elaborated when approaching the methodology, with the intent of both exploring and problematizing a distant reading approach.

(Ibid., 112). As such, they can be imported into formal analysis to observe larger configurations that result from the linkage between other forms discussed by Levine, namely, wholes, rhythms, and hierarchies. Not only do networks have forms and forms can generate networks, but the multiplicity, the nature, and the level of their interconnection can be also analyzed. In this research on the anthology form, networks will re-emerge in the fourth chapter as the invisible infrastructures that link the platform ecosystem.

2.5. Taxonomy

By observing recurrent design features of the anthology we can delineate a taxonomy of forms that has consolidated throughout the history of media, from the publishing industry to new media. In this section, I will list a preliminary morphology of the anthology form that will guide the rest of this study as we go into further depth by examining anthological practices in digital and algorithmic culture. First, it is worth distinguishing between anthologies created ex-ante and anthologies created ex-post. The scholarly studies that I have cited in relation to the definition of anthology in literature often refer to anthologies created ex-post, either through the act of collection or through the act of translation and re-contextualization. On the contrary, radio and television anthologies are most commonly produced ex-ante, in the actual process of writing and creating the narration – e.g. *Kraft Television Theatre* (NBC, 1947-1958), *The United States Steel Hour* (ABC, 1953-1955; CBS, 1955-1963); *Alfred Hitchcock Presents* (CBS/NBC, 1955-1965). Furthermore, in addition to a taxonomy based on modes of content production and distribution, we should consider a taxonomy based on the narrative structure itself, which, I argue, corresponds to three main categories in relation to their potential for narrative expansion: micro-anthologies; semi-anthologies; and macro-anthologies. Finally, I will briefly consider short story products that emerged in the interaction with traditional anthologizations practices, thus generating hybrid forms that contributed to the evolution of the anthology form in digital culture. The resulting taxonomy inscribes itself in a broader "morphology of media" (Soulez and Kitsopanidou 2015, 7), and draws attention to the contextual practices that exist around more structural conditions of the text. In this sense, the anthology on streaming platforms will be analyzed from a much more pragmatic standpoint – design-oriented, infrastructural, platform-based – than the definitions given so far.

In an endnote to his article "La double répétition. Structure et matrice des séries télévisées," Soulez discusses a pivotal difference between collections made a priori and a posteriori. He states that: "Inside the collection, we can distinguish the anthology, which is a collection a posteriori of disparate pre-existing objects (as we define an anthology of poetry), the collection itself, which corresponds to an editorial offer a priori addressed to future authors as well as to future readers-viewers" (Soulez 2011, online, my translation). For the purpose of a study on anthology forms and their affordances, I will borrow Soulez's distinction between a form constructed a priori and a form generated a posteriori, which I define respectively as ex-ante and ex-post anthologies, with reference to the design. Found across a variety of paper-based, audiovisual, digital media, ex-ante anthologies evolved into one of the main formal vehicles for producing contemporary narratives and media content. In opposition to ex-ante anthologies, ex-post anthologies are bound to editorial organization, subjected to distribution dynamics and tied to the contextual affordances of the platform interface. This first classification everages different practices for document collection and storage found across several media histories.

On the one hand, anthologies conceived ex-ante, in the process of production and with the active involvement of one or more writers in the design of the content, affect the development of the narratives –- their format, formula, genre. In media like radio or television, ex-ante anthologies influence the narrative structure along with a set of contextual production features (e.g., running time, actors' rotation, financial commitment, and budget constraints). This is the case for US anthology dramas adapted from radio to television, such as *Studio One* (CBS, 1948–1958), with live episodes containing different stories and literary adaptations each week. Unlike longer serialized narratives, in which the storytelling is highly dependent on viewing patterns and unforeseen events like writers' strikes or actors defections, thanks to a constant regeneration, ex-ante anthologies were able to reinvent their content and minimize the outcomes of external perturbations, while still generating a social discourse around certain themes.

On the other hand, I define ex-post anthologies as all collections generated after the process of actual creation of content. In this case, the anthology-making happens in the distribution phase. Ex-post anthologies do not necessarily have the same affordances as ex-ante anthologies. Their potential functions are mainly decided after the production phase, through attempts at anthologization that feed into processes of archiving, packaging, marketing, and circulation of content. Examples of anthologies created ex-post are television reruns like the 1980s collection originally curated for PBS, *The Golden Age of Television*, which was later turned into a DVD box sets of the same name, curated by the Criterion Collection. The anthology form proved to be particularly robust and effective for generating media reruns and for transitioning across different media supports. For instance, relying on digital data storage formats, DVD box sets are examples of curated ex-post anthologies, de facto being collections of stories previously released separately. Another interesting case of anthology often edited/distributed ex post is the made-for-TV movie collection. Most commonly presented under the "movie of the week" formula, it represents a peculiar media object, since it blends a filmic visual esthetic and style with the formal norms typical of television. What makes ex-post anthologies relevant in this discussion is the fact that they help connect and re-contextualize unrelated groups of narrative content (short stories, audio essays, TV episodes, files), making then ready to be rebranded and exported to foreign media markets.

Overall, while in ex-ante anthologies the anthological principle is involved in the very curatorial and creative production of narratives, in ex-post anthologies the affordances of the form rather emerge in mechanisms of editorialization and adaptation, whether historical or geographical, cultural or industrial. Ex-post anthologies imply a discourse on how culture is received rather than how it is produced. They raise questions on the epistemological impacts of exporting media content into a different context, through operations of resemantization, reorganization, and reordering, following a process of filtering, hierarchization, inclusion/exclusion, and centering/de-centering of material for transcultural, transhistorical, and transmedia audiences. In non-linear internet environments like streaming platforms, given the absence of seasonal release windows or reruns as traditionally conceived within a fixed programming schedule, such a process of anthology-making a posteriori lies behind the principles of categorization and clustering of content, usually driven by algorithmic recommendation systems. In traditional linear media these two anthological forms (ex-ante and ex-post) are associated with different uses and belong to separate actions, either in the programming schedule or in marketing operations. On the contrary, non-linear media allow not only a coexistence of both forms in the same virtual space, but also an interaction of both forms in relation to the same content. I will illustrate this point further in the following chapters, when going into detail on the media environment of online platforms and its functioning.

If on a pragmatic design level anthologies differentiate between ex-ante and ex-post, on a more structural design level they can be divided into micro-anthologies, semi-anthologies, and macro-anthologies. Such a distinction might seem irrelevant at first glance, as it simply states several degrees of serialization or magnitude of the work in the formation of anthologies.

However, the matter of scale in narrative forms is a crucial factor for the definition of the anthology and its affordances, since it influences more pragmatic dynamics related to production practices, modes of distribution, and even dynamics of content promotion and reception. The way micro-anthologies, semi-anthologies, and macro-anthologies function in the mediascape varies consistently. A semi-anthology acts in a different way than micro- or macro-anthologies, and micro- and macro-anthologies imply separate dynamics as far as their potential for creating franchises, transmedia occurrences, or a revival mechanism. More specifically, I define micro-anthologies as the most compact and rigid anthological form, where the length is usually predetermined, and the collection does not expand outside of such a prefixed length. Micro-anthologies tend to limit the possibilities for narrative dilatation by favoring narrative closure and completeness. In these anthologies, the accent is on the end of the narratives, in contrast with any attempt at reopening.

Factors that provide closure can be structural or contextual, meaning they can be related to the structure given to the raw narrative material itself or they can be linked to economic or cultural constraints. In the former case, the narrative structure generated by a composition of standalone stories is such that both within them and in their entity of body of works the dissemination of meaning is limited. That is to say, there is a containment principle – either topological, thematically, or even simply a lack of strength in the anthological framing – that makes the list of episodes definite by its very nature. In the latter, the containment principle is contextual, meaning it is not necessarily related to narrative barriers contained in the text. Rather, it is an effect of external limitations, like budget availability or social pressure, as in the case of outdated or controversial narratives. Of course, in the case of fluid objects, as narrative media productions are, micro-anthologies can emancipate themselves and transition to larger corpora, namely, to macro-anthologies. I use the term macro-anthologies with reference to anthologies that are open to expansion and tend to generate one of the following processes: franchising; revival; transmedia; serialization; adaptation; canonization. "Along similar lines, Patricia Odber de Baubeta suggests the consideration of anthology (in one volume) and macro-anthology (in several volumes) (2007, 29)" (Seruya et al., 3). She proposes to observe macro-anthologies as collections of content where "individual texts may be read on their own but are brought together to provide a far more inclusive vision of different periods, styles and authors" (Baubeta 2007, 76). This differentiation is useful for understanding tendencies in narrative development, in the imposition of a cultural canon and in the financial exploitation of content in the television market. It can also help us examine reception practices, as seen in active engagement of the audience through cult, fandom, and fan fiction phenomena.

Still connected to a cultural, commercial, and sometimes political phenomenon, a third typology of anthology is the semi-anthology, which is often excluded from a taxonomy of anthologies and traditionally enters the group of epical narratives or long-running radio and television shows. Semi-anthologies are more or less serialized narratives that adhere to a grand narrative and, at the same time, benefit from the alternation of formal closure and reiteration. This allows for a renewal of the narrative within certain parameters of repetition. Borrowing Alvey's (1995) definition, the term "semi-anthology" refers to television series where a framing narrative device contains a series of standalone stories. For instance, *Naked City* (ABC, 1958–1963) was originally conceived "not as a police procedural but rather as a dramatic anthology with a police backdrop [...] the series was never intended as a show about detectives or their activities, but rather as a series about the city and the people of New York" (Sabin et al. 2015, 32), in the same way that *The Dubliners* was a book about the city and the people of Dublin. The same episodic, self-contained structure is found in *77 Sunset Strip* (ABC, 1958–1964), which, in the wake of the great North American twentieth-century pulp literary tradition, replicated a semi-anthological form with different stories taking place in the same background location – Sunset Boulevard. Furthermore, with its episodic plots adapted from novels and short stories by Roy Huggins, which previously appeared in *The Saturday Evening Post*, this show is an interesting example of how the anthology form was able to efficiently transition from weekly magazines to radio or television.

Moreover, semi-anthologies introduce fluidity between narrative forms and genres, as they demonstrate how anthological and serialization processes can merge, coexist, and, ultimately, operate collectively. Such fluidity in the formation of narratives becomes even more evident with the multiplication of television networks, markets, technologies, devices, and platforms, which led pre-existing media like radio and television to undergo a series of mutations as a consequence of an increasingly competitive, interactive, global new media environment. In this scenario, the anthology form evolved into two major categories: the classic episodic anthology and the seasonal anthology. The distinction between episodic and seasonal anthologies is quite intuitive: in episodic anthologies, the narrative arc develops within the limits of an episode; in seasonal anthologies the narrative arc evolves throughout the span of a season. The division into sections or fragments – be they episodes, seasons, or chapters – lies at the basis of most televisual narrative structures, which are commonly framed in narrative sequences of various length with a beginning, a middle, and an end, or at least a shared setting or thematic background.

The reasons for the adoption of such rhythmical patterns in television narratives across various cultures and markets are to be retraced not so much in their narrative architecture (meaning how information and storytelling are structured), but in the need for a time-management system that involves –- albeit differently in linear and non-linear media – both industrial and technological mechanisms. The necessity of timing serial production and distribution in television responds to commercial, financial, and economic strategies, as well as to the affordances of the medium. Furthermore, the way episodes and seasons are arranged often mirrors the structure of the television industry in given local markets, which then lead to the emergence of specific narrative forms. Observing shifts in canonical episodic and seasonal structures can be helpful to gather more evidence about the evolution of television at different historical moments or in different geographical locations. Before discussing the seasonal shift in US television anthologies, the definition of episodic anthologies needs to be further explained in relation to the academic debate on media and television. For instance, even though television anthologies have existed in the episodic structure since the very beginning, in 1970 the US radio and television historian Erik Barnouw distinguished between a formula-based episodic series and the anthological form, which allows for creative experimentation. In particular, "whereas the episodic series had emerged from a radio tradition, the anthology series emerged from a theater tradition. From the start, artists from the theater were active in the anthology series" (Barnouw 1970, 26).

Elsewhere, Michele Hilmes states that early television carried over from radio "the medium's basic and distinctive characteristic of seriality – a system of episodic programs recurring on a regular weekly or daily basis [...]" (Hilmes 2012, 218). While Barnouw uses the term episodic to refer to a rigid genre-formula, Hilmes simply associates it with the timeframe for regular programming in television. The episodic frame, as intended by Hilmes, along with its frequency, affects narrative development, especially when it comes to traditional broadcasting television. For instance, products like telenovelas in Brazil or soap operas in the US became a serial form typically associated with daily programming, as opposed to anthological products commonly found in weekly schedules. The episodic shape of television anthologies can also change in relation to its location in different time slots, with impacts on reception. Even in non-linear media, the choice of scheduling an episode or an entire season daily or weekly, and releasing an anthology at different moments of the year can influence the economic success and cultural resonance of a serial product. The distinction between episodic and seasonal anthology is therefore intended here not as strictly narratological and formal, but also as economic, cultural, and historical.

As I have briefly shown in the previous chapter, where I analyzed the transformation of the anthology form as a consequence of mutations in media environments, television anthologies were influenced by such formal shaping and, over the course of their evolution, mutated into two different strands: episodic-based and season-based. As I argue in this book, US seasonal anthologies, otherwise known as anthology miniseries (e.g., *American Horror Story, True Detective, Fargo*), are the result of both a phase of reassessment in the media ecology on a macroscopic scale, as well as multiple processes of stylistic hybridization on a microscopic scale. The importance of this shift towards a seasonal anthology form can be understood not only in terms of economic development in business models for contemporary streaming platforms, but also in terms of creative contamination between forms. In the following chapters, I will discuss how television anthologies transitioned into algorithmic culture, by starting from an overview of basic concepts that regulate narrative experimentation

2.6. Concepts

Concepts such as world-building and world-narrowing, scalability, and connectivity need to be reconsidered when looking at a design-oriented taxonomy of the anthology form. For instance, a certain flexibility in processes of expansion and contraction of the narratives contained in the anthology form invites us to rethink the concept of world-building in media storytelling practices (Wolf 2014), in order to acknowledge an opposite tendency towards "world-narrowing." I use the term "world-narrowing" to account for cases of "limited world-building," where the imaginary world is pitched using processes of demarcation and a reboot of the story that prevents the potential for further "horizontal" developments of the narrative. On the one hand, world-building operates on three levels: it "brings a world to mind (setting) and populates it with intelligent agents (characters). These agents participate in actions and happenings (events, plot), which cause global changes to the narrative world" (Ryan et al. 2004, 337). On the other hand, world-narrowing in anthology series is based on the variation between different stories in a collection of at least two of these three levels:

setting, characters, and plot. Anthologies that change the setting and cast within the same core plot include crime dramas and anthology format adaptations like *Bron/Broen.* Other types of anthologies might opt for a more radical change of the setting and plot, while still maintaining the same set of characters in the wake of some police procedurals. Finally, anthologies might change both plot and characters while keeping the same setting, as in the television series *Room 104* (HBO, 2017–), which readapted the format of the British anthology *Room 101* (BBC, 1994–2007). In this case, the show rotates characters and situations against the background of the same hotel room. In more unusual examples, the change can happen on all three levels: setting, characters, and plot are constantly regenerated, and the organizing principle is provided by more abstract elements (main theme, tone, genre). Or else in hybrid forms like *Easy* (Netflix, 2016–), a set of characters might return in different situations and settings and interact with different plots as they progressively overlap in separate storylines.

A change in the setting is one of the most evident strategies to mark a variation in the story, such as the shifts in fictional locations that distinguish different seasons, with a tendency to set borders to the narrative ecosystem. Even in an anthology like *Fargo*, where the setting is recurrent, as suggested by the title itself, the configuration of the space varies depending on each season, in an effort to map different geographical and historical realities, namely, Duluth 2006 in season one, Fargo, North Dakota, 1979 in season two, St. Cloud 2010 in season three, and Kansas City in the 1950s in season four. *Narcos* (Netflix, 2015–) attempted to follow a similar path, as the setting was moved from Colombia to Mexico. Playing with the spatial and historical setting as a way to reboot the story is a common feature in contemporary US television anthologies. However, as I have showed, world-narrowing strategies based on the coexistence of innovation and repetition (Eco 1985) can also result in a spatial continuity that acts as a stable background for other variations – e.g., characters, plot. The rotation of characters typically adopted in horror stories to regenerate the plot over and over again. Horror anthologies usually provide closure by, quite abruptly, eliminating a set of characters (e.g., *Scream* [MTV, 2015-2016; VH1, 2019-]). Reasoning on the liminal category of closure in narratives is fundamental to describing an inner, structural property of the stories that constitute television anthologies, which always progress towards an ending.

Stressing this point, Shannon Wells-Lassagne distinguishes between a soap-opera form of seriality, where the end is constantly postponed, and a short-form seriality built on a foreseeable, pre-planned, pre-determined ending (Wells-Lassagne 2017). In this regard, not only horror, but also crime genres in their more traditional formulas tend to converge towards a conclusion, by fostering regenerative processes and other mechanisms of repetition typical of the crime series' tradition. I use the term closure in a pragmatic way: closure is where the narrative strands converge into a resolution and end. Instead of discussing a "phenomenological feeling of finality" (Carroll 2007, 1) found on a reception level in the audience, here I refer to practices of closure embedded in the narrative itself, as logical mechanisms of answering "all of the presiding macro-questions and all the micro-questions that are relevant to settling the macro-questions"[6] (Ibid., 6). In certain genres, this quest of the narrative plot for a conclusion is more evident. At the beginning of a horror or crime series, the audience is presented with a problem (i.e., a presiding macro-question), which is then usually solved in the end, with different possible outcomes. The eschatological structure typical of such genres appears to be functional to the anthology form. The process of narrowing, as opposed to world-building, other than being a formal and structural feature of serialized narratives, has effective outcomes on production. First, creating narrow worlds requires a lower commitment from the actors, who are not asked to sign a five-year (or longer) contract to return to the same series. Similarly, if narrowing happens in the setting, the financial investment on the location is likely to be lower. Finally, narrowing the plot allows for safer business models by opting for an anthological reboot.

In a platform economy, where there is a constant urge for new content to expand the library, anthologies create content quality and quantity, at once. Moreover, a long-tail economy (Anderson 2006) pushes internet-distributed television to invest in long-term success and niche audiences as much as –and sometimes even more than – in immediate sell-outs and mass audiences. Long-tail economy is a term commonly associated with digital platforms and it was first introduced by Chris Anderson, who used this term in an article in *WIRED* magazine to describe Amazon's business model.[7] The article states that, in a traditional economy, with high marginal costs, mass markets are sustained by a logic that privileges blockbusters, a phenomenon that David Hesmondhalgh defined as "the blockbuster syndrome" (Hesmondhalgh 2012,

---

6   Noel Carroll differentiates between "presiding macro questions," "macro questions," and "micro questions" contained in narrative plots. As Carroll explains, "[s]ome questions orchestrate our attention to the emerging story from one end to the other [...]. Questions that structure an entire text or, at least most of it, we can call *'presiding* macro questions'." Moreover, micro-questions are those "whose answers are required cognitively to render the answers to the macro-questions intelligible" (Carroll 2007, 10).

7   Chris Anderson. "The Long Tail." *Wired*. Last modified October 1, 2004. https://www.wired.com/2004/10/tail.

234). Referencing the Pareto principle, Anderson argues that, in mass media, only 20 percent of total content production is responsible for 80 percent of the revenues, meaning that the traditional television market, as well as other media and creative industries, were essentially based on mega-hit shows (Anderson 2006).

Internet aggregators like Amazon changed this logic by introducing a new model and significantly dropping marginal costs. online, what matters are not blockbusters that generate peaks in consumption, but niche products able to remain on the market in the long term, thus guaranteeing what Anderson calls a long-tail effect in terms of revenues. With the arrival of online platforms, television underwent a similar transformation, by favoring entertainment practices mainly based on the production of a diversified plethora of niche content. A fundamental strategy in the long-tail economy is therefore the expansion of the catalog and the overall offer, through the inclusion of niche products that used to be off-market due to distribution issues. Television anthologies show resilience at both a formal and production level. For instance, they can be canceled anytime, while preserving the possibility of a long-term benefit, which makes them a good option in moments of uncertainty and reassessment. The anthology form, as a way to collect narrow narratives containing a sense of closure, or else, more pragmatically, an ending, seems to grant the modularity and openness needed in this phase of technological transition and fast-paced media mutations.

The efficacy of a narrative-based anthological model in internet-distributed television can not yet be assessed clearly; however, we can advance some hypothesis about its future evolution and evaluate the current state based on previous transformations. For instance, the possibility of reinventing the story, while still offering a familiar narrative, allows screenwriters to gain greater control over the creative process. Television content creators can opt for the anthological form anytime: they can create a one-season long narrative with closure and decide to revive the story for a second season, then again they can close the plot once and for all and restart the show with a completely different story. Television anthologies today are both narrow and open: they can dynamically create infinite repetition and yet still guarantee variation where needed, by scaling narratives up and down based on an episodic, seasonal, or multi-seasonal rhythm. Unlike ancient anthologies, contemporary anthologies offer closure of content, without the need for a closure of the form.

The double affordance of the anthology form addresses to another concept: that of scalability. On digital platforms, anthology series generate scalable lists, streams of content, and, ultimately, organized databases, which operate as orienting maps for future recommendation and viewing. This anthological cycle starts from content production and it is brought to the fore during the online distribution and consumption phase. In computer science, the notion of the database has been discussed under several lenses, either considering archival and storage techniques, or the organizational structures (relational, networked) behind them. When translating this notion into media studies, Lev Manovich notes that "as a cultural form, database represents the world as a list of items and it refuses to order this list. In contrast, a narrative creates a cause-and-effect trajectory of seemingly unordered items (events). Therefore, database and narrative are natural enemies. Competing for the same territory of human culture, each claims an exclusive right to make meaning out of the world" (Manovich 1999, 87). As I argue, the anthology functions as a mechanism for the abstraction of narratives, by treating them as blocks of data and transferring them into a database system. By doing so, it bypasses the incompatibility stressed by Manovich between database and narratives. By blending narratives with a scalable model, the anthology typically provides a scheme, a form for conveying, organizing, and displaying content much like in a database.

Beyond the systemic perspective laid out by the metaphor of database-anthologies, to which I will return later, this term serves as a means for understanding certain properties that the anthology form shares with databases, notably scalability, and elasticity. Structural scalability refers to the capacity of a network, system or process "to expand in a chosen dimension without major modifications to its architecture" and the overall "ability not only to function well in the rescaled situation, but to actually take full advantage of it" (Bondi 2000, 195). Given the growing amount of content, an anthology series can be defined as scalable since it is able to handle and tolerate an increasing load of content thanks to its architectural characteristics. Structurally, anthologies can be subjected to vertical scaling and scaled up by adding resources – i.e., a new season can be added without changing the information architecture of the series. Scaling down would be equally possible – one could simply take away a season without affecting the remaining narrative content of the anthology – but neither desirable nor beneficial in terms of platform economy. Moreover, due to their fluid nature, as previously discussed, contemporary anthology series, in contrast with early anthologies, allow for horizontal scaling via the addition of nodes (i.e., another episode or season based on the same story) to the existing narrative ecosystem. In other words, standalone stories can be expanded

at any point, as we can see in the series *Easy*, an example of an open-ended
anthology that groups episodes by adding more to the same plot without
a formal ordering in the seasonal division (the same plot can be found in
episodes from different seasons). The idea of organizing narrative content
per main themes, or around characters and situations, contributes to this
particular use of the anthology as a scalable object. Indeed, scalability can
also be found in longer forms of serial storytelling, such as sit-coms. However,
sit-coms cannot be scaled down as effectively as short serial forms, due to
their innate tendency to always postpone the ending.

Furthermore, anthology series tend to favor space scalability as well: given
their short form, they can easily be moved to a range of different devices
and platform environments, in the wake of transmedia adaptations and
dynamics of media convergence. Another scalable element in the anthology form is time: the short-narrative structure can support short and long
marathon-viewing sessions alike. Anthologies can easily adapt to personal
viewing habits and time constraints, providing the freedom of managing
leisure time through content of different hours and lengths. This implies
a resilience and modularity of both form and content, as observed in the
ability of the anthology form to face changes and upgrades in the media
environment, without impacting users' access to the database/narrative
content. Together with numerical representation, automation, variability,
and transcoding, modularity is one of the five "principles of new media"
identified by Manovich "not as absolute laws but rather as general tendencies
of a culture undergoing computerization" (Manovich 2001, 27). In the context
of a modular structure inherent to the World Wide Web, modularity is the
key component of a digital, interactive environment. Anthology series
implement the principles of modularity and variability by favoring their
adaptation to such a non-linear, fractal structure made of "collections of
discrete samples" and "self-sufficient modules" (Manovich 2001, 51–52).
Such modules can act independently or together, with disparate outcomes
in the way they can make culture and meaning.

Of course, when talking about numerical databases, such properties
assume measurable values, which are not identifiable as easily when discussing cultural databases. However, even if we were to adopt the database
framework as a simple metaphor, it would be a relevant framework to test not
only the anthological model, but also the anthological extensibility (Doueihi
2009, 11) of certain televisual forms available in online libraries, in dialogue
with both a platform economy and an economy of nostalgia where media
franchises might be subjected to multiple reboots. The way anthologies are
scalable, modular, and variable makes them similar in nature to forms that

follow structural computer programming standards (Manovich 2001, 31). In line with technological advancements that eventually led to the Semantic Web, a web of data, the anthology form serves the purpose, on the one hand, of organizing content and information on digital platforms, and, on the other hand, of making sense of such content by actively affecting cultural production, distribution, and memory. If language and narratives already operate at scale, the anthology form in internet-distributed television helps boost this scaling paradigm found on the internet, by regulating content indexing on online platforms.

The rebooting mechanism typical of the anthology form creates a syntagmatic structure of repetitions and connections, while still generating a set of paradigmatic variations. Returning to these semiotic concepts (syntagmatic versus paradigmatic relations), as originally seen in Ferdinand Saussure (1986), might be useful for understanding how the anthological model is bound to the creation of a whole (the collection itself), of a rhythm (the episodic and seasonal division), and of a network of loose relationships between its parts (repetitions/variations). Reasoning in terms of syntagmatic (horizontal) and paradigmatic (vertical) processes in the use of world-narrowing strategies in anthology series can assist us in analyzing the surrounding social and cultural discourse. More specifically, the combination of these processes supports a canon through a collective, shared vision across episodes and seasons, as it also favors the rewriting a story episode by episode or season by season (syntagmatic). For example: what is the overall grand narrative conveyed by *Black Mirror* (e.g., the dystopian effects of technologies on human relationships and social structures) as opposed to the themes explored in each episode (e.g., queerness, non-normativity, and intersectionality in *San Junipero*)? Having already discussed on paradigmatic movements (world-narrowing, closure, scalability, discretion), the next paragraphs will briefly focus on syntagmatic tendencies found in anthologies.

Perhaps more than on discretion, streaming platforms rely on connection - notably, on the creation of a network of content in online catalogs, through algorithmic-driven recommendation systems. Connectivity not only plays a role in the large scale of a platform through a linkage of content, but it can also be found in the small scale of a serial narrative, as an interconnection of elements in the story-world. Within a narrative ecosystem framework, which I will discuss in the next chapter, vast serial narratives are, indeed, highly connected ecosystems. While it is evident that world-building involves a process of intra-textual connectivity and possibly even intertextual, transmedia citations, it is less evident to discuss practices of connection in world-narrowing, such as in the case of anthology series. Yet, despite their

discretional nature and their predilection for narrow worlds, contemporary
anthology series seem to aspire, even more than early television anthologies,
to the creation of a networked whole, capable of connecting standalone
stories in a homogeneous collection. Syntagmatic relationships between
episodes or seasons in contemporary US anthologies can be conventionally
found in the repetition of a shared genre, register, tone, or style, which
respond to an anthologizing principle, i.e., how the anthology is selected
through recurring themes. Some anthology series, however, present unusual
intertextual references between episodes or seasons. Examples may vary
from simple citations to the recovery of characters or narrative elements
transitioning between different episodes or between different seasons. These
connecting-the-dots mechanisms found in some television anthologies do
not affect the anthological structure. They act as repertoires of inner topoi
(Eco 1984, 119) and "links between texts, operating in the perception and
experience of audiences" (Ellis et al. 2016, 225), rather than operating on
a more profound narrative level that has affected the anthological form.

When observed in terms of industrial production and distribution
dynamics, intertextual citations, as in the case of the type of crossovers
that are internal to the anthology structure itself, do not emerge as relevant
components. They are perhaps more important for building a fandom, rather
than building a narrative complexity typical of long-running serials. On the
contrary, other syntagmatic relationships are related to the very process of
formation of the anthology, as in the definition of a structural recursivity,
which establishes the anthology form itself. Anthological ordering through
reiteration and connection of genre, register, tone, or style results in the
creation of specific anthological categories and clusters. *The Twilight Zone*,
for example, comes to define a specific, reproducible formula and not just
a generic sci-fi type, meaning that, while the anthology is not a format by
itself, it does show some formatting abilities to generate replicas. Instead of
demanding connectivity at a narrative level, like serials do, anthologies thus
show a connectivity at a production and distribution level. Connectivity in
production can happen in the recurring figure of a screenwriter or a director,
whereas at a distribution level, it results in the assemblage of snippets of
unrelated content. In this sense, the anthological practice is naturally embedded in the digital landscape, since "it responds to the nature of its objects and
supports, of their production, circulation and valorization" (Doueihi 2011, 170).
Beyond the inner anthological properties just outlined –world-narrowing,
scalability, modularity – and the related concepts discussed – intertextuality,
connectivity – we should therefore take a closer look at the ecosystemic
context in which the contemporary anthology form emerges and acts.

List of works cited

Abercrombie, Nicholas. 1996. *Television and Society*. Hoboken, NJ: Wiley.

Alber, Jan, and Monika Fludernik. 2010. *Postclassical Narratology: Approaches and Analyses*. Columbus, OH: Ohio State University Press.

Algee-Hewitt, Mark. 2017. *Canon/Archive: Studies in Quantitative Formalism from the Stanford Literary Lab*. New York: n+1 Foundation.

Allison, Sarah Danielle, Heuser, Ryan, Jockers, Matthew Lee, Moretti, Franco, and Michael Witmore. 2011. *Quantitative Formalism: An Experiment*. Stanford, CA: Stanford Literary Lab.

Altman, Rick. 1999. *Film/Genre*. London: British Film Institute.

Alvey, Mark Theodore. 1995. *Series Drama and the "Semi-Anthology": Sixties Television in Transition*. Austin, TX: University of Texas Press.

Anderson, Chris. 2006. *The Long Tail: Why the Future of Business Is Selling Less of More*. New York: Hachette Books.

Aveyard, Karina, Moran, Albert, and Pia Majbritt Jensen, eds. 2016. *New Patterns in Global Television Formats*. Bristol and Chicago, IL: Intellect Ltd.

Barnouw, Erik. 1970. *The Image Empire: A History of Broadcasting in the United States, Volume III–from 1953*. Oxford: Oxford University Press.

Barthes, Roland. 1975. "An Introduction to the Structural Analysis of Narrative." *New Literary History* 6 (2): 237–72. https://doi.org/10.2307/468419.

Bondi, André B. 2000. "Characteristics of Scalability and Their Impact on Performance." In *Proceedings of the 2nd International Workshop on Software and Performance*, 195–203. WOSP '00. Ottawa: Association for Computing Machinery. https://doi.org/10.1145/350391.350432.

Bordwell, David, and Noël Carroll. 1996. *Post-Theory: Reconstructing Film Studies*. Madison, WI: University of Wisconsin Press.

Buckingham, David. 2004. *Sorting Out TV: Categorization and Genre*. Vol. Children Talking Television: The Making Of Television Literacy. New York: Routledge.

Carroll, Noël. 2007. "Narrative Closure." *Philosophical Studies: An International Journal for Philosophy in the Analytic Tradition* 135 (1): 1–15.

Cawelti, John G. 1969. "The Concept of Formula in the Study of Popular Literature." *The Journal of Popular Culture* III (3): 381–90. https://doi.org/10.1111/j.0022-3840.1969.0303_381.x.

Cawelti, John G. 1972. "The Concept of Formula in the Study of Popular Literature." *The Bulletin of the Midwest Modern Language Association* 5: 115–23. https://doi.org/10.2307/1314918.

Cawelti, John G. 1976. *Adventure, Mystery, and Romance: Formula Stories as Art and Popular Culture*. Chicago, IL: University of Chicago Press.

Chalaby, Jean K. 2011. "The Making of an Entertainment Revolution: How the TV Format Trade Became a Global Industry." *European Journal of Communication* 26 (4): 293–309. https://doi.org/10.1177/0267323111423414.

Chalaby, Jean K. 2012. "At the Origin of a Global Industry: The TV Format Trade as an Anglo-American Invention." *Media, Culture & Society* 34 (1): 36–52. https://doi.org/10.1177/0163443711427198.

Chalaby, Jean K. 2016. *The Format Age: Television's Entertainment Revolution.* Hoboken, NJ: Wiley.

Doueihi, Milad. 2009. "Digital Objecthood and Scholarly Publishing," https://ecommons.cornell.edu/handle/1813/12020.

Doueihi, Milad. 2011a. *Digital Cultures.* Cambridge, MA: Harvard University Press.

Doueihi, Milad. 2011b. *Pour Un Humanisme Numérique.* La Librairie Du XXIe Siècle. Paris: Editions du Seuil.

Eco, Umberto. 1976. *A Theory of Semiotics.* Bloomington, IN: Indiana University Press.

Eco, Umberto. 1984. *The Role of the Reader: Explorations in the Semiotics of Texts.* Bloomington, IN: Indiana University Press.

Eco, Umberto. 1985. "Innovation and Repetition: Between Modern and Post-Modern Aesthetics." *Daedalus* 114 (4): 161–84.

Eco, Umberto. 1990. *The Limits of Interpretation.* Bloomington, IN: Indiana University Press.

Eco, Umberto. 2005. *On Literature.* Boston, MA: Houghton Mifflin Harcourt.

Ellis, John, Esser, Andrea, and Juan Francisco Gutiérrez Lozano. 2016. "Editorial. TV Formats and Format Research: Theory, Methodology, History and New Developments." *VIEW Journal of European Television History and Culture* 5 (9): 1–5. https://doi.org/10.18146/2213-0969.2016.jethc098.

Esquenazi, Jean-Pierre. 2014. *Les séries télévisées: L'avenir du cinéma?* Paris: Armand Colin.

Geertz, Clifford. 2008. *The Interpretation Of Cultures.* New York: Basic Books.

Genette, Gérard. 1983. *Narrative Discourse: An Essay in Method.* Ithaca, NY: Cornell University Press.

Gitlin, Todd. 1979. "Prime Time Ideology: The Hegemonic Process in Television Entertainment." *Social Problems* 26 (3): 251–66. https://doi.org/10.2307/800451.

Gitlin, Todd. 1982. "Television's Screens: Hegemony in Transition." In *Cultural and Economic Reproduction in Education.* New York: Routledge

Gitlin, Todd. 2000. *Inside Prime Time: With a New Introduction.* Berkeley, CA: University of California Press.

Herman, David. 2004. *Story Logic: Problems and Possibilities of Narrative.* Lincoln, NE: University of Nebraska Press.

Hesmondhalgh, David. 2012. *The Cultural Industries.* Newbury Park, CA: SAGE.

Hilmes, Michele. 2012. *Network Nations: A Transnational History of British and American Broadcasting*. New York: Routledge.

Hilmes, Michele. 2013. *Only Connect: A Cultural History of Broadcasting in the United States*. Boston, MA: Cengage Learning.

Keen, Suzanne. 2015. *Narrative Form: Revised and Expanded Second Edition*. New York: Springer.

Keinonen, Heidi. 2017. "Television Format as Cultural Technology Transfer: Importing a Production Format for Daily Drama." *Media, Culture & Society* 39 (7): 995–1010. https://doi.org/10.1177/0163443716682076.

Kindt, Tom, and Hans-Harald Müller. 2003. *What Is Narratology?: Questions and Answers Regarding the Status of a Theory*. Berlin: Walter de Gruyter.

Kramnick, Jonathan, and Anahid Nersessian. 2017. "Form and Explanation." *Critical Inquiry* 43 (3): 650–69. https://doi.org/10.1086/691017.

Levine, Caroline. 2006. "Strategic Formalism: Toward a New Method in Cultural Studies." *Victorian Studies* 48 (4): 625–57.

Levine, Caroline. 2015a. *Forms: Whole, Rhythm, Hierarchy, Network*. Princeton, NJ: Princeton University Press.

Levine, Caroline. 2015b. "Forms, Literary and Social." *Dibur Literary Journal*, Form (2). https://arcade.stanford.edu/dibur/forms-literary-and-social.

Levinson, Marjorie. 2007. "What Is New Formalism?" *PMLA* 122 (2): 558–69.

Levi-Strauss, Claude. 1955. "The Structural Study of Myth." *The Journal of American Folklore* 68 (270): 428–44. https://doi.org/10.2307/536768.

Levi-Strauss, Claude. 2008. *Structural Anthropology*. New York: Basic Books.

Lievrouw, Leah A.,, and Sonia M. Livingstone. 2006. *Handbook of New Media: Student Edition*. Newbury Park, CA: SAGE.

Lifschutz, Vladimir. 2015. "Series finale": Enjeux et théorie d'un compromis moderne." *TV/Series*, no. 7 (June). https://doi.org/10.4000/tvseries.284.

Linke, Uli. 2015. "Collective Memory, Anthropology Of." In *International Encyclopedia of the Social & Behavioral Sciences*, 181–87. Amsterdam: Elsevier. https://doi.org/10.1016/B978-0-08-097086-8.12036-7.

Manovich, Lev. 1999. "Database as Symbolic Form." *Convergence* 5 (2): 80–99. https://doi.org/10.1177/135485659900500206.

Manovich, Lev. 2001. *The Language of New Media*. Cambridge, MA: MIT Press.

Manovich, Lev. 2011. "What Is Visualisation?" *Visual Studies* 26 (1): 36–49. https://doi.org/10.1080/1472586X.2011.548488.

Odber de Baubeta, Patricia Anne. 2007. *The Anthology in Portugal: A New Approach to the History of Portuguese Literature in the Twentieth Century*. Lausanne: Peter Lang.

Propp, V. 2010. *Morphology of the Folktale: Second Edition*. Austin, TX: University of Texas Press.

Ryan, Marie-Laure. 2004. *Narrative Across Media: The Languages of Storytelling*. Lincoln, NE: University of Nebraska Press.

Sabin, Roger, Wilson, Ronald, and Linda Speidel. 2015. *Cop Shows: A Critical History of Police Dramas on Television*. Jefferson, NC: McFarland.

Saussure, Ferdinand de. 1986. *Course in General Linguistics*. Chicago, IL: Open Court Publishing.

Sayers, Jentery. 2018. *The Routledge Companion to Media Studies and Digital Humanities*. New York: Routledge.

Schnapp, Jeffrey T. 2014. *Knowledge Design: Incubating New Knowledge Forms, Genres, Spaces in the Laboratory of the Digital Humanities: Keynote Delivered Ath the Herrenhausen Conference "(Digital) Humanities Revisited – Challenges and Opportunities in the Digital Age"/ Jeffrey T. Schnapp. [VolkswagenStiftung]*. Hanover: Volkswagen-Stiftung.

Seruya, Teresa, D'hulst, Lieven, Assis Rosa, Alexandra, and Maria Lin Moniz. 2013. *Translation in Anthologies and Collections (19th and 20th Centuries)*. Amsterdam: John Benjamins Publishing Company.

Seyfert, Robert, and Jonathan Roberge. 2016. *Algorithmic Cultures: Essays on Meaning, Performance and New Technologies*. New York: Routledge.

Shahaf, Sharon, and Tasha Oren. 2013. *Global Television Formats: Understanding Television Across Borders*. New York: Routledge.

Soulez, Guillaume. 2011. "La double répétition." *Mise au point. Cahiers de l'association française des enseignants et chercheurs en cinéma et audiovisuel*, 3. https://doi.org/10.4000/map.979.

Soulez, Guillaume, and Kira Kitsopanidou. 2015. *Le levain des médias: Forme, format, média*. Paris: Editions L'Harmattan.

Todorov, Tzvetan. 1969. "Structural Analysis of Narrative." *NOVEL: A Forum on Fiction* 3 (1): 70–76. https://doi.org/10.2307/1345003.

Todorov, Tzvetan. 1976. "The Origin of Genres." *New Literary History* 8 (1): 159–70. https://doi.org/10.2307/468619.

Williams, Raymond. 1974. *Television: Technology and Cultural Form*. New York: Routledge.

Williams, Raymond. 1983. *Keywords: A Vocabulary of Culture and Society*. Oxford: Oxford University Press.

Wolf, Mark J.P. 2014. *Building Imaginary Worlds: The Theory and History of Subcreation*. New York: Routledge.

3. Infrastructures

Abstract

Taking an ecosystemic perspective, this chapter considers the anthology form in the context of archival and streaming practices, as it intersects with systems of knowledge organization and transmission. First, it provides a brief history of how classification evolved to define media and cultural objects. Starting from a discussion on human classificatory predispositions and abilities, it discusses how data-management systems transitioned towards machine-aided computational practices. It then considers more closely the infrastructural, geographical, and temporal dimensions of non-linear media ecosystems that make streaming processes functional and operational. The final aim is to understand how different modes of data and content distribution in online repositories or platform environments might affect both content organization and industrial strategies.

Keywords: Anthology; Media Ecology; Cultural Studies; Classification Systems; Streaming Media; Infrastructure Studies

3.1. Ecosystemic Perspectives

The study of anthological modes of content classification in relation to narrative forms requires an understanding of cultural and media ecosystems. An ecosystemic perspective is notably concerned with the technological and media-ecological infrastructures surrounding cultural production, as the physical spaces where culture is generated, stored, exhibited, and experienced. As an interdisciplinary concept and method developed by the American anthropologist Julian Steward (1969), the framework of cultural ecology acknowledges a correlation between cultural configurations and their proximate environments. This adaptive methodology, which looks at cultures as super-organic manifestations (Kroeber 1917), encompassing hereditary distinctive individual traits, derives from a theory of multilinear evolution that searches for recurrent patterns in cultural change and refutes cultural universalism (Steward 1972). While Steward's work refers

Taurino, Giulia. *The Anthology in Digital Culture.* Amsterdam: Amsterdam University Press, 2023.
DOI: 10.5117/9789463724265_CH03

to pre-industrial societies, the bulk of his theory can be effectively applied to post-industrial societies to account for the ways in which contextual infrastructural and industrial landscapes influence societal dispositions and cultural formations.

In practice, applying a "cultural-ecological (or systems-theoretical)" (Kelleter 2017, 3) approach to a multilinear genealogy of the anthology form from pre-digital to post-digital culture means observing norms and regularities in the evolution of systems of content classification. This allows us to observe similarities in cross-cultural phenomena, while not necessarily assuming that the anthology form is universal per se. The media scholar Frank Kelleter employs the concept of cultural ecology in order to stress the dependence of popular narratives on "coevolving conditions of cultural environments" (Kelleter 2017, 3). This means using a system-oriented inquiry to analyze the relationship between narrative records existing in connection with cultural habitats. Echoing previous theorizations in anthropology and social sciences, this ecological perspective solicits the analysis of cultures as ecosystems made of several interacting and overlapping components, which are organized into economic, political, social, and technological forms. Such a system-oriented thinking finds several points of convergence with the neo-formalist theory outlined by Levine, where forms are observed as being context-sensitive and embedded into systems of various kinds and nature that can themselves be arranged into forms (i.e., networks). The association of culture with ecologies, systems, and networks motivates the adoption of a macroscopic approach, where the anthology form is analyzed in interaction with surrounding mediascapes.

A few years after the introduction of the notion of cultural ecology, in *A Thousand Plateaus*, the French philosophers Gilles Deleuze and Félix Guattari explored system theory in relation to culture, by advancing their own "assemblage theory," a framework that accounts for socio-cultural, evolutionary dynamics of self-organizations into networks, thus cutting across technological determinism and social constructivism (Bousquet 2014). Assemblage theory observes culture as a constellation of elements – i.e., a network of systems – participating in processes of coding, ordering and stratification. Deleuze and Guattari call this model "rhizome," a net that "ceaselessly establishes connections between semiotic chains, organizations of power, and circumstances relative to the arts, sciences, and social struggles" (Deleuze and Guattari 1987, 7). Furthermore, in this heterogeneous multiplicity, "what counts are not the terms or the elements, but what is 'between' them, the in-between, a set of relations that are inseparable from each other" (Deleuze and Parnet 1987, viii). This postmodern perspective on the study of cultural systems as assemblages is particularly interesting in application to digital culture and the diffusion of the internet, where the emphasis is on networked dynamics, fluidity, and interoperability between systems.

Assemblage theory and the rhizomatic paradigm were adopted, among others, by the philosopher Manuel DeLanda, who advocates that, instead of reducing social analysis to either a microscopic or macroscopic view, it is necessary to consider social phenomena as multi-scalar (Delanda 2006, 32), comprised of components linked together within a complex and non-linear network forming an assemblage – or assemblages of assemblages, in a larger scale case (Ibid., 33). DeLanda's model suggests that, whereas assemblages are historically contingent, components exist in a relation of exteriority with the assemblage, meaning they do not change their essence as they are moved from one assemblage to another through processes of encoding/decoding (Ibid., 19). In this perspective, forms appear as both cross-historical and historically contingent. As single entities they present the same potential set of affordances. By contrast, as assemblages – i.e., systems – they become contingent on historical scenarios, since they are defined by the actuality of their uses and interactions with economic, technological, and industrial infrastructures. To this point, the literary scholar Hubert Zapf describes the notion of "evolution of aesthetics and imaginative forms of textuality as double-coded" (Zapf 2016, 141) – that is to say, as both transhistorical and cultural-specific. These ecosystemic perspectives are very useful for understanding the anthology form, on the one hand, as a persistent feature across Western societies for the storage, organization, and circulation of culture, and, on the other hand, as a contingent entity that manifests itself in the relationship with other systems – i.e., digital infrastructures and media technologies.

Taking a cultural-ecological, system-theoretical standpoint offers solid ground for the analysis of the anthology form in relation to digital environments and algorithmic culture at a theoretical level. However, it still lacks a connection to the materiality of media ecosystems, which is necessary for defining an effective methodology in application to the infrastructural landscape behind media configurations. As Peter Finke stresses out "information and communication have become major driving forces of cultural evolution (see Finke 2005, 2006)" (Finke, cited in Zapf 2016, 79). In the study of media culture, the very notion of culture as a structured, complex, and dynamic ecosystem therefore needs to be expanded to include information and communication ecosystems. Theories in media ecology were able to address this need.

A media ecological approach accounts for changes that happen over time in techno-infrastructural ecosystems. In this framework, media are to be interpreted as the physical, technological, and economic systems where a series of assorted cultural forms are created and leave social traces. By adopting a media-ecological approach, the present chapter takes into consideration system theory in application to media studies, as it poses the premises for understanding the connection between media and cultural forms. Niklas Luhmann, one of the sociologists who addressed complex mechanisms of communication and social behavior in mediated environments, discusses the relationship between medium and form by observing forms as actualizations of the medium, which themselves mediate other forms in a recursive process. In other words, "media can be recognized only by the contingency of the formations that make them possible" (Luhmann 2000, 104). In this mutual relationship between media and forms, media impose non-arbitrary "limits on what one can do with them" (Ibid., 105) and yet they do not actively oppose the creation of formal variations: "forms are always stronger and more assertive than the medium" (Ibid.). Furthermore:

> The difference between medium and form implies a distinctly temporal aspect as well. The medium is more stable than the form [...]. No matter how short-lived or lasting they turn out to be, forms can be created without exhausting the medium or causing it to disappear along with the form. As we noted earlier, the medium receives without resistance the forms that are possible within it, but the form's resilience is paid for with instability. [...] The medium manifests itself only in the relationship between constancy and variety that obtains in individual forms. A form, in other words, can be observed through the schema of constant/variable, because it is always a form-in-a-medium.
>
> (Ibid., 106)

This state of instability, persistence, and dependence of the form in a medium has required us to analyze the anthology in its historic-genealogical evolution, as seen in previous chapters that deploy a comparative method to examine the temporal evolution of the anthology form as always existing within a media system. This method is convenient to monitor the form diachronically and define historical analogies able to highlight both the resilience and vulnerability of the anthology form in Western media cultures. If we understand media technologies as social constructs, shaped by human actions (Williams 1974), then we can say that over the years different technologies did not so much determine, but rather released certain affordances of the anthology form. As we observed, dynamics of emergence, proliferation, convergence, and divergence in the evolution of the anthology form are prompted by certain infrastructural, economic, and industrial configurations, in a way that is technologically contextual but not deterministic. No redefinition of a form – be it a narrative, media, or technological form – is without effect on the evolution of tastes, preferences, and social practices. At the same time, the proliferation of a particular form is made possible by the existence of techno-cultural conditions that make it circulate better than others.

Both media systems and their technologies "operate, and are operated upon in a complex social field," proving that "a relationship between technology and society cannot be reduced to a simplistic cause-and-effect formula. It is, rather, an 'intertwining'" (Murphie and Potts 2002, 21). In other words, to consider the anthology in the specific context of streaming platforms, where platforms are both technologies and cultural forms, we need to understand their techno-infrastructural and socio-cultural ecosystems of reference. The media-ecological framework can help us reason on this synchronous intertwining, by focusing, for example, on internet-distributed media in contemporary digital culture and the way the anthology form emerges and operates within it, in connection with creative (productional), industrial (distributional), and social (receptional) dynamics.

Media ecology famously finds a comprehensive theorization in the work of Marshall McLuhan, who, in 1964, outlined a vast theory of media apparatuses and filled the gaps of a content-oriented cultural analysis by inserting a discourse on media properties. In *Understanding Media: The Extensions of Man*, McLuhan (1994) discusses media as diverse as roads and print, clocks, and radio or television, observing how the content (message) tends to be shaped by the characteristics of each medium. Following McLuhan, the ecological perspective on media as environments or ecosystems was first publicly defined in 1968 by Neil Postman, who affirmed that "such information forms as the alphabet, the printed word, and television images are not mere instruments which make things easier for us. They are environments – like language itself, symbolic environments within which we discover, fashion, and express humanity in particular ways" (Postman 1979, 186). Over the years, media ecology was expanded into several scholarly formulations (Nystrom 1975; Strate 2006; Scolari 2012). In line with cultural ecology, the core assumption across different theories in media ecology is always that "the word ecology implies the study of environments: their structure, content, and impact on people. An environment is, after all, a complex message system which imposes on human beings certain ways of thinking, feeling, and behaving" (Postman 1970, 161).

In the remaining chapters, I will consider the interplay between affordances of media (i.e., streaming platforms), affordances of forms (i.e., the anthology form), and their actual uses within technological environments (e.g., data-driven, infrastructural, and industrial practices behind modes of production, distribution, and consumption on streaming platforms). For this purpose, I will opt for an approach to the study of digital culture that falls under the definition of "soft technological determinism" (Marx and Smith 1994), which observes technologies as potential enhancements and not as necessary constraints. Weak (or soft) technological determinism observes technological changes as entangled in historical contexts and ultimately "claims that the presence of a particular communication technology is an enabling or facilitating factor leading to potential opportunities which may or may not be taken up in particular societies or periods (or that its absence is a constraint)" (Lievrouw and Livingstone 2006, 331). As David M. Kaplan puts it, technology softly determines, it "mediates and steers a society, but it does not quite drive it" (Kaplan 2009, xvii). Similarly, I argue here that technology mediates forms, without necessarily driving them. The next paragraphs combine information studies, infrastructure studies, and media industry analysis (Holt and Perren 2011) to research the archival, infrastructural, industrial practices, as well as business models, involved in the delivery of over-the-top content. Complementing the media historiographical approach taken in the first two chapters, the cultural and media ecosystem frameworks are used to identify the contextual forces that influenced the emergence and consequent mutations of the anthology form in the current digital mediascape.

3.2. The Classificatory Mind

Understanding present-day non-linear media requires us to rethink the positioning of older media formations in the contemporary technological landscape, starting from one of the main features that characterize digital media: the reliance on computer data and classification systems. Since the first mass-produced analog media, and even before then, many human civilizations have been exposed to the issue of organizing, storing, and preserving cultural objects. Practices of recordkeeping have been studied in anthropological research with the intent of understanding how different societies archive documents and narrative content from an ethnographic, comparative, historical, and sociological perspective (Durkheim and Mauss 1963; Bausi et al. 2018). Catalogs and lists containing a systematic survey of items in some sort of order have been scrutinized by archivists, curators and scholars in search for information. A common concern for both those who create and those who seek to retrieve information from these inventories is how to tame the abundance of records that we produce. As the philosopher Umberto Eco points out in *The Infinity of Lists*, digital technologies have provided us with endless lists, a wealth of information that, despite the promises of connectivity, risks losing its meaning into a virtual labyrinth where truth and error are indiscernible (Eco 2009, 360). The result is a constant quest for new classificatory solutions.

Over the years, forms of content organization have colonized all human spheres and aspects of the Western world, as they have come to regulate the access to almost all types of media material and have contributed to the creation of physical and digital spaces for the storage of things. Among a variety of repositories and storehouses, spaces like archives, libraries, and museums became the preferential containers of collective knowledge and institutions of memory for "the classification society" (Ina Wagner, quoted in Bowker and Star 1999, 284). And yet, classification goes beyond an intuitive problem of epistemology and memory. It is a problem of the material accumulation of things as we struggle to keep a record of tangible and intangible human histories. It is a problem of permanence and impermanence, of the persistence of power and control over archival acts of construction, deconstruction, and the erasure of myths and identities. It is a problem of accessibility and inclusion.

The "classificatory mind" of contemporary Western societies is ultimately the symptom of a deeper, cognitive human need to collect and catalog objects in order to understand them. The necessity to regulate the cognitive load of accessing media content, along with that of archiving and preserving cultural production, emerged in several ways in practices of temporally and systematically organizing objects into space. In literature, while some attempts to explicate textual information can sometimes be seen in unstructured and informal comments, annotations or marginalia at the corners of ancient manuscripts, it can be more clearly observed in the formal structuring patterns that define narrative units. From ancient papyrus rolls or manuscripted codex formats to chapters and paragraphs found in contemporary culture, narrative forms tend to adapt to the affordances of each medium. Not only do these forms impose an ordering on cultural consumption, but they also define a framework for further interpretation and classification. In other words, classificatory intelligence usually leans on textual or perceptual evidence, which, together with normalized and shared categories passed on generation after generation, contribute to determining both the integrity of an artifact and its points of breakdown. In this sense, a classification system rests upon similarities and differences within a network of connectivity and collectivity, where objects exist only in relation to other objects.

Early occurrences of classificatory systems date back at least to the fourth century BC, when Aristotle theorized the existence of categories – forms of the highest kind – that would include increasingly generic classes marked by specific differences, in a hierarchical organization (Aristotle 1975). Since then, in Western culture, mental representations have been used to explain relational coordination and/or subordination in language, logic, nature and all formal objects of interpretation. Some of the most recent and foundational examples of classification schemes deployed for the categorization of cultural objects in pre-digital culture are found in libraries, which had been concerned with keeping an organized record of the items contained in their inventories, while also facilitating the access to it. Originally developed in the late 1800s, the Dewey Decimal Classification (DDC) is perhaps one of the most widely known library classification systems and one of the first to consider an alternative arrangement of volumes on a shelf to the formerly adopted ordering per date of acquisition. Dewey notably proposed to use decimals to arrange volumes on library shelves, using three-digit numbers and additional fractional numbers to distinguish publications based on general subject, relative location (topical order) and index (alphabetical order).

This hierarchical classification based on general subjects and specific topics, however, presented limits in the categorization and retrieval of items pertaining to interdisciplinary topics at the intersection of more than one area of knowledge. As early as 2014, a paper in the *Annual Report of the American Historical Association* exposed some of the challenges of applying existing library theory and practice to the emerging "science of archives", noting that "the modern library has developed a system of subject classification, which has made the contents of its shelves easily accessible to the average reader. But the close application of a similar system to collections of archives has not met with success" (Virtue 1914, 374). The paper mentions the cases of the Swedish Royal Archives and the National Archives of France, and cites Leland's warning: "Archives are the product and record of the performance of its functions by an organic body, and they should faithfully reflect the workings of that organism. No decimal system of classification, no refined methods of library science, no purely chronological or purely alphabetical arrangement can be successfully applied to the classification of archives" (Leland, cited in Virtue 1914, 375-376).

From the Dewey Decimal Classification to more recent library systems, the question of the location and context of the records for the purpose of content retrieval remains an underlying concern, especially when it comes to archives that are subjected to constant expansion and scaling. Among others, one of the proposed solutions was to opt for faceted schemes, based on fundamental categories – e.g., material, space, time – that can define item's properties (facets) in a relational way (Ranganathan 1950; Star 1998). Over time, classification practices in library and archival settings have become more and more sophisticated.

Although it might appear as the result of centuries of analytical training required to manage the amount of collected artifacts, this ubiquitous classificatory inclination is a modern acquisition for the human kind, dependent on cultural norms and technological advancements more than on individual skills. To this point, the French sociologists Emile Durkheim and Marcel Mauss bring our attention to the risks induced by the generalized belief that classification has always been an innate human capacity, rather than the result of societal organization. They argue that classificatory skills and functions have been socially constructed and absorbed through a process of education to identify roles, objects, symbols, and entities (Durkheim and Mauss 1963). In this perspective, classification systems are likely to mutate along with mental categories, which are subject to changes in cultural awareness, institutionalization, and adaptation. As such, they are also likely to reflect personal views or reproduce biases.

Beyond the individual and collective intellectual ability to classify, human societies have been building upon different systems of organization, more or less rigid, more or less fluid, in an evolutionary manner. This is particularly evident when we compare pre-digital forms of classification to their digital counterpart. As we will see in the next chapter, information scientists and engineers have designed complex computational systems by absorbing older forms of content organization and updating them to newly acquired cognitive and technological affordances. While tracing a history of classification, Geoffrey C. Bowker, professor of informatics, and the sociologist Susan Leigh Star (1999) discussed this tension between pre-existing and emergent classification systems, stressing the non-deterministic nature of digital classification and stating that pre-existing cultural grids converge with the affordances of new information technologies and infrastructures. Modern digital supports for content organization often inherit naming conventions and functions from analog media. Tablets, desktops, and folders, for instance, borrowed similar design or affordances to their pre-digital predecessor. Online digitized catalogs on streaming platforms function very much like bookshelves in a physical library, where items are usually grouped based on subject, genre, or theme with the common scope of facilitating the search for content and promoting its retrieval.

Yet, digital media have also fostered the emergence of unique and innovative processes of data collection, chronological recordkeeping, and content classification, which did not exist before or only existed as tasks performed manually at a much smaller scale. We can think, for example, of email triage, a form of automated or semi-automated sorting based on archiving emails into separate folders – inbox, sent, drafts, junk, and so on. By activating new computational functions, digital media enhanced human ability to manage classification systems, and made them pervasive in our lives, in a perpetual invitation to reason in terms of resemblances and dissimilarities. The cultural sociologist David Beer discusses collection practices in relation to new media as part of what he defines a "classificatory imagination" (Beer 2013), by pointing at the fact that classificatory processes "are now central to how culture circulates" (Ibid., 60) and that, to fully understand digital platforms, we need to consider "how classificatory processes work to order culture on commercial, organizational, informal and everyday levels" (Ibid., 62). In a broad sense of the term, classification might apply to temporal divisions, measures of spaces, or roles in society, with the intent of presumably making our social and communication systems more efficient. When it comes to organizing culture, however, matters of efficiency and automation become secondary to the ethical questions around the obsessive quest for classifying everything.

As discussed in previous chapters, processes of archiving narrative material in the form of anthologies had already revealed the risks of unifying cultural collections under principles of exclusion that often rely on power dynamics. These risks are amplified in digital culture, where classification systems on online platforms seem to respond primarily to commercial interests tied to high amount of data and automated recommendations. This financial implication is what makes, among other factors, forms of categorization behind algorithmic filtering on online platforms so controversial. The sorting of socio-cultural data is now used as the main driver for algorithmic indexing, personalization, and individualized segmentation, with the ultimate aim to generate dynamics of consumption and profit. With thousands of different categories and genres multiplying on platforms like Netflix, the predisposition of cultural objects to be classified has turned into a cultural imperative for sustaining the digital economy. Questions arise as to "what are these categories? Who makes them, and who may change them? When and why do they become visible? How do they spread?" (Bowker and Star 1999, 3)

Understanding what, whose, and for whom these classification systems are, which categories they overshadow or elevate, and how these decisions are made is part of an ethical obligation to unveil the hidden principles of cultural selection (Ibid., 5–6). It also reminds us that the Western civilization is increasingly unable to function outside of classification grids. While one can only speculate about the possibility of a non-classificatory human society, ever-present forms of classification can be invisible and disappear into "infrastructure, into habit, into the taken for granted" (Ibid., 319). An expanding body of academic work has raised crucial questions on how to prevent classification systems, big data, and emerging technologies from being invisible instruments of white, male predominance (O'Neil 2016; Noble 2018; Buolamwini and Gebru 2018; Benjamin 2019; Klein and D'Ignazio 2020; Crawford 2021). Building upon these studies, the following paragraphs investigate how this invisible infrastructure translates into systems of cultural production and distribution. Classification is both symbolic and material (Bowker and Star 1999, 39–40), metaphorical and physical, and, as such, it bears epistemological and pragmatical consequences. Classifying cultural artifacts in digital platform environments – whether by format, formula/genre, form, or media type – implies regulating their proliferation and transmission by means of both humans and machines. If, on the one hand, curatorial practices of anthologization leverage a predominantly human intervention, data-based classification relies upon a mix of software, hardware, lines of code, content stored via data centers or cloud computing, and other technical "*dispositifs*" (Foucault 1975; Agamben 2009).

3.3. From Humans to Machines

Internet-based media are "fluid assemblages" (Redström and Wiltse 2018) that exist in a system of infrastructures outside of the materiality of a single object, be it a phone, a tablet, or a computer. Most computerized machines we use nowadays in our daily activities are enhanced by the internet super-structure and, in some cases, they can only gain their affordances thanks to wi-fi connection. Even older media supports, like television screens, can be turned into smart devices, connected, amplified, and intelligent. This complex architecture based on the interconnectivity and interoperability of objects via a wireless network has been described as the "Internet of Things (IoT)," a circuit of systems and applications that "alters the equation from

human-based data input to both human- and machine-based data input"
(Greengard 2015. 19). IoT technologies rely on a constant supply and storage
of data provided by humans and managed by machines in the long-awaited
"global village" (McLuhan 1989). This exchange of information can occur
from human to machine or from machine to machine. One example of a
human-to-machine communication model is wearable devices that can
collect physiological data through sensors. A machine-to-machine model,
on the contrary, is based upon a direct exchange of information between
two computational devices, such as a personal computer and a remote
network of servers.

The transition from data cognitively or physically managed by humans to
data managed by or through machines has evolved to intersect with processes
of datafication (O'Neil and Schutt 2013), which, on digital platforms, often
result in real-time data collection about users habits and preferences. In the
production and distribution of cultural objects (e.g., textual, audiovisual, or
others), the process of generating data can take the form of digitization, that
is to say, when analog content is converted into a computer-readable format
for information retrieval, re-use, or manipulation. Even before data collection
infrastructures came into play in the context of online platforms like Netflix,
digitization had started to change the way we archive and access most
narrative-based cultural artifacts, through the "anthologization of knowledge
and communication" (Doueihi 2011a, 21, my translation). Another relevant
concept, closely related to that of digitization, is digitalization. Digitalization
stands for the "sociotechnical process of applying digitizing techniques to
broader social and institutional contexts that render digital technologies
infrastructural" (Tilson et al. 2010, 749). The scholars David Tilson, Kalle
Lyytinen, and Carsten Sørensen argue (Ibid., 750) that digitalization led to:
device convergence – i.e., different types of information stored on single
devices; network convergence – i.e., many types of information assembled
in the same internet network; and, eventually, to industry convergence – i.e.,
many activities integrated into one industry. But exactly how does digitalization affect data classification and cultural data flows? When it comes to
classification, both digitized and digitally born material follow the same
principles valid for analog systems of classifications as they intersect with
data, medium, message, infrastructural routines, and standards.

Bowker and Star summed them up into three main statements. A first
principle is that data entry always requires the demanding work of selection
and organization, which inevitably results in errors, omissions, or biases
dependent on the classification scheme itself as well as on cultural variation (Bowker and Star 1999, 108). As Ramesh Srinivasan remarks, "most

off-the-shelf systems follow precreated metadata and ontology standards and thus command how information about or for a local community is described, classified, and retrieved. This tends to favor the perpetuation of the standards of the software creator rather than support of diverse, local community based ways of thinking and knowing" (Srinivasan 2018, 47). A second principle that applies to both analog and digital classification is that of an insoluble relationship between the medium and the message, which is to say that the information that "gets stored is at best what can be stored using the currently available technology: the encyclopedia comes to mirror the affordances of its technological base" (Bowker and Star 1999, 108–109). This implies that a digital management of data can also provoke "digital fractures" (Doueihi 2011a) between objects existing solely in an analog form and digitized objects, with higher likelihood of aggravating digital inequality (Srinivasan 2018) and technological deficits (Jin 2021). A third point is related to digital information technologies and "infrastructural routines as conceptual problems" (Bowker and Star 1999, 109), meaning infrastructure and industry standards that not only promote efficiency, but also actively transform the way data collection and management work.

Since large-scale computing and other forms of digital automation are built upon a series of dependencies between infrastructures, the human capacity to grasp the operations behind these systems tends to become increasingly uncertain. Humankind "has built a civilization so complex that he needs to mechanize his record more fully if he is to push his experiment to its logical conclusion and not merely become bogged down part way there by overtaxing his limited memory" (Bush 1996, 46). To tackle both issues of cultural over-production and decadence of the human memory, digitalization has been forecasted in the form of a supplemental memory, "a sort of mechanized private file and library [...] a device in which an individual stores all his books, records, and communications, and which is mechanized so that it may be consulted with exceeding speed and flexibility" (Ibid., 43). In this sense, machine intervention in the management of cultural artifacts, from books to audiovisual material, came both as a solution and a challenge, in that it offers a viable path for large-scale recordkeeping, while also underplaying the fragility of digital culture as it increasingly escapes human understanding. In line with a medium–message convergence, it has been observed that forms of classification change into increasingly elaborated systems as archival technologies become more and more sophisticated. It was the case of the codex, ancestor of paper-based books, which prompted "encyclopedists [to] gradually develop more elaborate categories and deeper hierarchies" (Bolter 1991, 90), much like genres mutated and multiplied with the affordances of electronic media. "As we move into desktop use of hyperlinked digital libraries, we fracture the traditional bibliographic categories across media, versions, genres, and author" (Bowker and Star 1999, 26).

Milad Doueihi (2011b) warns us that the rapid adoption of digital forms of archiving, classification, and information retrieval might return ever more fragmented cultural systems, with proliferating bits of data vulnerable to the hazards of history and in need of additional organization systems. With digital platforms and algorithmic filtering in particular, systems of narrative categories, genres, and forms have, indeed, been brought to the fore in a tireless quest for personalization. The original intent of online classification systems was to define a measure for proximity between documents (Karlgren 1990), analogous to the methods used to arrange a bookshelf in a library. With the optimization of algorithmic filtering operations, classificatory practices evolved to represent one of the triggers of intellectual isolation, information silos and "filter bubbles" (Pariser 2011). While critiques over the biases and errors in machine-learning classifications are largely known, it also important to remember that there is still a human component in determining forms of content organization and that not all classification systems are governed via institutional or algorithmic means. A human tendency to sort, categorize, group, and divide memory, knowledge, and information is embedded in editorial as much as in storytelling practices. In this context, the anthology form evolved into a classification system of itself, branching into machine-based and human-based practices. Anthologies can be seen as forms of "data play" and "re-appropriation of data into cultural practices" (Beer 2013, 166), as ways to reintroduce human stories into machine classification. "Thus, the story bursts into digital culture. The narrative is both a curatorial technique and a means of communication which, in some cases, seems to give a more human, individualistic dimension to information and its circulation in a universe characterized by the exponential growth of data and the abundance of tools for reading and consultation, even production of content. But the story is also the production site of a mythology of the digital" (Doueihi 2011a, 139, my translation).

3.4. The Streaming Machine

The computerization of narratives and cultures covers a wide range of occurrences in digital platform environments. In the process of digitalization of textual and audiovisual material, a series of practices are involved from content production to content classification and clustering, up until algorithmic filtering and information retrieval. It is important to note that:

> Defining the meaning of a word, a sentence, a paragraph, or a whole news story is much more difficult than defining an account number, and consequently comparing text is not easy. Understanding and modeling how people compare texts, and designing computer algorithms to accurately perform this comparison, is at the core of information retrieval. Increasingly, applications of information retrieval involve multimedia documents with structure, significant text content, and other media. Popular information media include pictures, video, and audio, including music and speech. [...] These media have content that, like text, is difficult to describe and compare.
>
> (Croft et al. 2011, 2–3)

In the hard endeavor to understand how classification and filtering systems might work in the interaction with curatorial and editorial forms of content organization, I will consider the case of Netflix as one of the most diffused streaming platforms worldwide. While little has been disclosed by corporate sources about the specific technical functioning of its service, some useful information can be established from the analysis of the interface and matched with press releases and official accounts. Netflix notably utilizes genres, emotion categories,[1] actors, release year, and other metadata connected to each title[2] to construct a scheme of classification based on the content delivered through its platform. Some genre descriptors correspond to unique identifiers, amounting to over 3,500 category IDs[3] in a plethora of over seventy-thousand micro-genres (Madrigal 2014, online).

In a study of how Netflix online-DVD service's categories are articulated, Daniel Smith-Rowsey was able to compress the catalog into nineteen macro-genres and four hundred subgenres, pointing at the fact that Netflix seems to embrace Rick Altman's vision of genre as transhistorical and synchronic, rather than connected to a specific era (McDonald and Smith-Rowsey 2018,

---

1   Emotion categories associated with each title can be found under the section "This show is..."; cf. "This show is...Intimate, Emotional." https://www.netflix.com/title/81166770.

2   Netflix Help Center, "How Netflix's Recommendations System Works." https://help.netflix.com/en/node/100639.

3   Cf. https://www.whats-on-netflix.com/library/categories/.

66–69).[4] Yet, the fractured way the global streaming platform approaches its audiences, with thousands of micro-categories, is itself an attempt to historicize genres. In a way, the definition of "film noir" does have a timeframe to it. It alludes to the studio system in a specific movie or television era and to a type of rather "classic" content, which may or may not be complemented with other tags. Compressing the Netflix streaming library tags into the list of genres found on the DVD-delivery service platform could be a viable method to rationalize the catalog, but it is evident by now that computational modes of handling content classification on streaming platforms leverage precisely the possibility to manage a massive scale of material, data, and metadata. Similar tags and entrances often allow us to retrieve content through a multiplicity of varied, polyvalent, assorted options for search. It looks like Netflix's classification system builds upon different labeling systems, variations, and ambiguities, rather than on a fixed and trackable hierarchy of macro-genres and sub-genres. In order to understand content classification on streaming platforms we therefore have to abandon predefined ideas of genre as something that is imposed by verifiable categories based on industry structure, aesthetic evaluation, journalistic or academic criticism. Instead, we should embrace a blurred meaning of genre, intended as a self-generative formula for cultural communication and transmission, one that can be informed and deformed, formulated, de-formulated, and re-formulated again, in a continuous process of re-negotiation.

In this sense, a tag like "horror movies"[5] is not really an umbrella term that includes other tags like "vampire horror movies," but rather a way to "carve out generic, semantic/syntactic space" (McDonald and Smith-Rowsey 2018, 71–72). By doing so, it recuperates primitive categories, while also retrieving analogous occurrences in a much more diversified digital culture, where the parts do not necessarily stand for the whole, but they are rather adjacent to it. This brings us outside of traditional genre categories crystallized in a male-centric canon, and into a more inclusive notion of genre based on fluid practices, where categories coexist, overlap, and hybridize. One wrong assumption of classical narratology has been to interpret categories as static

---

4   Daniel Smith-Rowsey's research is based on a list of Netflix genres as found on dvd.netflix. com, the Netflix-owned DVD-by-mail service. To my knowledge, there is no evidence that proves that the genre classification system is the same for both Netflix DVD and streaming services, especially considering that "in 2011, Netflix spun off its DVD selection from its primary platform, eventually establishing streaming on demand as the status quo. Netflix promised to continue mailing out DVDs, but with a catch. They would be siphoned off to a separate service, now called DVD.com, fully divorcing the physical media from the digital" (Sisson 2020, online).

5   https://www.netflix.com/browse/genre/8711.

entities, stuck in an arbitrary hierarchy, framed in a network that should not be disturbed or betrayed. As the narratives that circulate across media became more heterogenous, the discrepancy between genres and hierarchy emerged clearly. It showed that the state of "classificatory inertia," which led to the stereotypization of narrative categories, was in the way the network was constructed, and not in a pre-constituted, inescapable hierarchy of genres. As the network changed, and with it the system of infrastructures and politics of power, the configurations of genres also mutated, along with their functions. On streaming platforms, these functions are tied to the practical decisions and technical constraints of mechanisms of content personalization based on algorithmic recommendation systems. Indeed, there will be a hierarchy of categories, but how that hierarchy is imposed has to do with the need to prioritize both human selection and an efficient automated sorting. This opens up a series of ethical questions about the decisions made by humans in the machine workflow.

Streaming platforms' genre-classification systems are not necessarily inclusive. Most algorithmic-based practices of content organization on online platforms are the result of overlapping layers of human-machine interventions, which are hard to grasp and retrace. For this reason, the contribution of platforms like Netflix to the classification of cultural objects appears ambivalent. On the one hand, by disclosing a variety of categories that were never publicly recognized before, Netflix finally opened up audiovisual narratives to a diversity of genres, releasing them from elitist visions of how stories should be formatted, formulated, and named. In this systematic activity of keeping track of all genres, both what is in the streaming library and what is outside of it, naming everything can almost be interpreted as an act of inclusion, rather than exclusion. On the other hand, Netflix's genres are categories built on non-binary labels, with potentially infinite labeling descriptions able to generate seemingly endless streams of personalized content in synergy with algorithmic filtering. Consequently, "the freedom entailed is that we can customize our own library spaces; but as Jo Freeman (1972) pointed out in her classic article, 'The Tyranny of Structurelessness,' this is also so much more work that we may fall into a lowest level convenience classification rather than a high-level semantic one" (Bowker and Star 1999, 26). If defining a structure has obvious ethical challenges in processes of exclusion, even structureless-ness in the form of an extreme specificity and complexity of ontologies has its risks.

In the seminal work *Search Engines: Information Retrieval in Practice*, W. Bruce Croft, Donald Metzler, and Trevor Strohman go in-depth into the mathematical, computational, and technical programming issues of information classification and retrieval in digital environments, explaining how these influence the very design and implementation of search engines. As they state in the chapter on clustering and categorization:

> since classification is a supervised learning task, it is important not to construct an overly complex ontology, since most learning algorithms will fail (i.e., not generalize well to unseen data) when there is little or no data associated with one or more of the labels. In the web page language classifier example, if we had only one example page for each of the Asian languages, then, rather than having separate labels for each of the languages, such as "Chinese", "Korean", etc., it would be better to combine all of the languages into a single label called "Asian languages". The classifier will then be more likely to classify things as "Asian languages" correctly, since it has more training examples.
>
> (Croft et al. 2011, 341)

In a similar way, higher degrees of generalization of Netflix's categories might exist precisely with the intent to facilitate classification for information retrieval (i.e., querying of content) and filtering (i.e., algorithmic selection of relevant items), in cases when specific micro-genre occurrences are limited and a vaguer tag is needed. Other forms of macro-labeling are used to market content, such as the "only on Netflix" category,[6] or the algorithmically curated categorical streams based on popular content, latest releases, top ten most-watched titles in each country, critically acclaimed shows, and so forth. These additional categories and streams only appear once users log into the platform, when they are also exposed to the design of the interface, which suggests an intuitive classification scheme into separate sections, under the banners "TV shows," "movies," "new & popular," "my list," and "browse by language."

The subdivision of the platform into separate sections is in itself some sort of classification system that defines different lists containing interlinked categories. Each one of these sections functions like an open anthology: while it can constantly be expanded or narrowed as the library changes, it is always organized on specific principles of organization, either by media type (televisual or cinematic), novelty, popularity, personal selection, or language. If some forms of classification are the result of data-driven decisions, as in the case of the language classifier described by Croft et al., the decision-making

6   https://www.netflix.com/browse/genre/839338.

process in the design of the interface is one of the human components embedded in the editorial organization of content on Netflix. Furthermore, the interface design draws upon the partially manual-input of the tagging system. These human-based forms of classification, emerging from the work of specialized designers and taggers, operate in conjunction with a proprietary machine learning system. As Netflix's Director of Enhanced Content, Mike Hastings, revealed in an interview, metadata analysts and taxonomists are "the human voice to the algorithm, or the ghost in the machine, that's basically providing the sense to what the algorithms is trying to determine" (Walker 2017, online). This human voice to the algorithm is what Beer calls "infrastructure of participative organization," a tagging process that governs digital culture and "how we categorise it, it shapes the distinctions we make in classification, and it also forms a part of our own engagement with and contributions to cultural ordering. Tagging is an embodiment of the classificatory imagination, it is how we find the material we are looking for, that is to say it is how we navigate these cultural archives" (Beer 2013, online).

3.5. Geographies of Streaming

Both machine-based and human-based practices of content organization are situated in an ecosystem of infrastructures that make up the spatial and time dimensions of streaming data. We can say that narratives, data and "classifications have habitats. That is, the filiations between person [or object] and category may be characterized as inhabiting a space or terrain with some of the properties of any habitat. It may be crowded or sparse, peaceful or at war, fertile or arid" (Bowker and Star 1999, 316). Examining the habitat and geography of online platforms might help us gain more insight into how categorized narratives, data, and media objects are classified, organized, and spread in spatial – virtual or physical – contexts in certain ways, and why. Building upon a media-ecological perspective, the scholar Ramon Lobato suggested that we analyze the economic and infrastructural components of platforms like Netflix, starting with the disaggregation of "the ecology of services, platforms, set-top boxes, and apps that constitute the field of internet-distributed television. Internet distribution of television content is not a unitary phenomenon; it involves a wide array of different services, institutions, and practices" (Lobato 2019, 7).

Drawing from Lobato's work, in this section I will discuss the practical implications that the media-infrastructure ecology has on the circulation of audiovisual narratives, data, and systems of classification over streaming platforms. In this approach, two spatial notions emerge as particularly relevant: that of mediascape and that of infrastructure. The concept of mediascape was first theorized by Arjun Appadurai (1996) as part of five scapes that define the mobility of cultural material in the age of globalization, namely, ethnoscapes, technoscapes, ideoscapes, financescapes, and mediascapes. All of these concepts seem suitable for a study of a geography of internet distribution. However, that of mediascape presents us with a more specific term that connects technoscape – i.e., global configuration of technology (Ibid., 34) – with ideoscape – i.e., landscapes of images (Ibid., 35). More specifically, mediascapes "refer both to the distribution of the electronic capabilities to produce and disseminate information (newspapers, magazines, television stations, and film-production studios), which are now available to a growing number of private interests throughout the world, and to the images of the world created by these media" (Ibid.). Although it pre-dates algorithmic culture, Appadurai's definition of mediascape is a perfect account of contemporary streaming media: narrative-based; image-centered; highly visual; metaphorical; and yet always intertwined with modes of transmission, computer machineries, dynamics of cultural reception, industrial and political interests, geographies, and timescales. In other words, a system of infrastructures. Infrastructure is "the invisible background, the substrate or support, the technocultural/natural environment, of modernity" (Misa et al. 2003, 191).

In today's mediascape, internet-based media coexist with "disconnected" media. While these two environments intersect, they are also functionally and operationally separate habitats. Similarly, the anthological model in streaming media does not emerge only as the result of an adaptive mechanism that connects analog to digital technologies, inheriting certain forms and genres. It also inscribes itself within a topology of infrastructures that is rather specific to data-driven cultures and industrial economies, both in the quality and the scale of a delivery system that fundamentally relies on internet functionality. "Originally designed as a research network, the Internet has evolved into a massive-scale platform for multimedia delivery" (Böttger et al. 2018, 1). In this massive internet habitat, over-the-top media platforms have emerged as new services that exploit over-the-internet signal to send data and deliver content across several internet service providers, which act as intermediaries, without having to rely on commercial content delivery networks made of cable, broadcast, or satellite technologies. Over-the-top services like streaming platforms are therefore part of complex techno-cultural apparatuses consisting of several media entities[7] (e.g., protocols, metatypes, specifications, roles, or attributes) and they entail their own digital geography of internet infrastructures, content distribution networks, data centers, or cloud computing services.

The refined physical infrastructure that sustains the network of online traffic is primarily based on internet exchange points (IX or IXP),[8] which allow internet service providers (ISPs) to exchange data. A vast network of internet connection points is fundamental for an efficient functioning of content-delivery platforms, especially when they reach a global scale. In order to build their own content-delivery networks, streaming companies can either place servers in correspondence with internet exchange points or they can opt for agreements with private networks of internet service providers, such as Time Warner, Verizon, AT&T, and Comcast in the United States. "Traditionally, content delivery services have chosen one strategy or the other. Akamai, for example, hosts a lot of content with Internet service providers, while Google, Amazon, and Limelight prefer to store it at IXPs. [...] Netflix uses both strategies, and varies the structure of its network significantly from country to country" (Nordrum 2016, online). A research conducted at the Queen Mary University of London, which evaluated the deployment of Netflix servers in the local internet ecosystem of the United States, mapped a number of servers distributed across more than twenty IXP and over two hundred ISP locations (Böttger et al. 2018, 6), with different degrees of infrastructural localization. But internet exchange points and service providers are not the only type of infrastructures involved in the geography of streaming.

Netflix alone is sustained by the functionality of many interdependent infrastructures and technologies, which themselves entail different levels of locality. Personal devices (smart TV, computer, mobile phone),

---

7   V.J. Hobbs and Diarmuid Pigott define a media entity "as representing the set of all media artefacts that are related to a particular entity for a particular purpose. We identify potential media entities by considering both the media metatype that is required (sound, image, video, etc.) and the role the particular media artefact is to play in the database. For example, in the Earth Sounds database, we wish to include recordings of sounds and photographs of the sites, and we identify the media entities Site Recording and Site Photo. An entity may have one, several or no associated media entities. An entity may also have more than one media entity of the same media metatype: in the Earth Sounds database, we have Site Photo, Site Map and Phenomenon Diagram, all images, but used to represent different things. A media entity is thus somewhat similar to the domain of an attribute, in that it represents not merely a data type, but a pool of allowable values from within a type" (Hobbs and Pigott 1999, 5).

8   For a spatial reference, a map of geo-localized Internet Exchange points can be found here: https://www.internetexchangemap.com/#/ (Source: TeleGeography).

modems, and routers needed to access internet platforms rely on intangible infrastructures, such as energy infrastructures that provide electricity, programming infrastructures hidden behind the production of code, and other hardware and software resources that sustain network protocols and regulate the operations behind transmission. At the same time, bits of data travel through telephone lines, fiber-optic cables, and content delivery networks to guarantee a fluid platform experience on the distribution, interaction, and consumption side. "And of course the power grids and undersea cables that make all this activity possible" (Lobato 2019, 73). Overall, Netflix's hybrid operational strategy adheres to what was defined as a microservices architecture. In practice, this means that the platform's functionality depends on a multiplicity of microservices that together enable a continuous content-delivery and communication process, by guaranteeing more efficiency, agility, and optimization, while also limiting fragility and exposure to system failures (Nadareishvili et al. 2016, 45-46). To further strengthen its resilience and capacity to control its operations, Netflix developed its own content-delivery infrastructure in 2011, under the name of Netflix Open Connect,[9] a "global network that is responsible for delivering Netflix TV shows and movies to [...] members worldwide."[10] The network functions like common content-delivery networks, in the sense that it distributes internet content via HTTP/HTTPS from specific sites to a wide variety of client devices located in different places around the world.

Netflix Open Connect is not only global, but also highly localized, which makes it "one of the highest-volume networks in the world."[11] Another interesting shift that has affected the streaming mediascape in recent years is the massive migration of the content delivered by over-the-top services towards the cloud provider Amazon Web Services (AWS).[12] Netflix decided to deploy AWS for safely storing its content and for supporting ever-growing volumes of data. This transition, completed in January 2016,[13] marked the definitive move from a storage system based on data centers, which were more exposed

9   https://openconnect.netflix.com/en/##.

10 "Open Connect Overview." *Netflix.* https://openconnect.netflix.com/Open-Connect-Overview.pdf.

11 "How Netflix Works With ISPs Around the Globe to Deliver a Great Viewing Experience." *Netflix Media Center.* Last modified March 17, 2016. https://media.netflix.com/en/company-blog/how-netflix-works-with-isps-around-the-globe-to-deliver-a-great-viewing-experience.

12 "Hulu Case Study – Amazon Web Services." *Amazon Web Services Blog.* https://aws.amazon.com/solutions/case-studies/hulu.

13 "Completing the Netflix Cloud Migration." *Netflix Media Center.* Last modified February 11, 2016. https://media.netflix.com/en/company-blog/completing-the-netflix-cloud-migration.

to damage, data losses, and shutdowns, to a system based on cloud comput-ing. As of today, Amazon Web Services is the main infrastructure behind the most important US streaming providers[14] – e.g., Amazon Prime Video, Netflix, Hulu – and an interesting example of interconnectivity. Behind user-center connectedness – or, simply put, internet access – hides a system of owner-centered connectivity (Van Dijck 2013, 54), which, at its core, involves elements sustaining platform infrastructures and economies. Platform systems are comprised of a web of infrastructures that are interconnected, interoperable, and interdependent, often leading to agreements between rival tech companies to access the services of their competitors (e.g., the strategic alliance between Netflix and Amazon Web Services), a dynamic that has been described as "coopetition" among coordinating competitors (Van Dijck 2021).

The centralized and yet shattered geographical presence of Netflix calls our attention to a geopolitical system of infrastructures that simultaneously stands upon a global network of technologies and intersects with the local interests of national broadcasting industries. As Lobato reminds us, radio and television have always been transnational media, inherently obeying a spatial logic (Lobato 2019, 54). When we discuss streaming platforms in the context of digital culture, it is important to understand that Netflix's international presence, under the appealing idea of ubiquitous availability and connectivity, does nevertheless come with local costs and compromises. As powerful competitors, able to trespass local borders and regulations thanks to over-the-top technology, US-owned, quasi-global streaming platforms posed important questions regarding the extent to which forms of cultural intrusion in local television markets should be tolerated (Ibid., 64–65). From Kenya and Russia (Ibid.) to Canada,[15] many countries raised concerns at the governmental level about the increasing influence of Netflix on national cultural industries and regulations, along with other forms of US expansionism and media imperialism (Boyd-Barrett and Mirelees 2019) that are perpetuated by international digital platforms and tech corporations. With its internal conflicts, triggered by concurring transnational decisions and national interests, the geography of digital distribution (Lobato 2019) is the sum of many geographies of streaming, at once ambivalent and ever-changing, local and global.

14   A map of AWS global infrastructure can be found at the following link: https://www.infrastructure.aws.

15   Kait Bolongaro. "Trudeau's Party Passes Bill to Regulate Social Media, Streaming," *Bloomberg*, 2021. https://www.bloomberg.com/news/articles/2021-06-22/trudeau-s-party-passes-bill-to-regulate-social-media-streaming.

At first glance, mapping the infrastructural habitat of streaming services does not seem to directly provide us with a clearer understanding of the anthology form and its positioning in digital culture. However, a more granular observation reveals the complex geo-technical network of infrastructures that underpins media industry strategies, financial decisions, and the constitution of hierarchies of power hidden behind major over-the-top players. From a general description of how Netflix infrastructural habitat plays out in the circulation of media content, some interesting remarks can be made even outside of purely geo-technical or geopolitical considerations. Observing a geography of streaming platforms sheds light on how a "network effect" behind internet-distributed television (Venkatesan and Lecinski 2021) might be activated by the scale, diversity, and endurance of its infrastructural ecosystem. Netflix's infrastructural reliability and global presence enlarge its web of content providers, thus incrementing the platform value for both existing and potential users, who are offered a smooth viewing experience and a quality content selection. In turn, as new subscribers join the platform from different locations, more diversified users' data is collected and fed into Netflix's recommendation system, with an expected increase in performance and efficacy in the personalization of content. This proves that infrastructural efficiency has positive trade-offs in terms of levels of users satisfaction. More data also means additional information available to make decisions on which original content presents a good investment or which new classification categories might be needed to fill up empty spaces and enhance cultural framing through micro-genres. In the digital circulation of media forms, infrastructural geographies of streaming are physical manifestations of the computerization of knowledge, and how it is "changing the way in which learning is acquired, classified, made available, and exploited" (Lyotard 1984, 4). Technological, computational, and industrial infrastructures in space – and time – demonstrate that "the proliferation of information-processing machines is having [...] as much of an effect on the circulation of learning as did advancements in human circulation (transportation systems) and later, in the circulation of sounds and visual images (the media)" (Ibid.).

3.6. Infrastructures of Time

Non-linear streaming media not only affected pre-existing geographies of infrastructures, but they also revolutionized traditional linear media consumption. Much like the spatial dynamics of data transmission are tied to infrastructural reliability, the making of temporalities in streaming media is itself infrastructural. In an article on contemporary urbanization and processes of acceleration in daily human life, Besedovsky et al. (2019) propose to observe time as infrastructure. "We understand temporalities themselves as infrastructures: they are structures that underlie and powerfully shape current forms of social organization and interaction" (Ibid., 581). Capitalistic and consumeristic narratives of hyper-efficiency, technological mobility, and simultaneous multitasking are all tied to visions of augmented time, where media solicitations alter socially constructed temporalities through enhanced mechanisms of digital production, distribution, and reception. Infrastructures of time built on accelerated rhythms are not only made as a consequence of material and geopolitical infrastructure efficiency, as I have shown, but they are also active makers of socio-cultural infrastructures in the form of content organization. Streaming television presents an interesting example of how non-linear temporalities have impacted the creation of algorithmic infrastructures that order, sort, and pre-package audiovisual content.

Streaming platforms are built on the idea that the moment of consumption does not need to align with the moment of release, and that viewers can freely navigate a library of content in much the same way as they would navigate an online archive. In other words, "nonlinear forms of television are understood to free viewers from the temporal logic of the broadcast flow, providing programmes within the fragmented and hyperlinked structure of the internet or personal video recorder" (Johnson 2019, online). Beyond each platform's specificities, streaming libraries commonly generate a series of personalized databases of audiovisual content with different levels of continuity and length, instead of imposing a pre-planned, uninterrupted flow through a linear programming schedule. As James Bennett explained, "the program as content on these services calls our attention to its embedding in a new, digital media context: instead of flow here we have an interface, hyperlinks and a database structure experienced via broadband rather than broadcasting" (Bennett and Strange 2011, 1).

Since they grant the audience access to content with a more flexible choice and higher control over their viewing experience, convenience, and customization (Lotz 2007), non-linear media are often thought to provide a new sense of autonomy and freedom measured via a more elastic use of "discretionary time" (Goodin et al. 2008). By letting the users personally pick their individual content selection and manage their own viewing time, internet-distributed television has marked a radical turn in the way we perceive mediated time. Each viewer can decide to watch a single unit of one episode separately, as a discrete item, or entire seasons online in a continuous loop without interruption. In this seemingly unlimited and unregulated access to content, choice turns into a burden (Cohn 2019), control becomes an illusion (Johnson 2019), and freedom a deceit. Jonathan Cohn has directed our attention to the fact that recommendation systems were originally born to propose a computational solution to the problem of choice, by assisting overwhelmed consumers to speed up and facilitate their decisions, supposedly making consumption easy, fun, and productive. The paradox of choice (Schwartz 2009) is not so much about the human inability to choose among a given set of options, but it is rather about an overload of inputs, information, and expectations that the consumeristic society had framed as necessary for success. Machine-aided choice became a solution against the perceived anxieties and failures of human decisions. "Through these recommendations, making a choice was framed as a 'burden,' while automated computer technologies became the solution. These recommendation programs taught the bourgeoisie to treat their privileges and options as a burden they could pleasurably cast off to technologies and technocrats" (Cohn 2019, 3). Stressing the pragmatic nature of the decision process associated with individual time costs, non-linear television implemented already established algorithmic infrastructures and practices for generating internal regulatory patterns through the use of data classification and automated content sorting.

Lacking a programming schedule with fixed blocks, as well as regular phases and rhythms typical of the old season cycle – which orders linear broadcasting in a daily, weekly, monthly, quarterly, or season-long schedule – non-linear television paved the way for potentially excessive modes of consumption that could only be regulated by the interface through forms of content organization. In the absence of a fixed, regulatory programming pattern and a rigid season-cycle model, we have assisted in the redefinition of social practices of over-consumption of television content, already existent in linear television but strongly enhanced by the ever-expanding space of easily accessible online environments. As William Trouleau et al. underlined, "easy accessibility can often lead to over-consumption [...]. On video on-demand services, this has recently been referred to as 'binge watching', where potentially entire seasons of TV shows are consumed in a single viewing session" (Trouleau et al. 2016, 1215). As much as we need to consider new standards and norms in the production and distribution of television series from a media industry perspective, we should also observe new individual and collective behaviors in streaming television consumption from a time-oriented standpoint. In March 2016, a Nielsen survey reported that "among those who watch VOD, more than three-quarters of global respondents (77%) agree they do so because they can view content at a time that is convenient for them. Users are also watching VOD content because it allows multiple people in the household to watch different programming on different devices at the same time"[16] (Nielsen 2016). Moreover, the study shows that, on online platforms, binge-watching is becoming an increasingly popular practice, and it now largely moves viewership: data suggests that catching up on multiple episodes at once is one of the main reasons for streaming audiovisual content among different age groups (Ibid.).

If we look at another research published in the tenth edition of Deloitte's digital democracy survey, carried out by an independent research firm in November 2015, it is reported that "70% of U.S. consumers binge watch TV content. Among those, nearly a third of consumers are binge watching shows weekly."[17] Deloitte also reveals that users watch an average of five episodes per week, and that TV dramas appear to be the most popular content to binge-watch, suggesting a possible relation between consumption practices and genres. Furthermore, 92 percent of spectators interviewed in this survey are carrying out additional activities while watching television, with only a quarter of multitasking activities directly related to the programs that consumers are watching.[18] Such phenomenon addresses the phenomenon of "time-deepening" (Godbey 1976), a consequential effect of multitasking practices involved in watching television as a secondary activity itself or while engaging in other, secondary activities (Robinson and Martin 2009, 82–83).

Overall, these data and surveys demonstrate that the main factors that drive the audience towards streaming television are convenient time management and a general flexibility in viewing. With the possibility of streaming serialized content in a personalized manner, modes of consumption become increasingly varied. Again, time-management infrastructures and modalities are central elements for investigating the transition of television shows from linear to a non-linear media and the range of consumption practices it generated. The availability of content in extensive online libraries seems to entail at least three main types of over-consumption habits: a continuous stream of several episodes (binge-watching); an accelerated

16   "Video on Demand." *Nielsen Ratings.* https://www.nielsen.com/wp-content/uploads/sites/3/2019/04/global-video-on-demand-report-mar-2016.pdf.

17   "Digital Democracy Survey | Deloitte | Research Project." *Deloitte.* https://www2.deloitte.com/tr/en/pages/technology-media-and-telecommunications/articles/digital-democracy-survey-generational-media-consumption-trends.html.

18   Ibid.

form of viewing (speed-watching); or both (binge-racing). Furthermore, viewers can watch more than one content at the same time on multiple devices, resulting in a sort of simultaneous watching. These are examples of an amplified consumption that tends to take the shape of excess. However, binge-watching, speed-watching, binge-racing, and other forms of excessive watching are far from being simple evidence of addictive human behavior. They are rather the consequence of the overlapping infrastructural systems, data schemes, and dispositions (Bourdieu 1977) offered by the platforms designs and infrastructures. As such, they can also move away from a tendency to over-consume and transition towards a more or less self- and hetero-regulated consumption, within a diversified set of practices that seem to suggest a link between time management and forms of content management.

In order to study such a diversified set of practices, in an experimental study published in 2016 (Trouleau et al. 2016), a research group from the École polytechnique de Lausanne proposed the possible application of data-mining methods to understand binge-watching habits and their inner variety. They notably delineated a data-driven definition of binge-watching, to underline the presence of different types of binge-watching. The study shows that while it is common that episodes are watched in a sequential order in a single session to catch-up on content, this is not always true for binge-watching (Ibid., 1222). For instance, users might watch episode 8 and then go back to episode 7 or jump to episode 12 in the same session. While regular sessions are almost entirely sequential (97 percent), 84 percent of binge-watching sessions and 76 percent of the hyper-binge-watching sessions are non-sequential, indicating that binge-viewers are likely to watch content out-of-order (Ibid., 1223). The connection between binge-watching practices and non-sequentiality brings us back to the very definition of non-linear television: non-linear systems tend to be non-sequential, and affected by phenomena of disjunction and disruption. Non-linearity, however, calls for mechanisms of self-regulation in the consumption of television content.

Mechanisms of induced self-regulation in television consumption can occur in products like television series on a formal and a structural level. In addition to the industrial and sociological perspective, consumption can be analyzed by taking into account a narratological perspective and rhythmic forms of chapter division. One of the ways in which streaming habits are regulated is the narrative infrastructure. By narrative infrastructure, I mean the traceable physical, organizational, and operational structures involved in storytelling mechanisms. In the formation of narrative infrastructures, designing and staging is key to moving from the chaotic nature of human thoughts and imaginaries to a formal, even material, shape. Over the years, theoretical and empirical studies on storytelling styles and logics (Gunter 1987, 196; Gross 1997, 272; Herman 2004, 215–216; Keen 2015, 12; Hogan 2020, 2) have suggested that narrative structures (e.g., narrative cues in the design layouts, forms, genres) might anticipate, to some extent, cognitive reception, memory, and comprehension, by guiding the audience through a series of strategic textual steps that direct the perceptual experience and understanding. Narrative segmentations, such as division into episodes, seasons, and other time units strictly related to storytelling, such as cliffhangers or closures, create boundaries, hiatuses, and pauses throughout the plot. Such time units have always existed in storytelling. However, strategies of narrative division are undergoing a process of adaptation to non-linear television, where the absence of commercial interruptions makes the viewing experience more fluid and dependent on personalized time management in similar ways to reading a paper book. The idea of a discrete television episode as a single unit existing in the television flow is now being revised and questioned (Van Arendonk 2019), as the process of waiting one week or more for the next episode is being replaced by the single-release strategy taken by many streaming platforms.

Temporal consumption patterns in connected viewing (Holt and Sanson 2013) are therefore the result of several overlapping infrastructures – material, narrative, and distribution. The viewers' need to make sense of the narrative as a block of several episodes or as an entire season is now tied to physical networks of technologies, storytelling techniques, as well as to industrial strategies for commercial release. To test how genres, forms, or formats fit into specific modes of viewing, streaming platforms have been experimenting with how much they can release simultaneously. For example, Hulu initially opted for weekly releases and some YouTube Originals were divided into several episodes uploaded on a monthly basis, whereas Netflix most often releases its series all at once. Together, these factors have outcomes not only on the reception of media content, but also on its production. In the public media discourse, it has been noticed that products like podcasts, which are now often adapted into television series, "gained popularity precisely because they filled a gap in people's busy lives and busy schedules. Where screens demand that we stop, sit still and watch, podcasts can be squeezed in between commutes, child care and cooking dinner."[19] Similarly, miniseries and other forms of short programming have transitioned quite smoothly to

19   "The Rise of the Podcast Adaptation." *The Economist*. Last modified October 12, 2017. https://www.economist.com/prospero/2017/10/12/the-rise-of-the-podcast-adaptation.

streaming television as a result of their capacity to fit interstitial moments of our daily lives and with content that can be easily managed in our schedules. Even more adaptable to the new infrastructural environment of non-linear media is the anthology form, with its peculiar way of affording a flexible experience of time by inserting some level of narrative modularity between single story and human- or algorithmic-curated collection.

In this chapter, I have shown how topologies of data, infrastructures, space, and time operate on several layers in the "culture of connectivity" (Van Dijck 2013) that engineered platform ecologies. I observed how the reliance on new digital technologies has generated hybrid – human and machine-computational – practices for data storage, classification, and transmission, reconfigured the infrastructural network behind media communication and redefined the spatial and temporal logics of distribution, which, in turn, are changing industrial models and narrative forms. Undoubtedly, along with infrastructural geographies of streaming, which granted Netflix global access to users' data, one of the most valuable resources in the platform economy, time has emerged as an important factor for understanding both the industrial practices related to streaming platforms, as well as the narrative forms that circulate in the context of non-linear media. In this dense info-sphere (Floridi 2002) of narratives, data, and knowledge, "traffic is not perceived spatially, e.g., in terms of an overcrowded area or a queue, but chronologically, in terms of the amount of time required to access a particular site/document (e.g., thirty seconds can be perceived as a very long time to wait when using a computer)" (Ibid., 64). Infrastructural efficiency and velocity speak of a "time when we all let our computer search, at fantastic speeds, for the required needles in those huge, well-ordered, electronic haystack that are our databases" (Ibid., 97) and platforms. But it also speaks for a "poetics of infrastructures" through the political, material, "aesthetic and the sensorial, desire and promise" (Larkin 2013) of order.

List of works cited

Abbott, Andrew. 2001. *Time Matters: On Theory and Method*. Chicago, IL: University of Chicago Press.

Agamben, Giorgio. 2009. *What Is an Apparatus? And Other Essays*. Stanford, CA: Stanford University Press.

Appadurai, Arjun. 1990. "Disjuncture and Difference in the Global Cultural Economy." *Theory, Culture and Society*. 7(2–3), 295–310. https://doi.org/10.1177/026327690007002017.

Appadurai, Arjun. 1996. *Modernity At Large: Cultural Dimensions of Globalization*. Minneapolis, MN: University of Minnesota Press.

Aristotle. 1975. *Categories and De Interpretatione*. Oxford: Clarendon Press.

Bausi, Alessandro, Brockmann, Christian, Friedrich, Michael, and Sabine Kienitz. 2018. *Manuscripts and Archives: Comparative Views on Record-Keeping*. Berlin: Walter de Gruyter.

Beer, David. 2013. *Popular Culture and New Media: The Politics of Circulation*. New York: Springer.

Beer, David. 2017. "The Social Power of Algorithms." *Information, Communication & Society* 20 (1): 1–13. https://doi.org/10.1080/1369118X.2016.1216147.

Beer, David. 2018. *The Data Gaze: Capitalism, Power and Perception*. Newbury Park, CA: SAGE.

Beer, David. 2019a. *The Quirks of Digital Culture*. Bingley: Emerald Group Publishing.

Beer, David. 2019b. "The Depths of Platform Culture." Medium. October 11, 2019. https://towardsdatascience.com/the-baffling-depths-of-platform-culture-f5648af8bc5b.

Benjamin, Ruha. 2019a. *Race After Technology: Abolitionist Tools for the New Jim Code*. Hoboken, NJ: Wiley.

Bennett, James, and Niki Strange. 2011. *Television as Digital Media*. Durham, NC: Duke University Press.

Besedovsky, Natalia, Grafe, Fritz-Julius, Hilbrandt, Hanna, and Hannes Langguth. 2019. "Time as Infrastructure." *City* 23 (4–5): 580–88. https://doi.org/10.1080/13604813.2019.1689726.

Bolter, Jay David. 1991. *Writing Space: The Computer, Hypertext, and the History of Writing*. Mahwah, NJ: Erlbaum.

Bousquet, Antoine. 2014. "Welcome to the Machine: Rethinking Technology and Society through Assemblage Theory." In *Reassembling International Theory: Assemblage Thinking and International Relations*, edited by Michele Acuto and Simon Curtis, 91–97. London: Palgrave Macmillan UK. https://doi.org/10.1057/9781137383969_11.

Bowker, Geoffrey C., and Susan Leigh Star. 1999. *Sorting Things Out: Classification and Its Consequences*. Cambridge, MA: MIT Press.

Bowker, Geoffrey C., Timmermans, Stefan, Clarke, Adele E., and Ellen Balka. 2016. *Boundary Objects and Beyond: Working with Leigh Star*. Cambridge, MA: MIT Press.

Bush, Vannevar. 1996. "As We May Think." *Interactions* 3 (2): 35–46. https://doi.org/10.1145/227181.227186.

Buyya, Rajkumar, and Amir Vahid Dastjerdi. 2016. *Internet of Things: Principles and Paradigms*. Amsterdam: Elsevier.

Crawford, Colin Jon Mark. 2021. *Netflix's Speculative Fictions: Financializing Platform Television*. Lanham, MD: Rowman & Littlefield.

Crawford, Kate. 2021. *The Atlas of AI: Power, Politics, and the Planetary Costs of Artificial Intelligence*. New Haven, CT: Yale University Press.

Croft, Bruce, Metzler, Donald, and Trevor Strohman. 2011. *Search Engines: Information Retrieval in Practice*. New York: Pearson Education.

DeLanda, Manuel. 2019. *A New Philosophy of Society: Assemblage Theory and Social Complexity*. London: Bloomsbury Publishing.

Deleuze, Gilles, and Felix Guattari. 1987. *A Thousand Plateaus: Capitalism and Schizophrenia*. Minneapolis, MN: University of Minnesota Press.

Deleuze, Gilles, and Claire Parnet. 1987. *Dialogues*. New York: Columbia University Press.

Doueihi, Milad. 2009. "Digital Objecthood and Scholarly Publishing," https://ecommons.cornell.edu/handle/1813/12020.

Doueihi, Milad. 2011a. *Digital Cultures*. Cambridge, MA: Harvard University Press.

Doueihi, Milad. 2011b. *Pour Un Humanisme Numérique*. La Librairie Du XXIe Siècle. Paris: Editions du Seuil.

Drucker, Peter Ferdinand. 1969. *The Age of Discontinuity: Guidelines to Our Changing Society*. New York: Harper & Row.

Durkheim, Emile, and Marcel Mauss. 1963. *Primitive Classification*. Chicago, IL: University of Chicago Press.

D'Ignazio, Catherine, and Lauren F. Klein. 2020. *Data Feminism*. Cambridge, MA: MIT Press.

Flichy, Patrice. 2007. *The Internet Imaginaire*. Cambridge, MA: MIT Press.

Floridi, Luciano. 2002. *Philosophy and Computing: An Introduction*. New York: Routledge.

Foucault, Michel. 1970. *The Order of Things: An Archaeology of the Human Sciences*. New York: Vintage Books.

Foucault, Michel. 1975. *Surveiller Et Punir*. Paris: Gallimard.

Foucault, Michel. 1976. *The Archaeology of Knowledge*. New York: Harper & Row.

Greengard, Samuel. 2015. *The Internet of Things*. Cambridge, MA: MIT Press.

Holt, Jennifer, and Alisa Perren. 2011. *Media Industries: History, Theory, and Method*. Hoboken, NJ: Wiley.

Holt, Jennifer, and Kevin Sanson. 2013. *Connected Viewing: Selling, Streaming, & Sharing Media in the Digital Age*. New York: Routledge.

Kaplan, David M. 2009. *Readings in the Philosophy of Technology*. Lanham, MD: Rowman & Littlefield Publishers.

Kelleter, Frank. 2017. "Media of Serial Narrative." 2017. Athens, OH: Ohio University Press.

Kroeber, A.L. 1917. "The Superorganic." *American Anthropologist* 19 (2): 163–213.

Lievrouw, Leah A., and Sonia M. Livingstone. 2006. *Handbook of New Media: Student Edition*. Newbury Park, CA: SAGE.

Luhmann, Niklas. 2000. *Art as a Social System*. Stanford, CA: Stanford University Press.

McDonald, Kevin, and Daniel Smith-Rowsey. 2018. *The Netflix Effect: Technology and Entertainment in the 21st Century*. New York: Bloomsbury Publishing.

McLuhan, Marshall. 1962. *The Gutenberg Galaxy: The Making of Typographic Man*. Toronto: University of Toronto Press.

McLuhan, Marshall. 1989. *The Global Village: Transformations in World Life and Media in the 21st Century*. Oxford: Oxford University Press.

McLuhan, Marshall. 1994. *Understanding Media: The Extensions of Man*. Cambridge, MA: MIT Press.

Murphie, Andrew, and John Potts. 2002. *Culture and Technology*. London: Macmillan Education.

Nieborg, David B, and Thomas Poell. 2018. "The Platformization of Cultural Production: Theorizing the Contingent Cultural Commodity." *New Media & Society* 20 (11): 4275–92. https://doi.org/10.1177/1461444818769694.

Noble, Safiya Umoja. 2018. *Algorithms of Oppression: How Search Engines Reinforce Racism*. New York: NYU Press.

Nordrum, Amy. 2016. "Researchers Map Locations of 4,669 Servers in Netflix's Content Delivery Network." IEEE Spectrum. August 30, 2016. https://spectrum. ieee.org/researchers-map-locations-of-4669-servers-in-netflixs-content-delivery-network.

Nystrom, Christine L. 1975. *Toward a Science of Media Ecology: The Formulation of Integrated Conceptual Paradigms for the Study of Human Communication Systems*. Ann Arbor, MI: University Microfilms.

O'Neil, Cathy. 2016. *Weapons of Math Destruction: How Big Data Increases Inequality and Threatens Democracy*. New York: Crown.

O'Neil, Cathy, and Rachel Schutt. 2013. *Doing Data Science: Straight Talk from the Frontline*. Sebastopol, CA: O'Reilly Media.

Pariser, Eli. 2012. *The Filter Bubble: How the New Personalized Web Is Changing What We Read and How We Think*. London: Penguin.

Poell, Thomas, Nieborg, David B., and Brooke Erin Duffy. 2021. *Platforms and Cultural Production*. Hoboken, NJ: Wiley.

Postman, Neil. 1970. *The Reformed English Curriculum*. Vol. High School 1980: The Shape of the Future in American Secondary Education. New York: Pitman Publishing Corporation.

Postman, Neil. 1979. *Teaching as a Conserving Activity*. New York: Dell.

Postman, Neil. 1993. *Technopoly: The Surrender of Culture to Technology*. New York: Vintage Books.

Postman, Neil, and Charles Weingartner. 1971. *The Soft Revolution: A Student Handbook for Turning Schools Around*. New York: Delacorte Press.

Ramsay, Stephen. 2011. *Reading Machines: Toward and Algorithmic Criticism.* Champaign, IL: University of Illinois Press.

Ranganathan, Shiyali Ramamrita. 1950. *Classification, Coding, and Machinery for Search.* Geneva: UNESCO.

Redström, Johan, and Heather Wiltse. 2018. *Changing Things: The Future of Objects in a Digital World.* London: Bloomsbury Publishing.

Schwartz, Barry. 2009. *The Paradox of Choice: Why More Is Less, Revised Edition.* New York: Harper Collins.

Scolari, Carlos A. 2012. "Media Ecology: Exploring the Metaphor to Expand the Theory." *Communication Theory* 22 (2): 204–25. https://doi.org/10.1111/j.1468-2885 .2012.01404.x.

Steward, Julian Haynes. 1969. *The Concept and Method of Cultural Ecology.* Indianapolis, IN: Bobbs-Merrill.

Steward, Julian Haynes. 1972. *Theory of Culture Change: The Methodology of Multilinear Evolution.* Champaign, IL: University of Illinois Press.

Strate, Lance. 2006. *Echoes and Reflections: On Media Ecology as a Field of Study.* New York: Hampton Press.

Thylstrup, Nanna Bonde, Agostinho, Daniela, Ring, Annie, D'Ignazio, Catherine, and Kristin Veel, eds. 2021. *Uncertain Archives: Critical Keywords for Big Data.* Cambridge, MA: MIT Press.

Tilson, David, Lyytinen, Kalle, and Carsten Sørensen. 2010. "Digital Infrastructures: The Missing IS Research Agenda." *Information Systems Research* 21 (4): 748–59. https://doi.org/10.1287/isre.1100.0318.

Van Dijck, José. 2013. *The Culture of Connectivity: A Critical History of Social Media.* New York: Oxford University Press.

Van Dijck, José. 2021. "Seeing the Forest for the Trees: Visualizing Platformization and Its Governance." *New Media & Society* 23 (9): 2801–19. https://doi. org/10.1177/1461444820940293.

Williams, Raymond. 1974. *Television: Technology and Cultural Form.* New York: Routledge.

Williams, Raymond. 1983. *Keywords: A Vocabulary of Culture and Society.* Oxford: Oxford University Press.

Zapf, Hubert. 2016a. *Literature as Cultural Ecology: Sustainable Texts.* London: Bloomsbury Publishing.

Williams, Raymond. 2016b. *Handbook of Ecocriticism and Cultural Ecology.* Berlin: Walter de Gruyter.

4. Platforms

Abstract

To account for most of the recent transitions that led to a post-network
(Lotz 2007), post-broadcast (Turner and Tay 2009), post-channel (Lotz
2016) phase "after television" (Olsson and Spigel 2004: 2) and "after the
media" (Bennett et al. 2011), this chapter offers an ecological perspective
to the study of internet environments as embedded in techno-cultural,
industrial, and media-design dynamics. The specific positioning of the
anthology form in the context of streaming media is analyzed through
the lenses of platform research. Taking a "sociological impressionist"
(Frisby 2013) approach, this section discusses in detail the mechanisms
of the platformization of culture, the logistics of streaming media, their
economic and commercial context, and the outcomes of algorithmic
systems on the curation of digital content.

Keywords: Anthology; Platform Studies; Algorithmic Culture; Streaming
Platforms; Recommendation Systems

4.1. Platform Ecology

Long before the term platform became a way to describe digital environments, it was used to indicate a physical space, or, better, the design of a
space. From geography and agriculture to transportation, architecture, and
politics, a platform is primarily a form imposed on a pre- or post-industrial
landscapes: a shaped surface, physical, material, or symbolic, which offers
a grounding, a support, a structure for collective use and social action.
Embedded in its etymology there is also a geometrical dimension, that of
a plane (cf. French: *plate*) – flat, even, leveled, two-dimensional. Digital
platforms can be described as the forms of seemingly flat screen spaces.
They are designed to cut off distinct areas from unordered internet signals
and turn the information chaos into organized web traffic, where data can
be tracked, monitored, and analyzed. With their datacasting transmission
model, platforms are where our social web presence can be most accurately

Taurino, Giulia. *The Anthology in Digital Culture*. Amsterdam: Amsterdam University Press, 2023.
DOI: 10.5117/9789463724265_CH04

collected, identified, and datafied. Users enter liminal platform spaces and inevitably leave a trace by clicking, logging in with their online identity and credentials, subscribing to their personalized platform experience, and constructing their virtual, computational selves.

Far from their linear media predecessor, digital platforms are layered in a way that makes them three-dimensional (Beer 2019b) and somehow uneven. Their ecology is multifaceted and complex; multi-layered surfaces (infrastructural and computational) overlap and adapt to each other, by bringing their own figurative indentations, irregularities, and defects. Interestingly, while they have expanded the unilateral flat-land vision of the display into multi-dimensional architectures, digital platforms have retained most of the original uses acquired across several "analog" traditions. For instance, a digital platform is topological, in that it is grounded in a geographical network of infrastructures and geolocated points of access. It is also agri-cultural in that it is an area for seeding and planting culture, for cultivation and culture-growth at the interface level, but also for metaphorical server farming and data harvesting if we observe its infrastructural composition. Moreover, a digital platform is a means of transportation, communication, and transmission through a digital pipeline that connects individuals to social communities, bridges the producers to the consumers, or carries and delivers objects. Finally, it is architectural, industrial, and political in the way that it designs and builds a structure that rests on the backbone of economic interests, group-based decisions, cultural value-systems, and forms of knowledge organization. While I have partially explored the geographical dimension of platforms in the previous chapter on streaming infrastructures, here I will focus on the nature of architectural, cultural, industrial, and political entities that contribute to shaping the "internet imaginaries" (Flichy 2007) of a virtual society and new ecologies of knowledge (Star 1995).

Beyond these metaphorical constructs, as a field of application and research, the study of platform technologies intersects with a number of interdisciplinary topics, from internet infrastructures and digital economies to interface design and algorithmic indexing, all of which are relevant to observing the anthology form as a model for content organization, storage, promotion, personalization, circulation, and reception. The term digital platform itself can be used to refer to either the interface of social networks like Facebook, Instagram, and Twitter or the online storage space of cloud services like Dropbox, Google Drive, and iCloud. More generically, it might be used to address any other virtual environment presenting a "computing system" (Bogost and Montfort 2009), "an infrastructure that supports the design and use of particular applications" (Gillespie 2010 349). While online platforms are certainly computational and infrastructural, they also respond to a techno-cultural dimension and logic (Langlois et al. 2009). Platform theory and research is therefore used here as complementary to a cultural and media ecosystemic perspective, as outlined in the previous chapter. In this process of exploring, I draw upon platform studies as applied to media and cultural research. The intent is to investigate digital culture as it creates its own set of human-based and machine-based practices on streaming platform environments.

In order to analyze "the connection between technical specifics and culture" (Bogost and Montfort 2009, 4), Jan Bogost and Nick Montfort propose to study digital media and computing systems with technical rigor and to pursue an in-depth investigation of their relationship with generative processes of creativity, expression, and culture (Ibid.). Notably, they call platform studies a discipline dedicated to the study of the "detailed technical workings of computing systems" (Bogost and Montfort 2007, 1), where the term platform stands for programmed environments supported by a hardware and a software component (Ibid.). Over the years, the term platform has assumed several domains of significance outside of the computer-science sphere. In new media studies, the study of digital environments now includes a variety of analytical approaches taking different levels of intervention: an operation level, which benefits from reception studies; an interface level, which deploys theories of remediation and human-computer interaction; a form/function level, one of the main interests of cybertext studies and narratology; and a code level, investigated by code studies, software studies, and code esthetics (Ibid., 2). Bogost and Montfort propose to integrate this list at a more-strictly platform level:

> the abstraction level beneath code, a level which has not yet been systematically studied. If code studies are new media's analogue to software engineering and computer programming, platform studies are the humanistic parallel of computing systems and computer architecture, connecting the fundamentals of new media work to the cultures in which they were produced and the cultures in which coding, forms, interfaces, and eventual use are layered upon them.
>
> (Ibid.)

For these same reasons, platform research also comes with challenges, especially when we examine streaming platforms. The use of coding and the presence of digital data open up alternative methods for understanding culture, such as web scraping, data collection, data analysis and analysis of algorithmic practices. However, platform data are not always publicly available, and companies like Netflix are particularly strict about sharing information. Following debates and controversies about users' rights and privacy, but also safeguarding their own corporate interests, most platforms shut down or put major restrictions on access to the data they collect (Rogers 2019, 156). This poses limitations to media scholars who intend to pursue a platform study of streaming services. Methodological tools like API retrieval are not always possible, or reliable (Lomborg and Bechmann 2014) and web scraping methods are not well grounded. Digital footprints, users' activity, and interaction are therefore hard to map, and so are the data related to content. Being aware of these obstacles is a fundamental premise for positing the need to integrate platform studies in cultural and media studies, with their ecosystemic perspectives, in order to minimize the risks of missing relevant information while pursuing platform research.

Despite the challenges in decoding the back-end, reasoning on the editorial and algorithmic forms inscribed in the ecologies and economies of platforms provides interesting considerations on the digital transformations occurring in contemporary media culture. Cultural, media, and platform ecological perspectives can together contribute to outlining a hybrid investigation into forms of content organization on streaming platforms. By analyzing more specifically the implementation of recommendation systems in platform environments and their interaction with pre-existing systems of content organization, I will show how, even in the scenario of media interconnectivity, the history of content classification is always and profoundly connected to the affordances of a specific medium, so much so that it created its own platform culture. Amorphous and hard to grasp (Beer 2019a), the concept of platform culture, as I define it here, appeals to a series of features activated by the platforms themselves and the applications behind their recommendation systems. It emerges as the result of the convergence of two forces: social habits inherited by previous cultural systems (e.g., the anthology form) and practices that are strictly related to platforms' affordances (e.g., algorithmic practices). As Manovich explained in his introduction to *The New Media Reader*, new media blend together existing cultural conventions and the conventions of software (Wardrip-Fruin and Montfort 2003, 18).

Considering this culture-software-code encounter, Tarleton Gillespie explains that the descriptive term "platform" came to indicate a variety of socio-technical meanings at once, combining a computational/technological dimension, an architectural/structural/operational dimension, a figurative/conceptual dimension, and a political/ideological one (Gillespie

2010, 249–250). The multifaceted nature of platforms makes them more than simple functional digital tools. Instead, they are active drivers in enabling – or disabling – socio-cultural practices. Accounting for this ontological complexity, Gillespie defines platforms as "online content-hosting intermediaries" (Ibid., 350), insofar as they regulate "what can appear, how it is organized, how it is monetized, what can be removed and why, and what the technical architecture allows and prohibits" (Ibid., 359). Borrowing this definition, what I define as platform ecology is both the coded environment as it is articulated on a platform's interface, and the techno-cultural, media environment in which a platform is embedded and reverberates. A platform-ecological framework is thus intended to explore the visible facade of invisible infrastructures. This visible facade can come in different forms in platform culture. If, on the one hand, the platform ecosystem is made up of sensible technologies, information architecture, and front-end design that can be traced and researched, then, on the other hand, platform economics should also be studied in order to understand the contextual industrial space articulated by over-the-top media services. Platform ecology and economy are not mutually exclusive. On the contrary, they are strictly interlinked in the final outcome of generating sustainable and profitable platform cultures, on both the user side and the corporate side.

Considering its impact on digital culture and anthologization practices, the rest of the chapter examines how Netflix's platform configuration brings together human-driven and machine-driven practices in the same media environment, by offering new modes of online content classification, digital distribution, and cultural platformization. To observe platform culture, I will take David Beer's (2019a) suggestion to borrow the theories of the sociologist David Frisby (2013 [1981]) for the study of online platforms. Frisby introduces the term "sociological impressionism" to describe a theoretical framework concerned with the "persistence of existence" (Frisby 2013 [1981], 178), with how immediate perceptions acquire stability. This view draws from George Simmel's formal, relational, and ontological social theory and he "argues that the process of abstraction through which we perceive society and social forms rests upon the distance that exists between 'a complex of phenomena and the human mind'" (Ibid., 152). With this in mind, the next paragraphs adopt both a distant and close reading with the intent to reconnect the abstract picture to the particular form, or else the totality of the image, the impression, the whole – infrastructural, industrial, economic – to a close observation of its granular cultural composition as it manifests and persists in platforms environments.

4.2. The Platformization of Culture

In recent years, the field of media studies intersected with platform studies as a consequence of the introduction of internet-based technologies, which are increasingly affecting the circulation of cultural content. In addition to favoring the emergence of a new network of infrastructures in the media industry, the digital has come to stimulate new debates, theories, and methodologies among media scholars. A common conversation, which has engaged academic communities from both media studies and digital humanities, regards the way digital technologies operate as drivers for cultural and social change. This perspective collides with scholarly traditions that observe technologies through the lenses of either a hard or soft determinism (Marx and Smith 1994). Although contested by many scholars, this theoretical framework advances a necessary debate on the causes and effects of past, present, and emerging technological advancements, and the ways they interact with previous socio-cultural, institutional ecosystems. Reasoning on the complexities and entanglements that digital technologies and the internet brought to the realm of media, the platform study presented in this chapter does not limit itself to tackling simple cause–effect mechanisms involved in the spreading of internet-distributed media. It rather aims at examining how a dynamic genealogy of the anthology form invaded platform environments, with its set of practices inherited from previous processes of analog anthologization, which eventually led to the current digital scape, through evolutionary processes and technological disruptions.

Academic scholarships engaged with platform research from a diversity of analytical perspectives, ranging from the study of the platform industry, economics, and management (Gawer 2014; Gawer and Cusumano 2014), to analyze platform technologies, infrastructures, and architecture design (Star and Ruhleder 1996; Hanseth and Lyytinen 2010). This broad interest for the multi-layered concept of platform has been rising across several disciplines in the past twenty years, as a result of media mutations that have affected several domains and that are part of a process of platformization of the web (Helmond 2015) and, eventually, of culture (Nieborg and Poell 2018). Platformization is "defined as the penetration of economic, governmental, and infrastructural extensions of digital platforms into the web and app ecosystems, fundamentally affecting the operations of the cultural industries" (Ibid., 2). To investigate processes of platformization, we should therefore start by looking at the economic, political, and industrial strategies that affect content delivery. Furthermore, the term platformization indicates not only the process of generating a platform environment on the web, but, more importantly, the process of making content "platform-ready" (Helmond 2015), meaning ready to inhabit a platform and circulate, non-linearly, through platforms. Here, I will show how the collection model in the form of an audiovisual anthology is, in fact, one of the ways content is made platform-ready. Distribution, in particular, is the focal point of this research, as the phase where the non-linear platformization of culture happened, in the in-between space that connects production with reception.

If the study of production is, for the most part, sufficient for retracing the history of the anthology form in mainly Western literature, radio, and television, as shown in the first chapter, then the latest evolution of the anthology form requires a study of modes of distribution. Recalling Levine (2015), in order to understand what platforms are, we need to understand what platforms do – that is to say, their design affordances. Joss Hands et al. approached the pragmatic, factitive dimension of platforms on cultural and social systems by discussing the term "platformativity," which includes a variety of virtual social spaces and practices.

> 'Platform' is a useful term because it is a broad enough category to capture a number of distinct phenomena, such as social networking, the shift from desktop to tablet computing, smart phone and 'app'-based interfaces as well as the increasing dominance of centralised cloud-based computing. The term is also specific enough to indicate the capturing of digital life in an enclosed, commercialized and managed realm.
>
> (Hands et al. 2013, 1)

This enclosed, spatialized digital life – that is, the ensemble of creative and social digital practices that make up platform culture – is appended to and induced by the platformization and platformativity of digital media objects. In this context, "with the archival form that decentralised media and platform take" (Beer 2019b, 53), the production, distribution, and reception dimensions of cultural objects are even more closely interconnected, particularly in the ways in which we experience a hyper-mediated, formatted, curated delivery of cultural artifacts. As Beer emphasized, "platform culture presents us with a new politics of remembering and forgetting" (Ibid.) in the form of accurately archived, edited, and organized content.

To conclude this introduction to streaming platforms, I will emphasize that practices of archiving, editing, and classifying represent the bulk of cultural platformization, and reflect digital media practices at several levels – industrial, economic, cultural, algorithmic. Since they are conceived for distributing platform-ready content that can be fed into metadata structures, streaming platforms can be described as content repositories, other than intermediaries. Taking Netflix as the main focus of this research, I will therefore observe how online libraries present interrelated media objects in the guise of lists, collections, and anthologies to create a network-repository of content. This archival affordance of platform is particularly evident if we look at digital processes of anthologization as ways of ordering and clustering content at the source, before the process of reception activates additional, algorithmic-driven streams of content. Indeed, platformization is reconfiguring the media industries by introducing new practices and uses. Such a mutating scenario demands an understanding not only of narrative and cultural forms, but also of the media and platform ecology that lies behind the dynamics of non-linear distribution in a digital economy. In the next section, streaming platforms will be observed as additional competitors in the media industry that are activating alternative options for producing, distributing, and consuming television content, outside of the traditional value-chain. I will notably consider how internet-distributed television evolved into creating an industrial system of its own, with its own business models and profit strategies.

4.3. Industrial Context

The study of evolutionary dynamics represents a large part of historical research in many humanities fields. Similarly, processes of evolution and variation in media systems are important for understanding how cultural forms take shape across different time spans and geographical areas. In particular, the analysis of cultural, economical, or technological disconti-nuities attracted a wide interest and raised questions concerning the state and predictability of such events, and the way they influence the course of evolution, perhaps more than fluid, foreseeable, linear processes. As the case of US-based streaming platforms demonstrates, new technological innovations that have occurred in the history of media did not operate as unique, isolated driving forces acting in the void left by a lack of pre-existent media industry practices. And yet, we can certainly detect the presence of a moment of discontinuity (Drucker 1969) and disruption (Lotz 2018) that affected broadcasting both as a process of transmission/communication and as a whole industry, market, and economy. On the one hand, the seemingly revolutionary nature of internet-distributed media has been influenced by pre-established power structures and other hierarchical industrial macro-dynamics. On the other hand, the introduction of streaming platforms did bring a new conversation to the study of media, by leveraging previously undefined – or only partially defined – concepts like digitization/digitalization (Tilson et al. 2010), "algorhythmics" (Miyazaki 2012, 2016), platformization (Helmond 2015; Nieborg and Poell 2018), and other terms that became part of a renewed vocabulary for humanities and social scholarships.

Furthermore, the emergence of telecommunication and information infrastructures in the post-industrial society moved the focus from tangible to intangible goods, where content produced for either knowledge, entertainment, or leisure entered local economies at all scales, thus showing an unexpected potential for financial investments and growth. The information society relies more and more on "knowledge economies" (Drucker 1969), where the introduction of new technologies resulted in the formation of additional industries, which eventually led to a global economy based on communication, transmission, and the circulation of ideas. The lack of a prompt response to this change, via targeted policies and ad hoc governmental institutions, resulted in the surge of major players that are dominating the media economy, generating a new socio-cultural and geopolitical reality, where the way knowledge, culture, information, dis-information, and mis-information circulate has profound impacts on social, cultural, and political assets. Dynamics of info-tainment and info-mediation have frequently been associated with platformization, with the aim of moving our attention, once again, from the amount of data and content available to "the way in which computers replaced humans in sorting and organising information" (Smyrnaios 2018). The term info-mediation, in particular, invites us to think about platforms as "infomediaries," instead of generic intermediaries, thus asking us to focus on their algorithmic, social, and applicational or transactional value (Smyrnaios and Rebillard 2019).

Before observing platform culture in its interaction with previous socio-cultural systems, we should therefore understand the industrial dynamics that have generated digital, weightless economies as systems relying on intangible goods. Observing media continuities and discontinuities is not a way to "forecast tomorrow; it looks at today. It does not ask, 'What will tomorrow look like?' It asks instead, 'What do we have to tackle today to make tomorrow?'" (Drucker 1969, x). As much as contemporary cultural industries are more multifaceted than the unitarian, standardized vision of the cultural industry described by Theodor Adorno, streaming media industries are still defined by an oligopolistic market structure, where few firms have a higher level of control over the industry. In 2014, the Observatorio Latinoamericano de Regulaciòn Medios y Convergencia

(OBSERVACOM) published the article "United States: The Instinctive Illusion of Media Diversity," problematizing the diffused perception of an existing diversity across contemporary media and presenting it as an illusory belief, incompatible with an industry having such a high concentration of power in just a few major players.

In particular, "one of the questions that must be addressed [...] is why concentration continues to be an important issue in today's seemingly disperse and chaotic media ecology. [...] The current situation of the US media industry reveals inequity under the illusion of media diversity."[1] The article points at the fact that the contemporary US mediascape is still dominated by mega-corporations, including large media conglomerates that combine production, distribution, and other activities in a single corporation, as in the case of AT&T/Time Warner or Comcast. To these should be added big tech companies, which now control media traffic and content distribution via the "big three" of the over-the-top media ecosystem streaming platforms, namely, Amazon Video, Netflix, and Hulu.[2]

While a widespread narrative around television suggests that we are in a moment of great diversity of content and increasing fragmentation of audiences, a quick look at the US mediascape will tell us otherwise.[3] Over-the-top technologies contributed to reversing the trend initiated by cable technologies towards a multi-channel landscape, and triggered the return to a hierarchical structure. In the constant hunt by platforms for information to profile their users demographics and tastes, we are witnessing a surge in the processes of merging, acquisition (Srnicek 2017b), and coordinated "coopetition" (Van Dijck 2021), where smaller start-up firms are either bought up by or dependent on bigger firms, which have the ultimate aim of expanding their access to data. This expansionary mechanism threatened the pre-existing industrial scenario and fostered a phase of reconfiguration:

> Firms that were operating in completely different areas are now converg-
> ing together under the pressures of competitively extracting data. [...]
> While overt antagonism between these major platforms is at a low ebb for

1   "United States: The Instinctive Illusion of Media Diversity." *Observacom*. Last modified November 26, 2014. https://www.observacom.org/united-states-the-instinctive-illusion-of-media-diversity.

2   Andrew Wallenstein. "The OTT View-Niverse: A Map of the New Video Ecosystem." *Variety*. Last modified April 29, 2015. https://variety.com/2015/digital/news/ott-map-video-ecosystem-1201480930.

3   https://www.vox.com/2018/6/12/17450196/att-time-warner-court-ruling-media-landscape-deals-murdoch-stephenson-cbs-viacom-disney-fox.

now, as they expand into new areas they will increasingly come into direct competition. The consumer Internet of Things is a good example here, with Amazon and Google making major plays in an effort to dominate this arm of their data extraction empires"

(Srnicek 2017b)

The academic Nick Srnicek (2017a) explores the details of this data empire in his book on platform capitalism, stating that "capitalism, when a crisis hits, tends to be restructured. New technologies, new organisational forms, new modes of exploitation, new types of jobs and new markets all emerge to create a new way of accumulating capital" (Ibid., 36).

As the global media economy seems to converge towards the perpetuation of capitalistic dynamics, further mutations in the industry might lead to another moment of re-assessment. At the current stage, streaming services are still subject to constant technological mutations, which drive industry practices and strategic decisions. In this unstable scenario, non-linearity has emerged as a property of media transmission as well as media production, with new hybrid business models designed to secure profit. "The media landscape used to be straightforward: Content companies – studios – made stuff – TV shows and movies – and sold it to pay TV distributors, who sold it to consumers. Now things are up for grabs: Netflix buys stuff from the studios, but it's making its own stuff, too, and it's selling it directly to consumers. That's one of the reasons older media companies are trying to compete by consolidating."[4]

With their predominant position, Netflix and Amazon have conquered a privileged place in the contemporary US media oligopoly, by acquiring old television programs and producing original content at the same time. "The platform has emerged as a new business model, capable of extracting and controlling immense amount of data, and with this shift we have seen the rise of large monopolistic firms" (Ibid., 6). By competing with a pre-existent institutional, industrial, political, and economic system, streaming platforms turned internet-distributed television into a data-driven media apparatus generating a much more complex industrial scenario. Considering the most influential US subscription-based streaming services, the over-the-top industrial ecosystem appears to be an evolving system functioning by itself, with its own set of techno-industrial infrastructures, and ultimately

---

4   Rani Molla. "Here's Who Owns Everything in the Media Today." *Vox*. Last modified January 23, 2018. https://www.vox.com/2018/1/23/16905844/media-landscape-verizon-amazon-comcast -disney-fox-relationships-chart.

disconnected from former media power dynamics. Following the introduction of streaming technologies, former US television networks have adapted in order to offer both a linear and a non-linear viewing experience. In addition to streaming natives like Netflix, several over-the-top services are sprawling from their linear antecedent, with so-called skinny bundles options, born from a selection of larger cable and network catalogs.

On the one hand, US cable and network channels reacted to over-the-top services by increasing merger and acquisition activities, in order to create an oligopolistic environment made up of media conglomerates. On the other hand, they activated a mirroring effect and started offering themselves as platforms for non-linear distribution of content, such as HBO Now (HBO) or CBS All Access (CBS). It is now evident that the US television industry is traversing a second disruption, a shift in the paradigm (Lotz 2016). Some observable transformations, in partial continuity or discontinuity with previous industrial systems, occurred with the rise of the platform capitalism and can be summed up as follows. Platformization led to processes of recentralization and consolidation, in the form of privatization of knowledge, unequal access to infrastructures, and, therefore, uneven opportunities to enter and survive in the streaming market. This then resulted in a concentration of power in fewer players. The tendency towards centralization also generates concerns regarding unregulated manipulation of personal data, issues of privacy, and ecological implications in the use of digital technologies, as the digitization and the consolidation of the industry makes it easier for a single company to track users with greater detail and consistency. Narratives of users' empowerment, content democratization, and diversification widely adopted by streaming giants are, to some extent, misleading in a system that is much more centralized than we think.

Platform economies reflect platform power as much as infrastructural power. "The ultimate objective of internet companies [...] is to provide the infrastructure through which humans encounter the world. [...] When the mind wants to know something, it will go to Google; when it wants to communicate with someone, it will turn to Facebook. When we want to be somewhere else, we click on Uber, and when we simply want something; Amazon will make it arrive" (Davies 2018, 186). Some online platforms primarily act as amplifiers: they are advertisement-based platforms with no direct content creation and the aim to retain users on the platform as long as they can, via sentiment-based algorithms that increase engagement and interaction. On the contrary, companies like Netflix have a completely different operational system: they are subscription-driven services whose main mission is to provide access to audiovisual content. In the platform's

Interests to deliver quality of content and quality of experience. The commercial interests behind content-delivery platform, along with their process of adoption of data and algorithms, are substantially different than those of other platforms. Streaming platforms are to be understood as, simultaneously, networks of technologies and infrastructures, as systems of convergent socio-cultural practices, as media industry apparatuses, and archival repositories. This requires further analysis as to exactly which industrial practices and profit-driven strategies are impacting streaming platforms' decision-making approaches and business models.

4.4. Streaming Practices

Streaming technology, a delivery method that allows content to be distributed over the internet from a server to a client, was made available in telecommunications a few years after the invention of the World Wide Web. Much like any other media devices and infrastructures, from radio transmitters to satellite television, it took a few years before streaming reached a level of quality and efficiency able to sustain mass distribution. When the first popular video hosting and sharing services like Google Video and YouTube appeared in 2005, broadband penetration in the United States was nowhere near as widespread as it is today, despite its leading position in the global internet scape. A 2006 Pew study shows that the percentage of US adults with a high-speed connection at home was still lower than fifty percent.[5] By the end of the 2000s, when the streaming services Amazon Unbox (2006) and Netflix (2007) had become popular by launching their own platform, broadband penetration started a rapid growth, which led the US to achieving one of the highest broadband internet penetration rates worldwide within a ten-year span (2007–2017).[6] While digital divide is still an issue in many countries, over time, thanks to the spread of large-scale internet adoption and access, streaming services were able to create an advanced transnational network with a global reach. This paved the way for a new geography of communication infrastructure and opened up new

---

5   John B. Horrigan. "Part 1. Broadband Adoption in the United States." *Pew Research Center: Internet, Science & Tech (blog)*. Last modified May 28, 2006. https://www.pewinternet.org/2006/05/28/part-1-broadband-adoption-in-the-united-states.

6   "Internet Penetration Rates are High in North America, Europe and Parts of the Asia-Pacific." *Pew Research Center's Global Attitudes Project (blog)*. Last modified June 14, 2018. https://www.pewresearch.org/global/2018/06/19/social-media-use-continues-to-rise-in-developing-countries-but-plateaus-across-developed-ones/pg_2018-06-19_global-tech_0-01.

horizons for the circulation of content, making it efficient, cost effective, and reducing the time of media distribution.

Furthermore, from data collection to the storage and organization of content, the possibility of streaming media on internet platforms created a space for new industrial practices. A wide range of media streaming experiences and formats has been introduced, offering a variety of content-delivery and viewing options, and allowing users to stream content on personal computers and mobile supports. The process of streaming media on online platforms involves several elements: the establishment of a transnational geography of the internet (Warf 2012); the development of a back-end-to-front-end data transmission system and content delivery service (Lobato 2019); a reconfiguration of the global value chain able to sustain the flow of media content through international production, trade and investments. In its practical routine, the logistic of streaming is organized into interacting components operating at the intersection between infrastructure and technology. As the media scholar Ramon Lobato explains, "streaming platforms, as 'over-the-top' video delivery services, are naturally reliant on telecommunications infrastructure – the vast networks of fibre and coaxial cable, copper telephone wires, and satellite data links that form the internet's underlying foundation" (Warf 2017, 180). At the operational level, we can describe the streaming process as the result of two components: a software and a hardware component. On the one hand, the software component of streaming platforms consists of a web of infrastructures (e.g., browsers, protocols, data, algorithms, code, and so forth), which allow and facilitate the transmission of content. On the other hand, the hardware component is made up of a set of technologies that can host such content, namely, computers, tablets, and smartphones, but also television interfaces like Chromecast or Amazon FireTV.

Taking a more specific case study as the focus of this chapter, Netflix's platform architecture can be dissected into three parts: the server (back-end); the client (front-end); and the content delivery network. When the client computer requests to stream content, it does so through the platform interface, which is the primary gateway available to the user for accessing audiovisual content. The incoming content is provided by a back-end – in the case of Netflix, a cloud computing service like Amazon Web Services (AWS), where the library's content is stored. When the user presses play, the content is made ready to stream by the content delivery network (Netflix Open Connect[7]), via a transcoding process that makes the video format –

---

7   See: https://openconnect.netflix.com/en.

previously encoded in the cloud – readable through the internet. After the video streaming, the information relative to each user's profile and activity is stored on a scalable distributed database (Netflix adopted DynamoDB and Cassandra). The collected data is processed and analyzed by the streaming service via algorithms that then return personalized "streams" of content. In computer science, a data stream is "a sequence of data elements that are made available to the processing system over time" (Buyya and Dastjerdi 2016, 148). In streaming media, these streams make up the narrative, cultural, and commercial forms of the platform economy.

As a socio-cultural, industrial practice, "from the audience perspective, streaming is very much an extension of the television experience" (Warf 2017, 178). Even before streaming platforms were born and consolidated in the media industry, illegal streaming had impacted the circulation of television content, so much so that by the time digital distribution was put in place in contemporary cultural industries, practices of streaming content were already diffused among audiences as non-institutionalized ways of consuming television content online. Legal streaming in the form of video-on-demand services created an institutional structure for this type of illegal consumption, so that, in the end, what drove the shift to non-linear television was not just a technological and socio-cultural process, but also an industrial one. The constitution of a media industry and a legal economy officially acknowledged the potential of streaming to be a pervasive technology and a ubiquitous social practice. Streaming platforms are now part of digital industries and markets relying on economies of scale, where an increase in the network leads to a decrease in the average cost. In the case of Netflix, with its transnational distribution outreach, streaming, webcasting, and scaling dynamics are essential. Supporting a global geography of content circulation demands a system of infrastructures for distribution and a well-organized set of metadata for efficient retrieval. This requires a large investment up-front in server-side technologies that guarantee an efficient streaming experience to millions of users. The margins for revenues behind a company like Netflix will be therefore higher as the network expands through additional subscribers.

In the attempt to secure a solid customer base, Netflix abandoned the traditional Nielsen ratings points/share model and opted for alternative ways for measuring viewership based on the analysis of data collected via the platform itself. With this system, Netflix is able to profile viewers' interests, habits and demographics and gather relevant information on which content might be appealing for the subscribers. Using data to catch users' attention is one of the main strategies adopted by subscription-based streaming services, which rely on algorithmic recommendation systems to compute personal preferences. Unlike their non-linear television antecedent, the goal of streaming platforms is not to fill the programming time and saturate the daily schedule with a flow of content, but rather to offer enough good content to motivate subscriptions' renewal and enough interaction with the platform to gather data. Traditional network television programming was originally built on trying to interpolate viewers' expectations at specific times – e.g., Monday night football, daytime soap operas, peak comedy shows – while trying to maximize revenues via advertising. Thus, each time slot came with an opportunity cost versus other options. By contrast, Netflix business model allows users to decide when to watch content with enough flexibility, by simply providing them with sufficient audiovisual material to motivate them to maintain the subscription.

Because the investment in content creation is relatively low compared to the infrastructural costs, Netflix has been able to experiment with both content creation and release, by adopting alternative workflows for media production and distribution. For instance, to fit the needs of the platform economy and its reliance on data streams, among other practices, Netflix introduced a new straight-to-series business model, which reframed existing rules in the US television industry via a shorter circuit of production. As Netflix's Chief Content Officer Ted Sarandos declared, in the straight-to-series model the season tends to replace the pilot as a test for assessing the potential value and profit of the series.[8] Blocks of several episodes are produced and then released at once. The reasons for this strategy are many. On the one hand, the straight-to-series model offers more hours of content with similar marginal costs to the pilot model and higher creative freedom for narrative experiments. On the other hand, the negative outcomes of an unsuccessful full-season release are less impactful on the overall platform environment, in that the negative feedback is traded off by capturing additional viewing data. Even a lack of viewing data might itself provide relevant information with no direct revenue losses.

This innovative business model sparked the trend of "mini-rooms" with less writers, and a shorter production timeframe, which replaced the pilot development model by offering more flexibility and reducing the overall costs in the long term. While mini-rooms are not necessarily associated to anthology series, they do support short-term, season-based productions over

8   VanDerWerff, Emily Todd. "Netflix Is Accidentally Inventing a New Art Form – Not Quite TV and Not Quite Film." *Vox*. Last modified July 29, 2015. https://www.vox.com/2015/7/29/9061833/netflix-binge-new-artform.

long-running shows. As a result, the tendency of most recent fictional television series is to condense an entire season into an average of ten episodes.
As the long-time dominant US television business model of over twenty
episodes per season has been challenged in various ways by industrial and
technological changes in recent years, more heterogeneous short-narrative
forms are now emerging in addition to the traditional serial structures.
However, despite its current popularity, the mini-room practice is still a
source of debate. It has been recently brought to the media's attention that
mini-rooms pay less, thus adding to a widespread tendency of the digital sec-
tor to base their centralized models on "increasingly outsourced, contingent,
and precarious forms of work" (Rahman and Thelen 2019, 183). Outside of
Amazon's much-contested large-scale exploitation of labor (Alimahomed-
Wilson and Reese 2020), other digital platforms and streaming companies
rely on temporary positions to sustain the processes of content creation,
data collection, categorization, tagging, and even in software, algorithm,
and web development (Chen and Carré 2020, online). These "microtasks
are geared towards developing databases for big firms, which have the
potential of being used for automation or promoting products and services
(Rani and Furrer 2019)" (Ibid.).

While screenwriters are still demanding adjustments to safeguard their jobs,
other key occupations in the platform economy are starting to transition more
permanently into the corporate structure. For instance, Netflix has recently
advertised a position for "Editorial Creative Taxonomy Strategist," who "works
closely with the Product, Content and Marketing teams to define, develop,
maintain and govern common taxonomies that will allow Netflix to maximize
how we describe our titles to members and partners."[9] Other than defining
new taxonomies and metadata for audiovisual content along with teams of
engineers, responsibilities for this position include "auditing existing taxonomies
and improving their efficiency, reconciling disparate taxonomies and metadata
across teams, [...] ensuring metadata is defined such that its integrity will
not be compromised by cultural bias, working with subject matter experts to
define workflows and standards for metadata application, [...] establishing a
governance framework for taxonomies, establishing maintenance systems for
taxonomies, creating and maintaining documentation to support taxonomies."[10]
The establishment of these roles in the platform industry marks a positive
shift towards the regulation of the practice of content classification and data
collection, which stand at the basis of the business models previously outlined.

9   https://jobs.netflix.com/jobs/159322776. Last retrieved December 19, 2021.
10   Ibid.

After several requests to ensure more inclusive and diverse datasets (Gebru et al. 2021), some streaming companies are finally adopting workflows to minimize the risks of biases generated by their reliance on data for content creation and distribution. Yet, the automation, mechanization, and computerization of labor into algorithmic practices still provokes doubts when it comes to the ethical aspects of the streaming economy. Contemporary forms of content anthologization fall into this ethical dilemma: how can AI and human creativity coexist in the cultural industry? Interestingly, traditional anthologization practices found a fertile ground in this technological, infrastructural, industrial media landscape, and became more and more present among the content available on over-the-top services. By offering branded content and a reproducible narrative template, the anthology form turned out to be an interesting model for Netflix's streaming ecology both in terms of commercial interests and at the level of interface design. On the one hand, the anthology form aligns with the straight-to-series business model that supports the platform economy; on the other hand, it perfectly fits a modular "information architecture" (Baldwin 2008) generating snippets of content organized into collections. From production to distribution, whether human or algorithmic, practices of content organization are omnipresent in internet-distributed television. To understand how Netflix's content sorting plays out at the nexus of editorial and algorithmic practices, we need to expose and deconstruct digital culture in its post-digital evolution, where both human and computational agents partake in the decision-making processes and algorithms are simultaneously perceptual and permanent.

4.5. Algorithmic Culture

Data extraction empires (Srnicek 2017b) need automation. On the internet, Automation often comes in the form of algorithms. Broadly speaking, algorithms are "computerized method[s] of calculation" (Jaton 2021, 5), or else lists of coded instructions for the performance of specific tasks and computational problem-solving. Over the years, they transitioned from this purely mathematical definition to practical applications in mechanical computing devices, becoming synonyms of optimization, efficiency, velocity, control, and order. Building on this historical and cultural foundation, algorithms are now evolving into dynamic, fluid, swift, and distributive devices (Ibid., 6), meaning they quickly circulate, wear down, break, and change, simultaneously scattered and united, in the process of "modifying a network of relationships" (Ibid.). Both code-dependent and data-dependent, the operational functioning of algorithms becomes fundamental for guaranteeing controlled access to knowledge and information on the internet, as more and more content and data are made available via platform interfaces. As the researcher Ravi Sekhar Chakraborty reminds us, "many dimensions of contemporary culture are governed now largely by algorithms. Their recommendations, classification, and other modes of organization govern everything from political opinion to product choices, from taste in music to the field of medicine" (Chakraborty, in Hristova et al. 2020: 70). Most contemporary online platforms opt for automated, computational systems that operate as filtering classifiers for identifying content, running queries, and moderating media reception. A continuous process of data collection and machine-learning serves as the basis for building hybrid systems for content organization – human and computer-driven – and for dividing online catalogs into a variety of selected, personalized queues.

In this miscellanea of algorithmic practices, queues or streams of content are reconfigured in order to *expose* specific audiovisual products to the user via a machine-mediated archival process that gives the illusion of order and self-organization. One way content can be "exposed" is through algorithmic practices; and yet, the influence of algorithms on culture is not so deterministic that we can track its direct effects. Several scholars anticipated a conversation about algorithms and culture, by reasoning on a broad algorithmic turn (Uricchio 2011) in the media and creative industries. Among others, a detailed theorization of algorithmic culture is found in Ted Striphas (2010, 2015), who seeks to understand how data-driven, machine-based information-processing algorithms are affecting "the automation of cultural decision-making processes" (Striphas 2015, 408) and altering "how the category culture has long been practiced, experienced and understood" (Ibid., 396) Even more, Rob Kitchin suggests that algorithms are "contingent, ontogenetic, performative in nature and embedded in wider socio-technical assemblages" (Kitchin 2017, 16). A culture of algorithms is therefore visible both in the ways they impact culture as well as in their own algorithmic condition. The algorithmic condition is much like a human condition: it goes through birth, growth, conflict, transition, decay, and mortality. It can be explored from many points of view – human, physical-material, industrial-economic, professional or artistic, socio-cultural, ethical, and even biological-genetical – as algorithms persist, degrade, and mutate in a dynamic way in a variety of platform environments.

The question of the platformization of culture (Nieborg and Poell 2018), that is to say, the digitalization, formatting, and classification of content on online platforms, intersects with algorithmic culture at different levels of machine intervention. The very concept of algorithmic culture appeals to a series of design features activated by platforms' interfaces, which results in the creation of networks of affinities and filiations between media artifacts. "Important questions about filiations and their ecology [...] are: How many ties are there? That is, how many other categories are tied to this person [object], and in what density? Do these threads contradict or complement (torque versus boundary object of cooperation)? That is, are the threads tangled, or smoothly falling together?" (Bowker and Star 1999, 316). Questions relevant to the study of algorithmic culture include not only the density, quality, and fluidity of this system of media kinships, but also the ways it is constructed and who – or what – controls it. A specific concern for the digital circulation of cultural content on online platforms notably arises as we observe its ever deeper impact not only on the way we design a network of digital, encyclopedic knowledge, but also on the hierarchical, often biased form that this knowledge takes under the semblance of a personalization process. In this sense, algorithmic culture is both the product and the creator of a "data gaze" (Beer 2018), constructed via data analytics and other data-led, algorithmic forms of imposing order on a chaotic mass of data (Ibid.).

Considering the connection between platform environments and the algorithms embedded in them, the rest of this chapter responds to Nick Seavers' (2017) solicitation to observe algorithmic functions not as strictly procedural, mathematic formulas, but as broader socio-technical systems and as culture themselves. Seavers notably advocates for an ethnographic approach (Ibid.) to the study of content filtering algorithms, which can offer a solution to the shortcomings of attempting to access the black box of large-scale computational operations. What we call the Google algorithm or the Facebook algorithm is, in fact, the result of many algorithms operating at once (Bucher 2018), an interlinking of coded instructions, programmed commands, and dependencies that are almost impossible to unravel. As many algorithms concur to form invisible technical assemblages enclosed in one sophisticated model, which silently regulates our access to culture on streaming platforms, they can also become visible cultural forms in the shape of machine-curated indexed content, streams, and queues. While "we can only imagine the density of algorithmic processes and the complex ways that they are now a part of the ordering, structuring and sorting of culture" (Beer 2013, 63), we can still track their possible effects by looking at the reflections of algorithmic culture on content creation and organiza-tion. In the following section, I will discuss in more detail how algorithms interoperate with platform ecosystems at different levels in the shape of recommendation systems.

While the first academic studies on recommendation systems date as far back as the 1990s (Karlgren 1990; Resnick and Varian 1997), it is only more recently, with the large-scale introduction of broadband internet connections and a more democratic access to digital platforms, that we have witnessed the mass conversion of cultural industries and related practices to a new socio-technical media ecosystem, highly reliant on users' data, collected online, and machine-learning operations. During the past decade, cultural production, distribution, and reception have been extensively reshaped by algorithmic filtering systems and infrastructures, which now govern the sorting and filtering of content on most digital platforms by generating streams of data and recommended playlists. Another, less pervasive and self-regulatory way of configuring cultural content for algorithmic processing, as I argue here, can be accomplished through modes of classification that are designed at the time the content itself is produced, as in the case of the anthological model. On many digital platforms, the anthology operates as an aggregator of content, by generating a conceptual space for grouping self-standing episodes or seasons based on different stories, which can be piled up in the same anthological group and algorithmic stream. As we have anticipated in the first chapter, Together with tagging and algorithmic filtering, content creation in the form of prepackaged anthologies stimulates a double process of content index-ing and sorting. Indeed, the algorithmic infrastructure of video streaming websites creates new affordances for the anthology form and other processes of editorialization (Vitali-Rosati 2018) based on the collection model.

Similar to the work of a content creator, designers, taxonomy experts, data scientists, and engineers create formal objects – visual elements, code, algorithms – that simulate human understanding and preference. In the overlapping of pre-digital and post-digital media cultural practices that we find on platform environments, both the anthology form and algorithmic processes partake in the ordering, structuring, and sorting of content in internet-distributed media "recommended for you" to watch or rewatch. In contemporary algorithmic culture, the anthology model in narrative forms is not coming back as a massive and homogeneous presence. Instead, it differentiates in scope and extent based on a variety of processes of plat-formization (Nieborg and Poell 2018) and editorialization (Vitali-Rosati 2018) of content as part of different platform strategies. In this context, even though it does not appear as a uniform and predominant tendency, the anthology form is growing and diversifying to fit an increasingly non-linear media environment. The anthological model as a practice at large, one that involves both human and algorithmic curation, is becoming a constant, recurring component of major US streaming platforms dedicated to content delivery. On the one hand, short-form and anthology-form fictional, scripted content offer content that can be easily tagged, binged, re-watched, or screened on mobile devices, making it platform-ready. On the other hand, the anthological model is where the impact of algorithmic culture can be more evidently seen, with its topical clusterization of content in the form of streams, lists, and collections in the platform architecture. The breadth of anthologies to include multiple topics within the same macro-genre or style, and to reiterate identifiable categories across episodes and season, while also adding variations, is likely to result in a better classification criteria, as opposed to longer-running serialized content that is often hard to grasp outside of very formulaic genres. Furthermore, such an anthology-based classification avoids the risks of canceling content after one season, which, in platform environments, might create issues when cataloging and indexing content. By creating a finished product and providing a sense of narrative closure, standalone episodic or seasonal anthologies can afford to become part of longer collections and more efficient streams of anthologized content that can be scaled up and down as needed.

In the platform ecosystem, traditional and hybrid anthology products contribute to overcoming the limits of manual tagging and algorithmic indexing, in a moment when content is increasingly diversified, with much less rigidity in the production of genre-formulas and a variety of different serial narratives that are not easy to encapsulate in sharp categories. As we find ourselves at a moment of "narrative exhaustion,"[11] the short-form anthological model might be a way to generate an additional level of categorization on online streaming platforms and minimize the cultural bias of external, machine-dependent classification. One wrong assumption is that algorithms are static, imposed, normative technical forms. On the contrary, observing them as culture (Seaver 2017) allows us to conduct more comprehensive research on their cultural capacity, range, scope, and social outreach. In the previous chapters, I discussed the anthology form as deeply embedded in digital cultures, technologies, and economies from three main perspectives: historical; design-oriented; and infrastructural. In this final chapter, I observe the anthology form as a model in its broader sense, following its transition to platform and algorithmic culture. By considering how

---

11   Daniel Holloway. "FX Boss John Landgraf Talks 'Narrative Exhaustion' in TV's 'Gilded Age.'" *Variety*. Last modified August 3, 2018. https://variety.com/2018/tv/news/fx-boss-john -landgraf-tca-netflix-1202894641.

cultural artifacts are datafied and typified on internet-distributed media, I examine them not as self-existent objects, but rather as parts of designed and coded algorithmic environments. Drawing upon the historical, formal, infrastructural, technological, industrial, and socio-cultural implications of streaming platforms outlined so far, I will focus on a more detailed analysis of Netflix and explain how creation, classification, design, and reception strategies relate to anthological practices in algorithmic culture.

4.6. Recommendation Systems

Online recommendation systems are information filtering systems that provide users with streams of prioritized content based on expected individual preferences. While they can be of different types – e.g., collaborative, content-based, or hybrid filtering – they typically share the use of machine learning as a type of artificial intelligence able to perform predictions and profile personal taste" (Taurino 2022). These systems are responsible for the infrastructural, economic, design-operational sustenance of most streaming platforms. A well-engineered content filtering system is key for turning platforms' habitats into organized, manageable, and intuitive online libraries that can attract users, making the access to ever-growing and heterogeneous information easier. Even the most rudimentary recommenders rely on algorithmic operations designed to exploit the data available in order to arrange content in some kind of preferential order, contributing to both the conceptual and visual framing of each cultural record. With the aim of exploring the performative dimension of algorithms (Seyfert and Roberge 2016) on streaming platforms, let us considered the specific case of Netflix's proprietary recommendation engine and analyze the different levels of interplay between human and machine-driven content organization. At the platform level, Netflix's interface activates a series of data-led and algorithmic practices that overlap with pre-digital forms of classification: it collects data; connects metadata; predicts preferences; and informs choices, all while maintaining more traditional archival strategies. The study of such a hybrid structure requires us to take a digital ethnography approach, via the regular monitoring of the platform itself, as well as of the surrounding media discourse. For this reason, the following analysis uses a mix of sources, including press releases, press articles, and interviews with media professionals and practitioners, which together contribute to assessing the positioning of anthology-like forms on Netflix as part of a broader platform strategy. Supported by existing research on digital culture, this case study is ultimately intended to be a starting point for further consideration of the role of anthological collections across a variety of online content-hosting services and archive architectures.

At first glance, the mechanism of anthologization on Netflix appears to be closely related to the platform's specific ecology and economy. In fact, both practices of editorial and algorithmic indexing are symptoms of the same need to organize content into clusters and audiovisual itineraries, in order to guide the viewer into repeatable and predictable consumption patterns. In this context, we can identify four formal levels of content organization, ordered as follows from content production to content distribution, but really operating in a circular loop: (1) a content-creation level; (2) a meta-data level; (3) an interface-design level; and (4) an algorithmic level. These interacting organizational components are tied together via reception. During the reception, the acts of encoding and decoding occur at both ends. As the media text reaches the audience, users leave traces on the platform (e.g., personal data, engagement data, behavioral data), which are gathered and analyzed by recommendation algorithms that use machine learning to generate personalized ranking, searches, image selections, and other customized features. The result is that the original audiovisual text is now encoded in adjustable queues and its message re-contextualized. This process of encoding–decoding is particularly evident in instances where Netflix's recommendation algorithms return unexpected results. Often perceived as errors, these results have occasionally led to alternative interpretations of the text. Cohn (2019: 9) offers an example of these unusual, algorithmic-induced reception practices by citing the case of *The Babadook* (2015), which unpredictably appeared on Netflix among "LGBT Movies Recommendations" and became a queer icon.

Overall, Netflix's approach to the automated generation of collections brings about new layers of content categorization when compared to its anthological predecessors. For instance, while it intervenes in the "final" phase of media dissemination, it is worth taking a closer look at the algo-rithmic level first, as the innovative features found in many contemporary anthologies, to then reconstruct Netflix's classification cycle backwards. As anticipated, on most streaming services, individual viewing choices are quantified, compared, systematized, and reinserted in this human-algorithmic categorization circuit. Although the filtering algorithms operate as the outcome of human-directed classification linked to content, metadata, platform design, and user interaction, the machine-computational information processing is what ultimately unites all these categorization layers in a single cultural experience on the web interface. In a way, the algorithmic level functions as a dynamic and composite classification super-structure. Thanks to the algorithmic level, the expansive online library is tailored to each member's profile, where records are grouped and categorized into rows of content based on a specific organization principle (e.g., "continue watching," "my list," "trending now," "because you watched") and on different algorithms (e.g., Continue Watching Ranker, Personalized Video Ranking, Trending Now Ranker, Video-Video Similarity Ranker). As Amanda Lotz explains, "personalized queues in combination with recommendation algorithms [are] valuable tools for navigating an environment of post-network programming abundance" (Lotz 2007, 79, my parenthesis) As of 2015, Netflix queues were generated by "a variety of algorithms that collectively define the Netflix experience." (Gomez-Uribe and Hunt 2016, 2). "To give an impression of the many algorithms that play into designing this overall Netflix experience, Gomez-Uribe and Hunt list at least eight different algorithms, including the personalized video ranker (PVR), which orders the entire catalog of videos for each number in a personalized way; the Top-N Video ranker, which produces the recommendation in the Top Pick; and the page generation algorithm, which works to construct every single page of recommendations" (Bucher 2018, online).

A more detailed overview of how Netflix's recommendation engine works can be found on the platform's website.[12] Collectively, the algorithms embedded in the recommendation system rely on several parameters that calculate likelihood and proximity. As previously mentioned, these measures are estimated by evaluating data on a single user's interactions with the platform (e.g., content viewing history, ratings, and other activities including viewing time, duration, and device used) and similarity metrics based on other users' preferences, as well as by accounting for metadata related to the content – such as genre, cast, year and country of release, and so forth. Having mapped, collected, combined data and metadata, the recommendation system returns a series of collections that weave the classification fabric. This process differs from early examples of anthologization in digital culture, for two reasons. First, on Netflix, each user is exposed to a distinct selection. Due to their reliance on personal data, these systems of algorithmic anthologization do not constitute a public, shared media and narrative experience, as opposed to more traditional digital-anthology forms that mimic literary references generating a common canon. Second, unlike more static digital anthologies, where the order is usually non-hierarchical and fixed, Netflix's algorithms continuously re-order the records suggested

---

12   https://help.netflix.com/en/node/100639.

in each row, following a range of criteria for content prioritization. In addition to filtering the records to include in the rows on the homepage, a computational apparatus curates "each title within the row, and then ranks the rows themselves, using algorithms and complex systems to provide a personalized experience [...] designed to present the best possible ordering."[13]

The entirety of these algorithmic operations is made visible and "graphically enabled" (Drucker 2014b) through the interface-design level. On the one hand, algorithmically curated collections offer a hyper-personalized approach to the practice of anthology-making that help improve the platforms' functionalities and respond to users' needs, i.e., managing large amounts of content. On the other hand, they introduce a new esthetics of classification practices, by leveraging visible anthological features – rows and queues – on the interface, as well as on personalized and automated visual branding. To this aim, a computer-vision algorithm, recently introduced, prompts Netflix to categorize content with personalized promotional-image picks. Each artwork chosen to market a selected title,

> highlights the specific visual clue that is relevant for each individual member. [...] Different images are randomly assigned to different subscribers, using the taste communities as an initial guideline. This translates into hundreds of millions of personalized images continuously being tested among its subscriber base. For the creation of the artwork, machine learning also plays a critical role; thanks to a computer vision algorithm that scans the shows and picks the best images that will be tested among the taste communities.
>
> (Kathayat 2019, online)

What we think of as a given, intuitive platform esthetics is, in fact, the result of an assemblage of visual forms of information production and representation (Drucker 2014b), a carefully edited knowledge design (Drucker 2014a; Schnapp 2014), and information architecture (Morville and Rosenfeld 2006). In our "screen-saturated culture" (Drucker 2014b), "digital technology depends on visual presentation for much of its effectiveness. The ubiquitous graphical user interface and the design of icons for navigation, daily activities and functions, are familiar graphic structures" (Ibid.).

The design of the platform interface on Netflix offers a space of mediation for presenting to the users not only audiovisual content, but also the system of knowledge curated by the algorithms in the back-end. The division

---

13   Ibid.

into multiple, parallel lines or rows represents the ergonomic, graphical expressions of the platform's algorithmic affordances. Once they log-in via a computer or a smart TV, users are guided by esthetic cues through a plethora of content that has been methodically organized and ordered to facilitate their front-end experience. Along with personalized, ranked, labeled rows, different banners at the top of the interface suggest macro-categories that remain fixed across different users, like "TV Shows," "Movies," "New & Popular," "My List," and "Browse by Language." Additionally, drop-down menus located in the top-end area of the website allow users to both access their account settings and navigate the system of macro-categories into more specific genres (e.g., drama, comedy, documentary). Everything is designed to facilitate the choice of a compelling title, by alleviating the time and effort needed for decision-making and possibly preventing subscribers from abandoning the platform or service (Gomez-Uribe and Hunt 2016, 2).

So far, I have focused on two main data-led and human-led classificatory processes as seen in the interface of services like Netflix, namely, algorithmic filtering and platform design. However, other levels of content organization are present in the making of the streaming experience. For instance, in order to function properly, algorithmic recommendation systems found on most streaming platforms are usually based on a preliminary process of manual annotation and content tagging. This phase precedes algorithmic organization of content into curated streams, which is entirely machine-driven on the basis of personal data, metadata descriptors, content categories, and ontologies. The philosopher Milad Doueihi (2011a: 521) points at the fact that, in the context of digital culture, tagging practices have redefined processes of classification, dissemination, and selection of previously unrelated snippets of content, thus generating new forms of knowledge production and meaning-making. In other words, annotation and tagging "systems are active creators of categories in the world as well as simulators of existing categories" (Bowker and Star 1999. 321). Even more, these systems are part of a broader digitization process that makes content computationally readable and ready to undergo algorithmic treatments. Content in algorithmic culture is interpreted as an ensemble of metadata to process via large-scale computation. Extracting data, metadata, and other attributes from audiovisual stories turns records into topical, categorical information that can be queried, retrieved, interlinked, and grouped.

> The story will have some attributes, such as the headline and source of the story, but the primary content is the story itself. In a database system, this critical piece of information would typically be stored as a

single large attribute with no internal structure. [...] To do this search, we must design algorithms that can compare the text of the queries with the text of the story and decide whether the story contains the information that is being sought. [...] The current technology for searching non-text documents relies on text descriptions of their content rather than the contents themselves, but progress is being made on techniques for direct comparison of images, for example.

(Croft et al. 2011, 2–3)

On Netflix, the process of assigning metadata to media content is performed by a number of human agents – let us call them "taggers" – and supervised by teams of taxonomists, engineers, and data scientists, who create a pre-defined taxonomical grid. The result is an organized cultural archive that blends a set of pre-defined abstract categories with individual understanding. In this sense, Netflix operates in ways that are similar to other types of archival curation based on tagging, such as user-generated tagging, "with an immanent classificatory system produced in the collective classificatory imagination of the users [taggers]" (Beer 2013: 62). This act of anthologization is interesting precisely because it emerges at the convergence of multiple, collective processes of classification, thus mediating between a data-oriented, computational framework and human intelligence and cognition. In this context, an additional level of human intervention operates in the form of content creation as the bearer of the story itself. "Like previous major technological breakthroughs, the Internet is also having a profound impact on storytelling. Netflix lies at the intersection of the Internet and storytelling" (Gomez-Uribe and Hunt 2016, 1). By taking Netflix as a primary object of study, we can observe how AI-based recommendation systems interact with editorial forms of anthologizations on multiple levels, not least by means of the anthology form as we know it from pre-digital practices. The hypothesis outlined here is that television storytelling in the anthology form might be useful in the platform ecology to optimize the manual process of tagging metadata: once the anthology is tagged, each episode or season is likely to return with the same metadata, by exploiting a structural recursivity that is inherent to the anthological model.

As Netflix proposes thousands of different genres,[14] commissioning anthology content that is easy to sort into clusters contributes to creating: (1) a collective experience by generating a homogenous flow that can

14   Chris Lilly. "Netflix Genre List: 23,458 More Secret Genres Not in Other Lists." *Finder.* https://www.finder.com/uk/netflix/genre-list.

be followed from everyone more or less in the same way – since it is not personalized in individual streams – and (2) a canon, or a brand created under an umbrella title – meaning, everyone knows what to expect when people discuss an episode of an anthology like *Black Mirror*, even if they did not watch that same episode. The anthology form in internet-distributed television seems to provide a production-based narrative classification framework generated ex-ante, before data-led content indexing into streams operates as a secondary anthological classification ex-post. It declares the creation of a group, of a cluster of content, such as *dystopic narratives set in the near future about the impacts of technologies on human relationships*. And instead of keeping this long metadata description, it initiates a list of content – a collection – and classifies it as *Black Mirror*. We can think of a library shelf where we put all the content fitting into a specific description or category, instead of having to open the door onto a library of sparse, unorganized objects with different genres and forms. Thus, instead of searching for a "British TV show," halfway between "thriller," "drama," "sci-fi & fantasy," which is both "mind-bending" and "chilling," Netflix users will simply query "Black Mirror.".

Unlike content filtering, as seen in the design of the interface of media providers like Netflix, which fosters a wide variety of individual, personalized consumption patterns that are constantly changing as soon as consumption happens, the editorial creation of tagged collections or anthologies is a practice that can increase regularity and homogeneity in consumption. By pre-selecting an anthology principle that applies to content independently from personal choices, audiovisual anthologies open up to the possibility of a collective viewing experience in platform environments. For instance, if we observe the source code or the URL resulting from running a query on a streaming platform, pre-formatted anthological records are often organized and identified as collection-types,[15] showing that they can easily adapt to a platform ecosystem as a way to structure content. As already mentioned, this narrative form

---

15 When accessing a web page related to an anthology series, the content is often organized on the interface into collections. For instance, when searching for the TV series *Weird City* (2019) on the video sharing platform YouTube, the response returns a list of episodes coded as "web_modern_collections":true and "web_modern_playlists":true (raw HTML source code: view-source:https://www.youtube.com/results?search_query=weird+city+). On Netflix, the collection-type can be traced via the URL itself, such as in these examples from queries run in 2019, where the label "collection" follows the ID associated with the title searched for: https://www.netflix.com/search?q=american%20crime%20story&suggestionId=3066731_collection or https://www.netflix.com/search?q=black%20mirror&suggestionId=2939970_collection.

may also be part of a strategy for expanding and scaling the catalog, by responding to a broader need to automatically assign metadata to an increasingly higher amount of content. Indeed, in a platform dynamic where "75% of what people watch is from some sort of recommendation,"[16] even long-running shows, franchises, and other branded television content can be arranged into profitable collections in the broader sense of the term. Nevertheless, as previously outlined when discussing the industrial practices of streaming, anthology series, with their shorter runs, combine the potential for a continuous rebooting (and therefore, more content) with a safer production model. Furthermore, in terms of distribution and reception, the anthology form allows a more customizable consumption speed, at a moment when viewers' habits are in the process of adapting to a mutating non-linear mediascape – with practices of long-viewing (binge-watching), fast-viewing (binge-racing), multitask-viewing (carrying out secondary activities while watching), and non-sequential-viewing (watching episodes out-of-order).

Mapping the occurrences of the anthology form as part of a larger corpus of streaming platforms' productions returns an even more complex picture. While digital platforms' infrastructures and technologies are prone to welcoming and even inducing processes of anthologization that facilitate content indexing and retrieval in the long term, some over-the-top services seem to have adopted this model more radically than others. In general, different platforms are doing it for different reasons. For instance, streaming services heavily relying on a community of users, like Vimeo on demand and YouTube Prime, did not implement the production of anthology series as a predominant commercial strategy for content creation. On these platforms, the anthology form rather appears in online collection practices loosely based on the anthological model. It is still too early to evaluate to what extent the strategy of other emerging platforms is based on an anthology-making process. However, the case of Netflix shows that both algorithmic and anthological practices are closely related to the platform's environment. On July 16, 2019,[17] Netflix implemented a recommendation system based on a collection model on its DVD-delivery platform (not for streaming). As forms of editorialization and marketing, these collections are examples of ex-post anthologies. Quoting from the DVD Netflix' blog: "Collections are

---

16   "Netflix Recommendations: Beyond the 5 Stars (Part 1)." *Medium – Netflix Technology Blog.* Last modified April 18, 2017. https://medium.com/netflix-techblog/netflix-recommendations -beyond-the-5-stars-part-1-55838468f429.

17   See: https://twitter.com/dvdnetflix/status/1151285397911212037.

curated lists of movies centered around certain topics of themes. They're a convenient way to browse all the James Bond movies (without looking up each movie individually) or add our top 10 rented classic films at once. On the desktop website, you can hover over Browse, then click 'Collections' in the dropdown menu."[18] By simply entering the collections tab, users can add blocks of content to their queue of movies to rent.[19]

Technically, DVD Netflix is not a streaming platform; it is a platform for movie rental in different formats (DVD, Blu-Ray). However, this example suggests that the collection model, or anthology model, is something that both coexists with physical media and is present on a variety of digital platforms even beyond streaming, in the larger permeation scheme of algorithmic culture. Overall, both Netflix DVD-delivery and the Netflix streaming service adopted a content acquisition and distribution strategy that tends to follow a fundamental principle: it aims at covering a broad variety of people's taste to guarantee a personalized stream for each individual user.[20] On the one hand, the company does so by opting for shows with a wide, long-established audience; on the other hand, it invests in niche shows that offer a smaller, yet loyal pool of subscribers. As the 2018 annual report outlines, Netflix's estimates are based "on historical experience and on various other assumptions [...]. For example, we estimate the amortization pattern, beginning with the month of first availability, of any particular licensed or produced television series or movie based upon factors including historical and estimated viewing patterns."[21] Aside from the company's internal strategies, a conversation on the anthology form in relation to streaming platforms is arising among its content creators. For instance, *Black Mirror*'s creator Charlie Brooker suggested that standalone episodes can be considered as "short, individual films" (Landau 2015, 286), thus becoming part of a double stream: the one attached to the anthological collection *Black Mirror* and the other linked to the flow of algorithmic recommendations sparking from single episodes – "if you just watched… then." "So, in a way, these services that stack everything up are kind of made for anthology shows" (Ibid.).

18   "Collections: Now Available on IOS and Android." *Netflix DVD Blog.* http://blog.dvd.netflix.com/new-dvd-releases/collections-in-dvd-netflix-app.

19   "Introducing Collections." *Netflix DVD Blog.* http://blog.dvd.netflix.com/new-dvd-releases/introducing-collections.

20   "Netflix – Overview – Long-Term View." *Netflix Investors.* Last modified January 22, 2018. https://www.netflixinvestor.com/ir-overview/long-term-view/default.aspx.

21   Netflix Inc.'s Annual Report: https://s22.q4cdn.com/959853165/files/doc_financials/annual_reports/2018/Form-10K_Q418_Filed.pdf.

In this sense, Netflix's choice to acquire *Black Mirror* is quite easy to profile. Netflix might have looked at the data and identified certain viewing patterns, detecting an audience potentially interested in certain content. This might have helped isolate a series, namely *Black Mirror*, which was likely to attract viewers based on the data available. This series fits at least within three networks of related content: *Black Mirror*'s own collection of episodes; the broad sci-fi genre category; and a cluster of nostalgic content from a dystopian narrative tradition. In addition to these three groups, the anthology structure allows for other associations, based on single-episode topics. Other examples of the same anthological type made of standalone episodes in a greater series were undertaken by Netflix Original productions, which repurposed macro-anthological and semi-anthological designs. For instance, the anthology collection of documentaries *Chef's Table* (2015–) inserts itself in the renewed televisual interest for food-driven storytelling, which can be expanded into a macro-group of interrelated episodes. As the creator of the show, David Gelb, put it, "it's about how do we balance the chefs, how do we make it so each story is different, so that the different stories complement each other. While each film can stand alone, together they should form a greater whole."[22]

Another example is *Easy* (2016–), an anthology comedy-drama that turns into semi-serial with multiple separate narrative strands. *Easy* represents an interesting experiment, because it shows interconnected characters in different stories and builds on the reprise of narrative strands in sparse order, making a statement on the non-linearity of streaming platforms, where the viewer can afford to skip episodes or watch them in an arbitrary order. This television series is a good case of scalability and elasticity in the contemporary anthology form, which cleverly redefines the rules for making audiovisual narratives in unprecedented ways. Furthermore, this show was created collectively, as an improvised, choral experience based on pitching a recurring scenario in the background (all narratives are based in Chicago). In an interview with Indiewire, the creator Joe Swanberg explained: "I leaned really heavily on the actors [...] to help me craft that story and to bring their own belief systems to it so that I'm not overly informing the episode as a straight, white guy and that I'm really having their voices be present in the writing process."[23] Some additional affordances of narrative

22   Daniela Galarza. "Netflix's 'Chef's Table' Returns for Second, Third, and Fourth Seasons." *Eater*. Last modified March 8, 2016. https://www.eater.com/2016/3/8/11175948/netflix-chefs-table-davidgelb-second-season.

23   Ben Travers. "Joe Swanberg Wants You to Know a 'Straight White Guy' Isn't the Sole Creative Force Behind 124 'Easy'." *IndieWire*. Last modified December 21, 2017. https://www.indiewire.com/ 2017/12/easy-season-2-joe-swanberg-interview-netflix-1201910035.

anthologies emerge from this close reading, which offers a new approach
to anthology-making as a fluid process: the presence of a cultural setting
that helps shape the narrative; the predominance of actors as themselves
creators of the story; the portrayal of non-normative, non-conforming stories
depicting social issues and minorities through hybrid genres or nonlinear
storylines; and finally, the possibility to challenge the white male canon
through a multiplicity of stories, visions, and perspectives.

The metaphor of a scalable database as applied to the anthology form
finds evidence precisely in the fact that anthology series can be consumed
on the platform in a modular way: as the narrative arc can spread outside of
the single episode, while still fitting into shorter seasons and even shorter
episodes, in anthology series blocks of content can be easily identified, thus
improving the user experience. When the televisual content produced and
made available overcomes viewers' capacity to consume it and absorb it, or
even to simply make a choice about what to watch, the industry needs to
rethink its strategy. These overlapping machine-based and human-based
classificatory systems found on Netflix, which portray examples of either
collaborative classification, algorithmic-driven classification, or a mix of
both, produce clusters of content that are somehow similar to anthologies in terms of their aim. From algorithmic systems to design practices,
from metadata management to content creation and reception, in today's
mediascape the anthology form breaks down into millions of pieces of code,
visual information, data, and content. These anthological snippets are all
directed to maintaining a long-term platform logic, ecology, and economy.
In terms of production, distribution, and reception, the anthology appears
as a malleable and ductile form that emerge at all levels – at the algorithmic,
interface, metadata, content, and user interaction levels – to create resilient,
adaptable, predictable narratives tailored to the viewers' taste.

List of works cited

Alimahomed-Wilson, Jake, and Ellen Reese. 2020. *The Cost of Free Shipping: Amazon in the Global Economy*. London: Pluto Press.

Beer, David. 2013. *Popular Culture and New Media: The Politics of Circulation*. New York: Springer.

Beer, David. 2017. "The Social Power of Algorithms." *Information, Communication & Society* 20 (1): 1–13. https://doi.org/10.1080/1369118X.2016.1216147.

Beer, David. 2018. *The Data Gaze: Capitalism, Power and Perception*. Newbury Park, CA: SAGE.

Beer, David. 2019a. *The Quirks of Digital Culture*. Bingley: Emerald Group Publishing.

Beer, David. 2019b. "The Depths of Platform Culture." *Medium*. October 11, 2019. https://towardsdatascience.com/the-baffling-depths-of-platform-culture -f5648af8bc5b.

Bowker, Geoffrey C., and Susan Leigh Star. 1999. *Sorting Things Out: Classification and Its Consequences*. Cambridge, MA: MIT Press.

Bennett, James, and Niki Strange. 2011. *Television as Digital Media*. Durham, NC: Duke University Press.

Bennett, Peter, Kendall, Alex, and Julian McDougall. 2011. *After the Media: Culture and Identity in the 21st Century*. New York: Routledge.

Bogost, I., and Nick Montfort. 2007. "NEW MEDIA AS MATERIAL CONSTRAINT: An Introduction to Platform Studies." 2007. https://www.semanticscholar.org/paper/ NEW-MEDIA-AS-MATERIAL-CONSTRAINT-An-Introduction-to-Bogost-Mon tfort/7647d84e00696504c7c94a49ca8a82d59bed89f1.

Bogost, Ian, and Nick Montfort. 2009. "Platform Studies: Frequently Questioned Answers," December. https://escholarship.org/uc/item/01rok9br.

Bucher, Taina. 2018. *If...Then: Algorithmic Power and Politics*. Oxford: Oxford University Press.

Buyya, Rajkumar, and Amir Vahid Dastjerdi. 2016. *Internet of Things: Principles and Paradigms*. Amsterdam: Elsevier.

Croft, Bruce, Metzler, Donald, and Trevor Strohman. 2011. *Search Engines: Information Retrieval in Practice*. New York: Pearson Education.

Chen, Martha, and Françoise Carré. 2020. *The Informal Economy Revisited: Examining the Past, Envisioning the Future*. New York: Routledge.

Doueihi, Milad. 2011a. *Digital Cultures*. Cambridge, MA: Harvard University Press.

Drucker, Peter Ferdinand. 1969. *The Age of Discontinuity: Guidelines to Our Changing Society*. New York: Harper & Row.

Drucker, Johanna. 2014a. *Graphesis: Visual Forms of Knowledge Production*. Cambridge, MA: Harvard University Press.

Drucker, Johanna. 2014b. "Knowledge Design." *Design and Culture* 6 (1): 65–83. https://doi.org/10.2752/175470814X13823675225117.

Flichy, Patrice. 2007. *The Internet Imaginaire*. Cambridge, MA: MIT Press.

Frisby, David. 2013. *Sociological Impressionism: A Reassessment of Georg Simmel's Social Theory*. New York: Routledge.

Gawer, Annabelle. 2014. "Bridging Differing Perspectives on Technological Platforms: Toward an Integrative Framework." *Research Policy* 43 (7): 1239–49. https://doi.org/10.1016/j.respol.2014.03.006.

Gawer, Annabelle, and Michael A. Cusumano. 2014. "Industry Platforms and Ecosystem Innovation." *Journal of Product Innovation Management* 31 (3): 417–33. https://doi.org/10.1111/jpim.12105.

Gebru, Timnit, Morgenstern, Jamie, Vecchione, Briana, Wortman Vaughan, Jennifer, Wallach, Hanna, Daumé III, Hal, and Kate Crawford. 2021. "Datasheets for Datasets." *ArXiv:1803.09010* [Cs], December. http://arxiv.org/abs/1803.09010.

Gillespie, Tarleton. 2010. "The Politics of 'Platforms.'" *New Media & Society* 12 (3): 347–64. https://doi.org/10.1177/1461444809342738.

Gomez-Uribe, Carlos A., and Neil Hunt. 2016. "The Netflix Recommender System: Algorithms, Business Value, and Innovation." *ACM Transactions on Management Information Systems* 6 (4): 13:1–13:19. https://doi.org/10.1145/2843948.

Hands, Joss, Elmer, Greg, and Ganaele Langlois. 2013. "Vol. 14 Platform Politics." *Culture Machine* (blog). https://culturemachine.net/platform-politics/.

Helmond, Anne. 2015. "The Platformization of the Web: Making Web Data Platform Ready." *Social Media + Society* 1 (2). https://doi.org/10.1177/2056305115603080.

Hristova, Stefka, Daryl Slack, Jennifer, and Soonkwan Hong. 2020. *Algorithmic Culture: How Big Data and Artificial Intelligence Are Transforming Everyday Life*. Lanham, MD: Rowman & Littlefield.

Jaton, Florian. 2021. *The Constitution of Algorithms: Ground-Truthing, Programming, Formulating*. Cambridge, MA: MIT Press.

Karlgren, Jussi. 1990. "An Algebra for Recommendations: Using. Reader Data as a Basis for Measuring Document Proximity". Cyberjaya: SYSLAB. Technical Report

Kathayat, Vinod. 2019. "How Netflix Uses AI for Content Creation and Recommendation." *The Startup* (blog). September 18, 2019. https://medium.com/swlh/how-netflix-uses-ai-for-content-creation-and-recommendation-c1919efc0af4.

Kitchin, Rob. 2017. "Thinking Critically about and Researching Algorithms." *Information, Communication & Society* 20 (1): 14–29. https://doi.org/10.1080/1369118X.2016.1154087.

Landau, Neil. 2015. *TV Outside the Box: Trailblazing in the Digital Television Revolution*. New York: Focal Press.

Langlois, Ganaele, Elmer, Greg, McKelvey, Fenwick, and Zachary Devereaux. 2009. "Networked Publics: The Double Articulation of Code and Politics on Facebook." *Canadian Journal of Communication* 34 (3): 415-434. https://doi.org/10.22230/cjc.2009v34n3a2114.

Larkin, Brian. 2013. "The Politics and Poetics of Infrastructure." *Annual Review of Anthropology* 42 (1): 327–43. https://doi.org/10.1146/annurev-anthro-092412-155522.

Levine, Caroline. 2006. "Strategic Formalism: Toward a New Method in Cultural Studies." *Victorian Studies* 48 (4): 625–57.

Levine, Caroline. 2015a. *Forms: Whole, Rhythm, Hierarchy, Network*. Princeton, NJ: Princeton University Press.

Lobato, Ramon. 2019. *Netflix Nations: The Geography of Digital Distribution*. New York: NYU Press.

Lotz, Amanda D. 2007. *The Television Will Be Revolutionized*. New York: NYU Press.

Lotz, Amanda D. 2018. *We Now Disrupt This Broadcast: How Cable Transformed Television and the Internet Revolutionized It All.* Cambridge, MA: MIT Press.

Lynch, Paul A. 2005. "Sociological Impressionism in a Hospitality Context." *Annals of Tourism Research* 32 (3): 527–48. https://doi.org/10.1016/j.annals.2004.09.005.

Marx, Leo, and Merritt Roe Smith. 1994. *Does Technology Drive History?: The Dilemma of Technological Determinism.* Cambridge, MA: MIT Press.

Morville, Peter, and Louis Rosenfeld. 2006. *Information Architecture for the World Wide Web: Designing Large-Scale Web Sites.* Sebastopol, CA: O'Reilly Media.

Miyazaki, Shintaro. 2012. "Algorhythmics: Understanding Micro-Temporality in Computational Cultures | Computational Culture." 2012. http://computationalculture.net/algorhythmics-understanding-micro-temporality-in-computational-cultures/.

Miyazaki, Shintaro. 2013. *AlgoRHYTHMS Everywhere: A Heuristic Approach to Everyday Technologies.* Amsterdam: Rodopi. https://doi.org/10.1163/9789401208871_010.

Miyazaki, Shintaro. 2016. "Algorhythmics, Media Archaeology and Beyond." *Medium* (blog). https://medium.com/@algorhythmics/algorhythmics-archaeology-and-beyond-2eff6595e6ab.

Nieborg, David B., and Thomas Poell. 2018. "The Platformization of Cultural Production: Theorizing the Contingent Cultural Commodity." *New Media & Society* 20 (11): 4275–92. https://doi.org/10.1177/1461444818769694.

Olsson, Jan, and Lynn Spigel. 2004. *Television after TV: Essays on a Medium in Transition.* Durham, NC: Duke University Press.

Rahman, K. Sabeel, and Kathleen Thelen. 2019. "The Rise of the Platform Business Model and the Transformation of Twenty-First-Century Capitalism." *Politics & Society* 47 (2): 177–204. https://doi.org/10.1177/0032329219838932.

Resnick, Paul, and Hal R. Varian. 1997. "Recommender Systems." *Communications of the ACM* 40 (3): 56–58. https://doi.org/10.1145/245108.245121.

Seaver, Nick. 2017. "Algorithms as Culture: Some Tactics for the Ethnography of Algorithmic Systems." *Big Data & Society* 4 (2). https://doi.org/10.1177/2053951717738104.

Seyfert, Robert, and Jonathan Roberge. 2016. *Algorithmic Cultures: Essays on Meaning, Performance and New Technologies.* New York: Routledge.

Smyrnaios, Nikos. 2018. *Internet Oligopoly: The Corporate Takeover of Our Digital World.* Bingley: Emerald Group Publishing.

Smyrnaios, Nikos, and Franck Rebillard. 2019. "How Infomediation Platforms Took Over the News: A Longitudinal Perspective." *The Political Economy of Communication* 7 (1). https://www.polecom.org/index.php/polecom/article/view/103.

Srnicek, Nick. 2017a. *Platform Capitalism.* Hoboken, NJ: Wiley.

Srnicek, Nick. 2017b. "The Challenges of Platform Capitalism: Understanding the Logic of a New Business Model." IPPR. September 20, 2017. https://www.ippr.org/juncture-item/the-challenges-of-platform-capitalism.

Striphas, Ted. 2011. *The Late Age of Print: Everyday Book Culture from Consumerism to Control*. New York: Columbia University Press.

Striphas, Ted. 2012. "What Is an Algorithm? – Culture Digitally." 2012. https://culturedigitally.org/2012/02/what-is-an-algorithm/.

Striphas, Ted. 2015. "Algorithmic Culture." *European Journal of Cultural Studies* 18 (4–5): 395–412. https://doi.org/10.1177/1367549415577392.

Tilson, David, Lyytinen, Kalle, and Carsten Sørensen. 2010. "Digital Infrastructures: The Missing IS Research Agenda." *Information Systems Research* 21 (4): 748–59. https://doi.org/10.1287/isre.1100.0318.

Turner, Graeme, and Jinna Tay. 2009. *Television Studies After TV: Understanding Television in the Post-Broadcast Era*. New York: Routledge.

Uricchio, William. 2011. "The Algorithmic Turn: Photosynth, Augmented Reality and the Changing Implications of the Image." *Visual Studies* 26 (1): 25–35. https://doi.org/10.1080/1472586X.2011.548486.

Van Dijck, José. 2013. *The Culture of Connectivity: A Critical History of Social Media*. New York: Oxford University Press.

Van Dijck, José. 2021. "Seeing the Forest for the Trees: Visualizing Platformization and Its Governance."

Van Arendonk, Kathryn. 2019. "Theorizing the Television Episode." *Narrative* 27 (1): 65–82. https://doi.org/10.1353/nar.2019.0004.

Vitali-Rosati, Marcello. 2018. *On Editorialization: Structuring Space and Authority in the Digital Age*. Amsterdam: Institute of Network Cultures.

Wardrip-Fruin, Noah, and Nick Montfort. 2003. *The New Media Reader*. Cambridge, MA: MIT Press.

Warf, Barney. 2012. *Global Geographies of the Internet*. New York: Springer.

Warf, Barney. 2017. *Handbook on Geographies of Technology*. Cheltenham: Edward Elgar Publishing.

Conclusion

Narratives are metaphors. They generate the concepts we live by, they carry them over generation after generation. Anthologies, in turn, spatialize them, geolocate them, frame them temporally and conceptually. They assign them a meaning in a broader system of mutual relationships. They are, themselves, classification systems. "Today, with the emergence of new information infrastructures, these classification systems are becoming even more densely interconnected" (Bowker and Star 1999, 326). As a cultural form and organizational model, the anthology has represented an important editorial framework in the development, preservation, and retrieval of Western narratives, from paper-based media to audiovisual content, throughout a series of discontinued analog and digital technologies. Over time, even anthologies, like narratives, have become part of the "metaphors we live by" (Lakoff and Johnson 2008), figurative lenses through which we read, navigate, and interpret stories and organize human thoughts for better understanding. Perhaps more importantly, they have become a practice, evolving, mutating, yet persistent in the ultimate human attempt to make space for and sense of the culture we produce. Throughout the book, I have demonstrated that anthologies are bound to the things that they do, their potential affordances and actualized functions. I have also shown how these affordances and functions collide with surrounding cultural and media ecosystems. In looking at the evolutionary genealogy of the anthology form, I have tried to assess how it plays out in the creation of a symbolic value, of a cultural capital within social, technological, infrastructural, industrial, and algorithmic-platformed contexts. Because, like sociology, the cultural history "of art and literature has to take as its object not only the material production but also the symbolic production of the work, i.e., the production of the value of the work" (Bourdieu 1983, 37).

When addressing the symbolic production of this form, I therefore considered contextual media, economic and social environments, as well as historical evolutions. Across media histories, anthologies have always participated in the formation and preservation of cultural value, identity, and heritage. The presence of a directed, hegemonic cultural standard in early anthologies in literature, radio, and television was subjected to

Taurino, Giulia. *The Anthology in Digital Culture*. Amsterdam: Amsterdam University Press, 2023.
DOI: 10.5117/9789463724265_CONC

dynamics of authority, policymaking, or censorship that greatly influenced media industries. As a pragmatic way to formalize knowledge, the anthology form and its history reminded us that cultural categories have often served as systems of power and exclusion. For a long time, anthologization practices have represented unsettling sites for both defining and contesting a conservative idea of canon, of what should be central and marginal in our cultures. Similarly, in digital culture, the anthology has come to represent the canonical and the non-canonical, all while trying to situate itself in processes of knowledge formation in mediated environments. Today, the anthology is both material and immaterial, it can be read, seen, listened to, but it is also invisible. It can be actively created, navigated, interacted with, or passively retrieved. Understanding how to approach this multi-formal practice that derives from pre-digital culture means gaining oversight on the algorithmic invisibility of performative, computational machines. With an act of epistemological re-appropriation of the anthology form, as primarily human, and then algorithmic, this book highlights the instrumental role of anthologies in solving issues of storage and archival uncertainties (Thylstrup et al. 2021). It also stresses their potential generative affordances to either promote hierarchical networks or undermine the very concept of authority.

Despite its first publication in 2011, Milad Doueihi's work on digital culture and the anthological turn remains topical for the purposes of the research presented here. To insist on the extent of the anthological turn, Doueihi (2011) addressed the anthology as both a concept and a practice, a model and a methodology. By accounting for its affordances in digital culture, he offered an insightful vision of the anthological fragmentation on the web as something that feeds into the very way content is organized online. Building upon his work, my study serves as a starting point for understanding the importance of observing the anthology form in the continuity between analog and digital culture, which eventually led to its re-appearance in algorithmic media. As I have illustrated, from pre-digital to post-digital culture, the practice of anthologization operated towards the collection, organization, and diffusion of content, manifesting reiterative traits in its design. Using a genealogical method, I retraced the past, present, and future of anthology-making practices through a branching tree structure, which outlines "divergent lines and hidden relationships that point towards the present in critical ways; this includes the dead ends lost to the present" (Apprich and Bachmann 2017, 1). If a media genealogy (Ibid.) approach helped us draw a branching system that reveals processes of divergence, convergence, proliferation, and reciprocal relationships linked to actual uses, then a design-oriented framework contributed to framing the narrative,

cultural, and commercial types of the anthology form and its affordances, by
providing a partial taxonomy and list of concepts. Ex-ante/ex-post anthologies, micro-/semi-/macro-anthologies, and episodic/seasonal anthologies
are all abstract forms deriving from existing configurations and narrative
infrastructures in the mediascape. Here, they are deployed to orientate the
reader throughout different anthological prototypes and shapes.

Categorized by temporality, magnitude, and extension, these abstract
forms have returned in algorithmic culture in practical examples of "anthologization" (pre- or post-release) of the catalog as a whole, into (more
or less vast) sub-collections. Notably, we have witnessed the algorithmic
repurposing of the anthology form as a space of experimentation, as well
as a space of encounter between narrative materials, multimedia artifacts,
and classificatory imaginaries inherited from different pre-existing media
cultures. In digital and algorithmic culture, the production of anthologies
conflates with a complex set of infrastructures that motivates the existence
of a variegated selection of anthological forms and cultural repertoires in
the constitution of virtual archives (De Kosnik 2016, 65–67). After history
and design, infrastructure is therefore the third keyword deployed for
understanding the positioning of the anthology as a system of classification of narratives and data. In the midst of human-computer interactions,
classification systems stand on a precarious balance. Seemingly untethered
from the concrete reality and confined to the abstract symbolic worlds to
which they belong, they still rely on physical infrastructures for storage
and transmission. Beyond its historical and design uses, the contemporary
anthology is a state of this abstract classificatory human mind, but is also
embedded in an ecosystemic projection of data and machine operations. In
the streaming machine, geography and time play a pivotal role in redefining
the ways we spatialize and temporalize forms of classification into networks
of interrelated infrastructures. This network of infrastructures is also a vital
part for the maintenance of platform ecosystems, which today define the
very nature and meaning of digital culture as a data-driven space existing
in the internet superstructure. Additional concepts like scalability and
connectivity suggest a similarity between the anthology and a "database
model" (Manovich 1999) or a "database imaginary" (Thylstrup et al. 2021,
127–128), in that it enables and makes sense of cultural practices.

Even more than previous technological advancements and disruptions,
internet-based digital cultures and economies have had a pervasive impact
on a range of media practices, business models, and modes of representation, superimposing themselves onto pre-existing social and industrial
habits. As Manovich argues, while other technological revolutions affected

only specific stages and types of cultural communication, "the computer media revolution affects all stages of communication, including acquisition, manipulation, storage, and distribution; it also affects all types of media – texts, still images, moving images, sound, and spatial constructions" (Manovich 2001, 19). In television as much as in other media, the term "digital" notably came to address a rather complex intertwining of technological, economic, and social dynamics, which eventually affected the creation and circulation of, as well as the access to, information, narratives, and cultural forms at large. Such a digital turn (Svensson and Goldberg 2015) not only landed in media studies, by carrying an implicit call for the redefinition of traditional theories and methodologies in order to account for the most recent technological evolutions, but it also affected the creative industry as a body of infrastructures. Digital media initiated a broad reassessment of the very network of institutional entities, collective and individual players that concur in all phases of the assembly line, from production, to distribution, up until the reception of content. The idea of network represents a key component for understanding internet platforms and the way they function in the interplay with cultural forms. By explicitly referring to processes of digitization/digitalization, the sociologist Manuel Castells discussed the social entity arose with the introduction of digital technologies using the term "networked society" and describing how the internet has impacted human communication and activities at all levels of making and spreading culture.

"At the heart of these communication networks the Internet ensures the production, distribution, and use of digitized information in all formats. According to the study published by Martin Hilbert in *Science* (Hilbert and López 2011), 95 percent of all information existing in the planet is digitized and most of it is accessible on the Internet and other computer networks" (Castells 2014, online). In his work, Castells addressed topics as varied as the technological revolution and the new economy, dynamics of globalization, informational flows, and virtual culture, to account for a radical shift in the level of interconnectedness between contemporary human communities and techno-cultural systems. Media inhabit this network and fill it with "traveling narratives [...] *flows of symbolic mobile and mobilizing resources* that have the potential to widen the range of our imaginary geography, multiply our symbolic life- worlds, familiarize ourselves with 'the other' and 'the distant' and construct 'a sense of imagined places'" (Buonanno 2008, 108–109). This web of traveling narratives, internet infrastructures, data-driven and classification systems that glues together human activity at scale is what lies behind the platformization of culture, which reimplemented

the anthology form in its human and computational complexity as a structural annex. Contemporary anthologies are products inevitably nested in
algorithmic culture, obeying the logics of platform capitalism and global
distribution, appended to knowledge economies, info-mediation, data-driven
entertainment, and other industrial dynamics.

To give a clearer picture of how the anthology form is positioned in this
algorithmic present, I opted for a combination of distant reading – i.e., an
observation that encompasses the knowledge of a single object to account
for the knowledge produced by an ensemble of objects (Moretti 2013) –
with a more detailed close-reading of specific anthological formations in
streaming environments. The case of television, with its fast and evident
transition from a linear to a non-linear model, offered several close-ups on
the comparative evolution of the anthology form in different media and
infrastructural ecosystems, and contributed to anticipating and framing
its uses in platform ecosystems. As Lisa Parks suggests in an essay on cable
infrastructures, "if television technology is a historically shifting form and
set of practices, then it is necessary to consider more carefully how the
medium's content and form change with different distribution systems"
(Parks 2007, 114). From the analysis presented across the last two chapters
on infrastructures and platforms, it became evident that, although operating in an equally oligopolistic industrial landscape, streaming platforms
respond to different internal strategies from their media predecessors
and their ecology seems to follow a separate logic: the logic of data and
algorithms.

In this context, the anthology returns as a cultural form presenting a
certain set of affordances, but also as a practice, a model, and a process
for classifying and managing data. Finding themselves at the crossroads
between media histories and the digital, contemporary anthology forms
serve as linkages to previous media traditions, as much as they act as
medium-specific entities in the definition of classificatory systems on
online platforms. The case of Netflix indicates that the anthology form
can be exploited by streaming platforms not only in connection with genre
formulas, but also with more diverse cultural uses, while resuming previous uses of the anthology form in print or electronic media that predate
the internet revolution. This connection between form and content, form
and platform, in algorithmic-driven anthologization and classification is
constantly being redefined. For this reason, the modularity of its content
is a key property for the sustainability of the anthology form on streaming
platforms. Its formal division into discrete narratives modules – whether
in the form of algorithmic streams or curated story-collections – constantly

subjected to mechanisms of scalability and reproducibility, make it a highly resilient form in a non-linear, scattered, and disrupted environment. On Netflix, the anthology emerges as a multifaceted cultural form for the framing, organization, and diffusion of algorithmic knowledge, by preserving a classificatory equilibrium between single modules, algo-rhythms (Miyazaki 2012), and the whole. This reflects a vision of knowledge as multidimensional, encyclopedic (Eco 1976), non-linear, and rhizomatic, as in Deleuze and Guattari's (1987) view of culture as a system in constant need of a definition, collocation, and indexing.

The example of Netflix, a streaming platform based on recommendation and personalization systems, perfectly outlines how streams of algorithmically collected content can be capitalized on by sorting content into multiple lists, which operate "at massive scales under the contemporary conditions of a globalized economy" (Soon 2018, 195). Anthologization practices position themselves in algorithmic culture as attempts to find alternative strategies for content production, distribution, and reception that better fit a global content-delivery system. My research positions itself in such a technological, industrial, and cultural context, where media content is increasingly fragmented and virtually travels across borders and platforms, creating a transnational experience. Given such fragmentation and scale, the ways media content is categorized in the interaction between algorithmic-driven recommendation processes and more traditional editorial practices are pivotal to understanding the specific conditions that affect the emergence of some content over other in the media industry. Analyzing the anthology form in its various occurrences on a single platform is a way of trying to frame this process of hierarchization and emergence. To observe digital platforms, we need to rethink existing cultural forms, *re-define* them, in order to account for new geographies and spatialities, or better yet for new media ecologies, built on the principle of network interconnectedness.

As anthology-making practices are ceasing to exist in a solely human-regulated environment and become complementary to the operational functioning of algorithms in the sorting of content, one might ask how we can use the anthology as a form human and computational design intervention to imagine different categories. If we admit a view where classification schemes are acquired imaginative mindsets, as we have learnt to classify, can we unlearn to classify and learn to un-classify? Or better yet, learn to classify differently? Can a reflexion on the anthology form on streaming platforms help us change biased narratives, data, and classification systems? Can the digital anthology, as a hybrid practice, turn into a creative space for experimenting with the non-standard, non-canonical, and non classifiable? Taking up these questions, my research contributed to framing both the normative and subversive role of the anthology form, by looking at a set of uses over time. What stands out from the analysis I carried out throughout the chapters is that the anthology form in streaming media presents affordances that fit into a number of different categories.

For instance, initial observations of anthology-making practices presented *structural and narrative-oriented affordances* in the wide variety of Netflix's speculative fiction (Crawford 2021) and unlimited genre categorization. Anthological narratives are likely to develop starting from short narratives. Without the constraints of regulatory, institutional control, they tend to portray intersectional identities and address social or political issues. In more formulaic versions, they attract specific genres and generate canons. To these, we should add *industrial affordances*: anthology series afford cross-media adaptations, diversity, and scalability in production through rebooting, non-linear distribution, and a flexible experience of time when it comes to reception. Yet, to understand the anthology form and how it operates both in digital television and digital culture, we should look at a third group of affordances, which can be defined as *pragmatic* and *ecological*, in that they enable possibilities for action and find themselves in the *actuality* of uses, as well as in the interaction with a mediated *environment*.

By pointing at the pragmatic and ecological affordances of the anthology form in algorithmic culture, I notably refer to anthology series as objects that *afford* processes of editorialization, classification, organization, ordering, indexing, displaying, and marketing of content at the same time. As a traditional model for content organization, which overlaps with algorithmic forms, the anthology form in non-linear media interacts not only with narrative or industrial dynamics, but also with digital culture at large. The case studies examined in the last chapter suggest that the implementation of anthology series in internet-distributed media is based only partially on a defined and recurring business strategy, and mostly on a certain level of experimentation. Nevertheless, in the context of digital culture and economy, the pragmatic and ecological affordances of anthology forms operate as active forces in the wider process of the circulation of knowledge. While there are no clear data to verify whether the anthology form is more profitable and successful than other types of content classification, we can still track its peculiar interactions with platform ecologies. Anthological streams of content are generated by a constant negotiation, with "hundreds of hands reaching into them, tweaking and tuning, swapping out parts and experiencing with new arrangements" (Seaver 2019, 10). As my research currently stands, I am monitoring a larger sample of streaming profiles, in

order to collect more data about the tendency of anthological collections
to be exposed and amplified within Netflix's catalogs.

So far, algorithmic recommendation systems seem to superimpose
a rhythmic stream over the library, by interpreting data and metadata,
and translating them into a coded flow of content. When this content is
already grouped and organized into an anthological narrative, which already
presents internal classificatory affordances, the interplay between the
human-curated and algorithmic-curated collections generates interesting
outcomes in terms of circulation of content. Drawing upon previous research
on practices of anthology-making (Doueihi 2011), data classification (Bowker
and Star 1999), and platform infrastructures (Poell et al. 2021) for streaming
content, I pointed at the epistemological value of the anthology in digital and
algorithmic culture, as a primitive form of knowledge organization, which
has undergone an evolution in synergy with technology. Having defined a
techno-genesis (Hayles 2012) of the anthology form, it is worth discussing its
ontology as a classificatory model designed for framing cultural knowledge,
in addition to preserving it. As a form, a practice, and a cultural model,
the anthology creates a framework for the circulation and the access to
narratives. In contemporary media, it identifies and defines a reproducible
structure for each story module, thus creating a larger narrative based
on fragments of data and content. By putting together randomness and
systematicity, the anthology form feeds into the very process of indexing
content on streaming platforms, adapting to different interfaces. On streaming platforms, as much as in other media, anthologization proves to be a
form of categorization that gives shape to otherwise form-less narrative
content, lending itself to effectively adapting to digital environments on
the basis of standalone variations encapsulated within recurring patterns.

But even more so, both in analog and digital culture, the anthology
has proven to be an interpretationally primitive concept (Carey 2009), an
irreducible primitive notion and type. It is also a "boundary object" (Star
1988; Star and Griesemer 1989), a representational form – both plastic and
robust, weak and strong – that carves out and shapes a shared, habitual
reference – material or symbolic, with more or less granularity – between
communities holding different systems of understanding (Star 2010; Bowker
et al. 2016). As Susan Leigh Star emphasizes (Ibid.), boundary objects operate
at an organizational level with some degree of interpretative flexibility,
material scope, and infrastructural properties. Approaching the anthology
both as a primitive concept and boundary object allows us to comprehend
its pragmatic affordance of giving shape to the forms-less, unclassified,
and residual. "Over time, all standardized systems throw off or generate

residual categories. These are categories that include 'not elsewhere categorized,' 'none of the above,' or 'not otherwise specified.' As these categories become inhabited by outsiders or others, those within may begin to start other boundary objects […] and a cycle is born" (Star 2010, 614). Given its cross-historical, cross-cultural, cross-media relevance, I propose to insert "anthology" into a vocabulary of digital culture to account for both human-driven and machine-driven computational processes of cultural classification, in a broader attempt to expand the critical "keywords" (Williams 1983; Striphas 2015; Thylstrup et al. 2021) for the study of culture, society, and data. If we had to define it anew, we would say that the anthology is, first and foremost, a form of classification that partakes in the fundamental mechanism of labeling cultural records, and, as such, it transforms into a form of knowledge, understanding, interpretation.

Appendix

On Methods

Researching digital culture requires scholars to investigate a variety of media dynamics related to contextual technological, infrastructural, or economic mutations, as well as to pre-existing cultural, social, and institutional practices. Similarly, taking the anthology form as a means for exploring the transition from analog to digital culture required the mobilization of a wide range of concepts, theories, and methods. The invaluable works of Milan Doueihi, Caroline Levine, Susan Leigh Star and Geoffrey C. Bowker provided me with the conceptual tools to navigate this complex landscape and understand how digital culture is being constructed in terms of its forms, affordances, systems of relationships, and boundaries. As this book shows, the affordances of cultural forms like the anthology do not emerge only in relation to a specific medium, but rather occur throughout historical evolutions across several media by activating a series of connections between analog and digital environments. To gain insight into how practices of anthologization have transitioned to a post-digital landscape, where algorithmic occurrences coexist with the abstraction of ancient forms, I opted for a cross-media and cross-historical observation. A media genealogy approach helped me "point towards the present in critical ways" (Apprich and Bachmann 2017, 1), finding the pathways and dead ends of history that led us to the unveiling of algorithmic culture, via "an intuitive 'swimming' (Turner) in the complex contexts of the past, and from there back into the present" (Ibid.).

The volume opened up with references to media history, design and narrative theory, and expanded in subsequent chapters to include notions of media ecology, infrastructure studies and platform research. In the process of unraveling the multifaceted aspects of the anthology form, I adopted a comparative historical analysis and media industry analysis, via the qualitative survey of the data and information available (from media archives, interviews, newspapers articles and online sources), along with a thorough review of literature. For this approach I followed the periodization proposed by Lotz (2007), who theorized a "post-network era" of US television, or, as she later reframed it considering the most recent adjustments in the industry, a "post-channel era" (Lotz 2016). The study of media transitions that led to a post-network (Lotz 2007), post-broadcast (Turner and Tay 2009), post-channel (Lotz 2016) phase "after television" (Olsson and Spigel

2004: 2) and "after the media" (Bennett et al. 2011) necessitates of a series of interdisciplinary research methods able to account for their mutations over time in a more detailed way than traditional approaches to media analysis. For this reason, I integrated my research with tools from digital humanities and digital ethnography that could support a systematic review of anthological records.

Drawing upon digital humanities projects that study databases and archives through computational approaches, text analysis and data visualization (Schreibman et al. 2008), for this research I harnessed "digital toolkits in the service of the Humanities' core methodological strengths: attention to complexity, medium specificity, historical context, analytical depth, critique and interpretation" (Schnapp and Presner, quoted in Berry 2012, 3). Through acts of curation, editing and modeling of humanities data, digital methods opened up to new forms of interpretation: distant versus close; macro versus micro; surface versus depth (Burdick et al. 2012, 39). To distinguish different levels of analytical interpretation in digital humanities, Franco Moretti (2000, 2005a) proposed to differentiate between a "close reading," which operates on a small canon of texts, and a "distant reading," which approaches the study of literature and textual data at large. In this research, I used distant reading to tackle a large-scale database of textual and audiovisual records, and identify trends and patterns in the long term. This method allowed me to observe "units that are much smaller or much larger than the text: devices, themes, tropes – or genres and systems." (Moretti 2000, 57–58) Yet, "if we want to understand the system in its entirety, we must accept losing something. We always pay a price for theoretical knowledge: reality is infinitely rich; concepts are abstract, are poor. But it's precisely this 'poverty' that makes it possible to handle them, and therefore to know." (Ibid.)

To avoid the risks of macro-analysis (Jockers 2013), I have adopted an integrative model that combines distant reading with close reading through interactive visualizations. Interactive "distant reading visualizations [...] allow to interactively drill down to specific portions of the data" (Jänicke et al. 2015), they highlight patterns" and is able to "drill down on these patterns for further exploration" (Ibid.). In 2009, Monika Bednarek proposed a similar approach and reflected on a corpus-based methodology, taking into consideration a "three-pronged approach [*that*] involves a. large-scale computerized corpus analysis, b. semi-automated small-scale corpus analysis, and c. manual analysis of individual texts. As such, this is an approach that incorporates macro- (large-scale quantitative analysis), meso- (small-scale quantitative analysis), and micro- (individual text analysis) levels" (Bednarek

2009, 19). Focusing on both the history and design of the anthology form, I situated my research in this flexible analytical framework, bringing together the distant analysis of practices of anthologization across media with the more specific observation of substantial connections between cultural forms and digital infrastructures.

By utilizing both a close and distant reading for the study of the anthology form, I was able to bridge the gap between traditional media research and the analysis of digital platform environments. Looking at the anthology form from a distance provided a vantage point for understanding archival practices in relation to data-driven and algorithmic mechanisms underlying the platform ecology. The very process of doing digital methods required me to undergo a phase of data collection and discovery, and to define a corpus – perhaps an anthology in and of itself. This exploratory work led to a series of data visualizations that helped me navigate the complex landscape of cultural production and distribution. In the following paragraphs, I will provide a walk-through on the modus operandi I used for data collection, cleaning and discovery based on archival resources. Let us take as an example one of the corpora of anthology series that I used for this study. This particular corpus was selected by accounting for the following elements: medium (television); text type (anthology dramas); temporal frame (broadcasted between 1947 and 2019); and geographical location (United States). Data were preliminarily extracted, collected, and organized through research in physical archives (UCLA Film & Television Archive, AFI Louis B. Mayer Library, Paley Center for Media) and online databases (Wikipedia, Wikidata and IMDb). The information therefore came from an uneven set of databases, and included both institutional archives as well as user-generated catalogs.

The process of data collection was a fundamental one, as it defined the basis for subsequent data visualization and analysis. In the digital humanities, this process needs to be "rethought through a humanistic lens" (Drucker 2015, 238), where "capta is 'taken' actively while data is assumed to be a 'given' able to be recorded and observed. [...] Humanistic inquiry acknowledges the situated, partial, and constitutive character of knowledge production, the recognition that knowledge is constructed, taken, not simply given as a natural representation of pre-existing fact" (Ibid.). Furthermore, archival collections and online databases in the humanities often contain messy data, which make information retrieval problematic. To facilitate the understanding of the methodology I adopted here from data collection to visualization, I will provide an overview of the steps I followed for making sense of the data I gathered.

This study originally started from physical archives, with the intent of collecting information over a corpus of US television anthology series. The UCLA Film & Television Archive served as the main source for mapping early US television anthologies, and was integrated with complementary research at the American Film Institute's Louis B. Mayer Library and at the Paley Center for Media. The UCLA Film & Television Archive contains "over 160,000 holdings spanning the entire course of broadcast history,"[1] making it one of the largest television archive collections in the United States. If we browse for television anthologies in the archive's online catalog, the search returns over 1000 episodes from several anthology series. The list found in the online catalog, however, includes titles that cannot be screened due to the precarious state of their preservation. A close reading of each title in the entire catalog is therefore not possible, and, even if it was, the amount of content to retrieve and analyze would be very high, thus compromising the possibility to offer a complete overview of the corpus. I therefore decided to opt for other methods for information retrieval and use visualization as guide for navigating the database. Even though it was not possible to download metadata directly from the UCLA Film & Television Archive's online catalog through a .cvs or .json file, I was able to save a list containing all the data available for each entry: title, format, year, subject, publisher (e.g., television network), and other additional notes and descriptions. This list was then moved manually into a tabular form and incorporated with data found on Wikipedia, which was used to organize the UCLA catalog in a structured format.

In addition to the data collected from the UCLA Film & Television Archive's catalog, I downloaded data from online databases, with the aim of making the information more complete and minimizing the biases that a single archival source might present. I notably tapped into two online databases: Wikidata and IMDb. Having extracted the list of items contained in the Wikipedia page "American_anthology_television_series_by_decade"[2], I used Wikidata to filter all the items in the category "anthology series" and to select the following attributes: title, genre, production company, distributor, and original network. After cleaning the dataset, I matched this list with the UCLA list in order to group single episode-items into the corresponding series – e.g., "He's For Me" (S02E21) in *Alcoa Hour* (NBC, 1955–1957). I then proceeded to clean the data using Python to eliminate null values, compress duplicates in single attributes (e.g., "true crime" and

---

1   See: https://www.cinema.ucla.edu/collections/explore-collections.
2   https://en.wikipedia.org/wiki/Category:American_anthology_television_series_by_decade.

"crime" were collapsed under a single umbrella term), and filter out items
that were not relevant for the purpose of my analysis (e.g., films). A similar
process was adopted for cleaning the data extracted from IMDb. On the one
hand, the first dataset was the outcome of a manual process of assembling
data from the UCLA Film & Television Archive's catalog with information
found on Wikipedia about anthology series. On the other hand, the second
dataset was generated through a semi-automated process of data extraction
from online databases such as Wikidata and IMDb. For the final dataset, I
combined both datasets, which resulted in a final corpus that I could use
to create visualizations.

Once I had the dataset, I proceeded to data discovery. "Visual data discovery is the use of visually-oriented, self-service tools designed to guide
users to insights through the effective use of visual design principles [...]"
(Ryan 2016, 40). In this process, I explored several options to display my list
of cultural records and highlight historical patterns. The intent was provide
a visual chronology that could support the analysis of both evolutionary
patterns and media dynamics. In relation to questions of volume, quantity,
and temporal variation of the anthological form, I considered the following
factors as the basis for creating the visual models: on the one hand, the
density of anthology forms throughout different media, and, on the other
hand, its *temporal evolution* and *variation*. Among other attempts to visualize
the dataset, a configuration I generated using Knight Lab's tool Timeline JS
(Northwestern University) proved to be one of the most effective at showing
dynamics of emergence, convergence, proliferation, and divergence in the
evolution this form. In the timeline[3], the anthology form stands out as
the dominant form in the early years of its appearance in television. Its
emergence is immediately followed by a moment of convergence in which
the form conforms to a single model (e.g., episodic). In this phase, "there is
coherence with the mutation now being clearly distinct in its environment.
A critical mass of the entity now exists providing the chance of further
replication" (Kiel 2014, 73).

As we move to the right, the timeline shows a decline in the production
of anthologies. Once we reach the right edge, the density of anthology series
seems to increase again, signaling a new moment of proliferation, when "the
converged entity, now with some solid grounding in its environment, may
reach a stage of environmental fit in which it proliferates" (Ibid.). As we
can easily verify from more traditional historical analysis, after moments
of lower density in the use of this form across media, a stage of proliferation

3   https://goo.by/hpKNKK.

and divergence usually begins, with the diversification of "novel forms of the proliferant entity as it seeks new forms of adaptive fit" (Ibid.). Thanks to this visualization I was able to isolate more accurately the chronological limits of this last stage, marked by the introduction of innovative versions of the anthology form. While in a tabular form, major patterns of emergence, convergence, proliferation, decline, and divergence remain obscure and hidden in the substrates of data and metadata, the timeline brought them to the surface, to finally show the rate and the extent of the change. Measuring historical time and temporal progression in the evolution of the anthology form through a timeline allowed me to identify the timeframe during which this form emerged in a specific medium, such as television, (late 1940s), only to converge in an institutionalized formula (early 1960s). In television, the collection model went through a momentary crisis in the 1980s. Nevertheless, this decline witnessed the survival of the anthology in certain genres, which then sparked the rebirth of the anthology form in the twenty-first century, and initiated a path towards divergence, along with a whole new wave of algorithmic anthology-making practices.

On an abstract level, the timeline visualization shows the formation of *strata* of content. Instead of designing the timeline visualization as a single, linear, homogeneous, directional description of discrete intervals, I chose a visual rendering made of superimposed layers, to signal that "in the humanities time is frequently understood and represented as discontinuous, multi-directional, and variable" (Drucker 2014, 75). Considering the temporal structure as a chronostratigraphy of objects helps us to understand not only the positioning of anthological configurations, but also their stratigraphic relationships. A *chronostratigraphic visual model* for analyzing narrative-based anthologies represents a multilayered vision of culture. This visualization was ultimately meant to facilitate the analytical process and explore the corpus at different scales. It was specifically designed to tackle a dataset that cannot be handled solely through a close reading.

Furthermore, through this and other visual models, I was able to demonstrate that the occurrences of the anthology form in television evolved over time in relation to distribution networks, specific timeframes, and genres. By means of visual renderings showing temporal strata and flows of content, I observed the anthology form across media, production companies, genres, and delivery networks. Moreover, these visual operations helped me identify the case studies worth exploring further, in order to understand trends and patterns in broad industrial-cultural network. Even before performing a more attentive analysis, the very process of creation of a corpus set the premises for the production of knowledge. As Anna Maria

Lorusso remarks, this "cultural-type survey" (Lorusso 2015) poses questions related to the principle of selection of the corpus, as well as its size, density, complexity, and level of interconnectedness. A corpus aims to be "significant and representative," while avoiding "both the logic of *exemplum* (taking a single case and postulating a posteriori that it explains everything else) and the most extreme derivation of *constructivism* (by defining an ad hoc corpus that confirms the original hypothesis and that, therefore, does not really test it or have the ability to modify it)" (Lorusso 2015, 55). While the selection will always inevitably present a partial point of view, as one cannot escape from choosing criteria for collecting data or defining an interpretative hypothesis, the aim is to render the perspective as objective as possible. "In semiotic analysis we explain our research hypothesis and our own corpus building procedures, avoiding extraordinary examples and focusing instead on a series of *ordinary cases* that are significant because they demonstrate regularity" (Ibid.).

Mapping these regularities in literature, radio, and television was fundamental to making a case for the anthology form and its definition. Here, I use the term mapping not only in the abstract sense of the term, as a "function that creates a correspondence between the elements in two domains" (Manovich 2011, 11), but also as "any remapping is a reinterpretation of the original media map, which not just teases out but also creates new interpretation and meanings" (Ibid., 12). In this sense, the acts of building a corpus and creating a visualization are closely intertwined. Visualizations are not only a way for exploring the dataset, but also a way to present the outputs of a study for a better cognitive understanding of the dataset/corpus (Card et al. 1999, 7).

Once knowledge is collected in the form of data, in order to become understandable, it has to undergo a structural design, which establishes a point of access to the "information architecture" (Morville and Rosenfeld 2006) of the corpus. As Drucker explains, "visualizations are always interpretations – data does not have an inherent visual form that merely gives rise to a graphic expression" (Drucker 2014, 7). While large historical corpora might contain unrelated data, design contributes to defining relationships, trends, patterns, and a meaningful narrative. In my analysis of the anthology form, I used visual displays to gather possible interpretations about the density in production within a certain timeframe, networks of distribution and main industrial players, but also to infer a formal taxonomy of anthological practices through knowledge design (Drucker 2014a; Schnapp 2014). This design-oriented approach to the analysis of cultural corpora provided me with a tool to investigate the diversity of affordances, uses, and practices within the anthology form. With this I was able to define abstract models and outline a taxonomy. For the purpose of a taxonomic analysis, I paired digital humanities with the study of digital ecosystems and digital ethnography, by looking at the "a stratified hierarchy of meaningful structures" (Geertz 1973, 7). Via ecological (McLuhan 1994 [1964]; Postman 1979) or system-theoretical (Kelleter 2017) perspectives in cultural (Deleuze and Guattari 1987), media (Nystrom 1975; Strate 2006; Scolari 2012), and platform (Bogost and Montfort 2009; Gillespie 2010) studies, I sew the historical, formal, design study of the anthology form together with its contextual infrastructures.

The infrastructure-oriented research opened up onto "a deeper, networked media history" (Mattern 2016, 2), "embodied on a large scale" (Ibid., 4) of space, time, force, and social organizations (Edwards 2003, 186). It was a necessary addition to find proof of the discoveries found through data collection and visualization. The aim of a methodical study of the infrastructures behind streaming was, on the one hand, to create a bridge with the previous chapters, by analyzing historical continuities in the current industrial scape, and, on the other hand, to insist on the disruptions – technological, infrastructural, cultural – that marked the shift to non-linear television. Studying algorithmic culture and the way it organizes and distributes content has proven to be a challenging task for many scholars, due to the complex intertwining of infrastructures, information technology resources, content delivery networks, back-end software, and algorithmic functions involved in the streaming process. Some resources, such as the Netflix Research website or the Netflix Technology Blog, might help untangle this complexity.

However, the constant evolutions and implementations of new technologies, along with the control that media companies exert over the information they share, make it difficult to study the platform back-end and the infrastructural system it relies upon. When trying to assess the long-term socio-cultural outcomes of streaming platforms, looking at the front-end structure of the platform and its design remains the most viable option for humanities scholars. The observation of the anthology form as it appears on streaming interfaces might present evidences of structural and algorithmic dynamics hidden in the back-end. Yet, the challenges I encountered in advancing my research on streaming service algorithms were many. Turning to an interdisciplinary methodology solved such challenges only partially. If, on the one hand, historical analysis might pose problems with finding or accessing data, on the other hand, contemporary television streaming platforms often lock information up or else provide unreliable data. While the trading zone between media studies, distant reading, and digital ethnography leaves many questions unanswered, the hope is that this book can still represent a space of knowledge transfer and exchange between fields, in the attempt to help readers understand the hidden apparatus of mechanized libraries and describe the complex ecosystem of the information forest.

Bibliography

Abbott, Andrew. 2001. *Time Matters: On Theory and Method*. Chicago, IL: University of Chicago Press.

Abercrombie, Nicholas. 1996. *Television and Society*. Cambridge: Polity Press.

Agamben, Giorgio. 2009. *What Is an Apparatus?: And Other Essays*. Stanford, CA: Stanford University Press.

Alber, Jan, and Monika Fludernik. 2010. *Postclassical Narratology: Approaches and Analyses*. Athens, OH: Ohio State University Press.

Algee-Hewitt, Mark. 2017. *Canon/Archive: Studies in Quantitative Formalism from the Stanford Literary Lab*. New York: n+1 Foundation.

Alimahomed-Wilson, Jake, and Ellen Reese. 2020. *The Cost of Free Shipping: Amazon in the Global Economy*. London: Pluto Press.

Allison, Sarah Danielle, Heuser, Ryan, Jockers, Matthew Lee, Moretti, Franco, and Michael Witmore. 2011. *Quantitative Formalism: An Experiment*. Stanford, CA: Stanford Literary Lab.

Altman, Rick. 1999. *Film/Genre*. London: British Film Institute.

Alvey, Mark Theodore. 1995. *Series Drama and the "Semi-Anthology": Sixties Television in Transition*. Austin, TX: University of Texas Press.

Anderson, Chris. 2006. *The Long Tail: Why the Future of Business Is Selling Less of More*. New York: Hachette Books.

Appadurai, Arjun. 1990. "Disjuncture and Difference in the Global Cultural Economy." *Theory, Culture and Society*. 7(2–3), 295–310. https://doi.org/10.1177/026327690007002017.

Appadurai, Arjun. 1996. *Modernity At Large: Cultural Dimensions of Globalization*. Minneapolis, MN: University of Minnesota Press.

Apprich, Clemens. 2017. *Technotopia: A Media Genealogy of Net Cultures*. Lanham, MD: Rowman & Littlefield.

Apprich, Clemens, and Götz Bachmann. 2019. "Media Genealogy: Back to the Present of Digital Cultures." In *Digitisation*, edited by Gertraud Koch, 293–306. *Digitisation*. Abingdon-on-Thames and New York: Routledge. https://doi.org/10.4324/9781315627731-16.

Aristotle. 1975. *Categories and De Interpretatione*. Oxford: Clarendon Press.

Arnheim, Rudolf. 1936. *Radio*. Translated by Margaret Ludwig and Herbert Read. London: Faber & Faber.

Aveyard, Karina, Moran, Albert, and Pia Majbritt Jensen, eds. 2016. *New Patterns in Global Television Formats*. Bristol and Chicago, IL: Intellect Ltd.

Baldwin, Carliss Young. 2008. *The Architecture of Platforms: A Unified View*. Cambridge, MA: Harvard Business School.

Bardolph, Jacqueline, Viola, André, and Jean-Pierre Durix. 2001. *Telling Stories: Postcolonial Short Fiction in English*. Amsterdam: Rodopi.

Barnouw, Erik. 1970. *The Image Empire: A History of Broadcasting in the United States, Volume III–from 1953*. Oxford: Oxford University Press.

Barthes, Roland. 1975. "An Introduction to the Structural Analysis of Narrative." *New Literary History* 6 (2): 237–72. https://doi.org/10.2307/468419.

Bausi, Alessandro, Brockmann, Christian, Friedrich, Michael, and Sabine Kienitz. 2018. *Manuscripts and Archives: Comparative Views on Record-Keeping*. Berlin: Walter de Gruyter.

Bednarek, Monika. 2009. "Corpora and Discourse: A Three-Pronged Approach to Analyzing Linguistic Data." In *Selected Proceedings of the 2008 HCSNet Workshop on Designing the Australian National Corpus: Mustering Languages*, edited by Michael Haugh, Kate Burridge, Jean Mulder, and Pam Peters, 19–24. Somerville, MA: Cascadilla Proceedings Project. https://www.lingref.com/cpp/ausnc/2008/abstract2283.html.

Beecroft, Alexander. 2018. "Anthologies and Canon Formation in China and the West." *Orbis Litterarum* 73 (4): 341–47. https://doi.org/10.1111/oli.12186.

Beer, David. 2013. *Popular Culture and New Media: The Politics of Circulation*. New York: Springer.

Beer, David. 2017. "The Social Power of Algorithms." *Information, Communication & Society* 20 (1): 1–13. https://doi.org/10.1080/1369118X.2016.1216147.

Beer, David. 2018. *The Data Gaze: Capitalism, Power and Perception*. Newbury Park, CA: SAGE.

Beer, David. 2019a. *The Quirks of Digital Culture*. Bingley: Emerald Group Publishing.

Beer, David. 2019b. "The Depths of Platform Culture." *Medium*. https://towardsdatascience.com/the-baffling-depths-of-platform-culture-f5648af8bc5b.

Benjamin, Ruha. 2019a. *Race After Technology: Abolitionist Tools for the New Jim Code*. Hoboken, NJ: Wiley.

Bennett, James, and Niki Strange. 2011. *Television as Digital Media*. Durham, NC: Duke University Press.

Bennett, Peter, Kendall, Alex, and Julian McDougall. 2011. *After the Media: Culture and Identity in the 21st Century*. New York: Routledge.

Bennett, Peter, Slater, Jerry, and Peter Wall. 2005. *A2 Media Studies: The Essential Introduction*. New York: Routledge.

Berry, D. 2012. *Understanding Digital Humanities*. New York: Springer.

Besedovsky, Natalia, Grafe, Fritz-Julius, Hilbrandt, Hanna, and Hannes Langguth. 2019. "Time as Infrastructure." *City* 23 (4–5): 580–88. https://doi.org/10.1080/13604813.2019.1689726.

Bhaskar, Michael. 2013. *The Content Machine: Towards a Theory of Publishing from the Printing Press to the Digital Network*. London: Anthem Press.

Bloom, Harold. 1994. *The Western Canon: The Books and School of the Ages.* San Diego, CA: Harcourt Brace.

Bogost, Ian, and Nick Montfort. 2007. "New Media as Material Constraint. An Introduction to Platform Studies." 2007. https://www.semanticscholar.org/paper/ NEW-MEDIA-AS-MATERIAL-CONSTRAINT-An-Introduction-to-Bogost-Mon tfort/7647d84e00696504c7c94a49ca8a82d59bed89f1.

Bogost, Ian, and Nick Montfort. 2009. "Platform Studies: Frequently Questioned Answers." https://escholarship.org/uc/item/01rok9br.

Bolter, Jay David. 1991. *Writing Space: The Computer, Hypertext, and the History of Writing.* Mahwah, NJ: Erlbaum.

Boluk, Stephanie, and Patrick LeMieux. 2012. "Hundred Thousand Billion Fingers: Seriality and Critical Game Practices." https://doi.org/10.5900/ SU_9781906897161_2012.17(2)_14.

Bona, Mary Jo, and Irma Maini. 2012. *Multiethnic Literature and Canon Debates.* Albany, NY: SUNY Press.

Bondi, André B. 2000. "Characteristics of Scalability and Their Impact on Performance." In *Proceedings of the 2nd International Workshop on Software and Performance*, 195–203. WOSP '00. Ottawa, ON: Association for Computing Machinery. https://doi.org/10.1145/350391.350432.

Bordwell, David, and Noël Carroll. 1996. *Post-Theory: Reconstructing Film Studies.* Madison, WI: University of Wisconsin Press.

Böttger, Timm, Cuadrado, Felix, Tyson, Gareth, Castro, Ignacio, and Steve Uhlig. 2018. "Open Connect Everywhere: A Glimpse at the Internet Ecosystem through the Lens of the Netflix CDN." *ACM SIGCOMM Computer Communication Review* 48 (1): 28–34. https://doi.org/10.1145/3211852.3211857.

Bourdieu, P. 1983. "The Field of Cultural Production, or: The Economic World Reversed." https://doi.org/10.1016/0304-422X(83)90012-8.

Bourdieu, Pierre. 1977. *Outline of a Theory of Practice.* Cambridge: Cambridge University Press.

Bousquet, Antoine. 2014. "Welcome to the Machine: Rethinking Technology and Society through Assemblage Theory." In *Reassembling International Theory: Assemblage Thinking and International Relations*, edited by Michele Acuto and Simon Curtis, 91–97. London: Palgrave Macmillan UK. https://doi. org/10.1057/9781137383969_11.

Bowker, Geoffrey C., and Susan Leigh Star. 1999. *Sorting Things Out: Classification and Its Consequences.* Cambridge, MA: MIT Press.

Bowker, Geoffrey C., Timmermans, Stefan, Clarke, Adele E., and Ellen Balka. 2016. *Boundary Objects and Beyond: Working with Leigh Star.* Cambridge, MA: MIT Press.

Boyd-Barrett, Oliver, and Tanner Mirrlees. 2019. *Media Imperialism: Continuity and Change.* Lanham, MD: Rowman & Littlefield.

Braudel, Fernand. 1982. *On History*. Chicago, IL: University of Chicago Press.

Brown, Nik, and Brian Rappert. 2017. *Contested Futures: A Sociology of Prospective Techno-Science*. New York: Routledge.

Bucher, Taina. 2018. *If...Then: Algorithmic Power and Politics*. Oxford: Oxford University Press.

Buckingham, David. 2004. *Sorting Out TV: Categorization and Genre*. Vol. Children Talking Television: The Making Of Television Literacy. New York: Routledge.

Buolamwini, Joy, and Timnit Gebru. 2018. "Gender Shades: Intersectional Accuracy Disparities in Commercial Gender Classification." In *Proceedings of the 1st Conference on Fairness, Accountability and Transparency*, 77–91. PMLR. https:// proceedings.mlr.press/v81/buolamwini18a.html.

Buonanno, Milly. 2002. *Le formule del racconto televisivo: La sovversione del tempo nelle narrative seriali*. Florence: Sansoni.

Buonanno, Milly. 2008. *The Age of Television: Experiences and Theories*. Jerusalem, IL: Intellect Books.

Burdick, Anne, Drucker, Johanna, Lunenfeld, Peter, Presner, Todd, and Jeffrey Schnapp. 2012. *Digital_Humanities*. Cambridge, MA: MIT Press.

Bush, Vannevar. 1996. "As We May Think." *Interactions* 3 (2): 35–46. https://doi. org/10.1145/227181.227186.

Buyya, Rajkumar, and Amir Vahid Dastjerdi. 2016. *Internet of Things: Principles and Paradigms*. Amsterdam: Elsevier.

Caldwell, John Thornton. 1995. *Televisuality: Style, Crisis, and Authority in American Television*. New Brunswick, NJ: Rutgers University Press.

Cantril, Hadley, and Gordon Willard Allport. 1971. *The Psychology of Radio*. New York: Arno Press.

Card, Mackinlay, Mackinlay, Jock, and Ben Shneiderman. 1999. *Readings in Information Visualization: Using Vision to Think*. Cambridge, MA: Morgan Kaufmann.

Carey, Susan. 2009. *The Origin of Concepts*. Oxford: Oxford University Press.

Carroll, Noël. 2007. "Narrative Closure." *Philosophical Studies: An International Journal for Philosophy in the Analytic Tradition* 135 (1): 1–15.

Carter, Eli Lee. 2018. *Reimagining Brazilian Television: Luiz Fernando Carvalho's Contemporary Vision*. Pittsburgh, PA: University of Pittsburgh Press.

Castells, Manuel. 2011. *The Rise of the Network Society*. Hoboken, NJ: Wiley.

Castells, Manuel. 2014. "The Impact of the Internet on Society: A Global Perspective." *OpenMind* (blog). https://www.bbvaopenmind.com/en/articles/ the-impact-of-the-internet-on-society-a-global-perspective/.

Cawelti, John G. 1969. "The Concept of Formula in the Study of Popular Literature." *The Journal of Popular Culture* III (3): 381–90. https://doi.org/10.11119,525 mm/j.0022-3840.1969.0303_381.x.

Cawelti, John G. 1972. "The Concept of Formula in the Study of Popular Literature." *The Bulletin of the Midwest Modern Language Association* 5: 115–23. https://doi.org/10.2307/1314918.

Cawelti, John G. 1976. *Adventure, Mystery, and Romance: Formula Stories as Art and Popular Culture*. Chicago, IL: University of Chicago Press.

Chalaby, Jean K. 2011. "The Making of an Entertainment Revolution: How the TV Format Trade Became a Global Industry." *European Journal of Communication* 26 (4): 293–309. https://doi.org/10.1177/0267323111423414.

Chalaby, Jean K. 2012. "At the Origin of a Global Industry: The TV Format Trade as an Anglo-American Invention." *Media, Culture & Society* 34 (1): 36–52. https://doi.org/10.1177/0163443711427198.

Chalaby, Jean K. 2016. *The Format Age: Television's Entertainment Revolution*. Hoboken, NJ: Wiley.

Chen, Martha, and Françoise Carré. 2020. *The Informal Economy Revisited: Examining the Past, Envisioning the Future*. New York: Routledge.

Cheney-Lippold, John. 2017. *We Are Data: Algorithms and the Making of Our Digital Selves*. New York: NYU Press.

Childs, Peter, Zhao, Ying, and Joanna Grigg. 2013. "Narrative in Design Development." *DS 76: Proceedings of E&PDE 2013, the 15th International Conference on Engineering and Product Design Education, Dublin, Ireland, 05-06.09.2013*, 108–13.

Chomsky, Noam. 1969. *Deep Structure, Surface Structure, and Semantic Interpretation*. Bloomington, IN: Indiana University Linguistics Club.

Clements, Jonathan, and Motoko Tamamuro. 2003. *The Dorama Encyclopedia: A Guide to Japanese TV Drama Since 1953*. Berkeley, CA: Stone Bridge Press.

Cohn, Jonathan. 2019. *The Burden of Choice: Recommendations, Subversion, and Algorithmic Culture*. New Brunswick, NJ: Rutgers University Press.

Colman, Alison. 2005. "Un/Becoming Digital: The Ontology of Technological Determinism and Its Implications for Art Education." *Journal of Social Theory in Art Education* 25 (1): 278–305.

Cooper, Grosvenor W., and Leonard B. Meyer. 1963. *The Rhythmic Structure of Music*. Chicago, IL: University of Chicago Press.

Cramer, Florian. 2014. What is 'post-digital'. *APRJA (A Peer-Reviewed Journal About)* 3/1: 10-24.

Crawford, Colin Jon Mark. 2021. *Netflix's Speculative Fictions: Financializing Platform Television*. Lanham, MD: Rowman & Littlefield.

Crawford, Kate. 2021. *The Atlas of AI: Power, Politics, and the Planetary Costs of Artificial Intelligence*. New Haven, CT: Yale University Press.

Croft, Bruce, Metzler, Donald, and Trevor Strohman. 2011. *Search Engines: Information Retrieval in Practice*. London: Pearson Education.

DeLanda, Manuel. 2019. *A New Philosophy of Society: Assemblage Theory and Social Complexity*. London: Bloomsbury Publishing.

Deleuze, Gilles, and Felix Guattari. 1987. *A Thousand Plateaus: Capitalism and Schizophrenia*. Minneapolis, MN: University of Minnesota Press.

Deleuze, Gilles, and Claire Parnet. 1987. *Dialogues*. New York: Columbia University Press.

D'Ignazio, Catherine, and Lauren F. Klein. 2020. *Data Feminism*. Cambridge, MA: MIT Press.

Dobson, W.A.C.H. 1964. "Linguistic Evidence and the Dating of the 'Book of Songs')." *T'oung Pao* 51 (4/5): 322–34.

Doueihi, Milad. 2009. "Digital Objecthood and Scholarly Publishing," https://ecommons.cornell.edu/handle/1813/12020.

Doueihi, Milad. 2011a. *Digital Cultures*. Cambridge, MA: Harvard University Press.

Doueihi, Milad. 2011b. *Pour Un Humanisme Numérique*. La Librairie Du XXIe Siècle. Paris: Editions du Seuil.

Drucker, Johanna. 2014a. *Graphesis: Visual Forms of Knowledge Production*. Cambridge, MA: Harvard University Press.

Drucker, Johanna. 2014b. "Knowledge Design." *Design and Culture* 6 (1): 65–83. https://doi.org/10.2752/175470814X13823675225117.

Drucker, Peter Ferdinand. 1969. *The Age of Discontinuity: Guidelines to Our Changing Society*. New York: Harper & Row.

Dunning, John. 1998. *On the Air: The Encyclopedia of Old-Time Radio*. Oxford: Oxford University Press.

Durkheim, Emile, and Marcel Mauss. 1963. *Primitive Classification*. Chicago, IL: University of Chicago Press.

Eco, Umberto. 1976. *A Theory of Semiotics*. Bloomington, IN: Indiana University Press.

Eco, Umberto. 1984. *The Role of the Reader: Explorations in the Semiotics of Texts*. Bloomington, IN: Indiana University Press.

Eco, Umberto. 1985. "Innovation and Repetition: Between Modern and Post-Modern Aesthetics." *Daedalus* 114 (4): 161–84.

Eco, Umberto. 1990. *The Limits of Interpretation*. Bloomington, IN: Indiana University Press.

Eco, Umberto. 2005. *On Literature*. Boston, MA: Houghton Mifflin Harcourt.

Eco, Umberto. 2009. *The Infinity of Lists*. New York: Rizzoli.

Edgerton, Gary Richard. 2007. *The Columbia History of American Television*. New York: Columbia University Press.

Edwards, Paul N. 2003. "Infrastructure and Modernity: Force, Time, and Social Organization in the History of Sociotechnical Systems." In *In Modernity and Technology, Eds Misa*, 185–226. Cambridge, MA: MIT Press.

Ellis, John, Esser, Andrea, and Juan Francisco Gutiérrez Lozano. 2016. "Editorial. TV Formats and Format Research: Theory, Methodology, History and New Developments." *VIEW Journal of European Television History and Culture* 5 (9): 1–5. https://doi.org/10.18146/2213-0969.2016.jethc098.

Esquenazi, Jean-Pierre. 2014. *Les séries télévisées: L'avenir du cinéma ?* Paris: Armand Colin.

Essmann, Helga, and Armin Paul Frank. 1991. "Translation Anthologies: An Invitation to the Curious and a Case Study." *Target* 3 (1): 65–90. https://doi.org/10.1075/target.3.1.05ess.

Fitzpatrick-Martin, Iris. 1985. *Social Implications of Informediation.* Montreal: Institut Gamma.

Flanders, Julia. 2014. "Rethinking Collections." In *Advancing Digital Humanities*, edited by Paul Longley Arthur and Katherine Bode, 163–74. London: Palgrave Macmillan. https://doi.org/10.1057/9781137337016_11.

Flichy, Patrice. 2007. *The Internet Imaginaire.* Cambridge, MA: MIT Press.

Floridi, Luciano. 2002. *Philosophy and Computing: An Introduction.* New York: Routledge.

Foucault, Michel. 1970. *The Order of Things: An Archaeology of the Human Sciences.* New York: Vintage Books.

Foucault, Michel. 1975. *Surveiller Et Punir.* Paris: Gallimard.

Foucault, Michel. 1976. *The Archaeology of Knowledge.* New York: Harper & Row.

Frankel, Hans Hermann. 1976. *The Flowering Plum and the Palace Lady: Interpretations of Chinese Poetry.* New Haven, CT: Yale University Press.

Franzosi, Roberto. 2010. *Quantitative Narrative Analysis.* Newbury Park, CA: SAGE.

Frey, Mattias. 2021. *Netflix Recommends: Algorithms, Film Choice, and the History of Taste.* Berkeley, CA: University of California Press.

Frisby, David. 2013. *Sociological Impressionism: A Reassessment of Georg Simmel's Social Theory.* New York: Routledge.

Frye, Northrop. 1957. *Anatomy of Criticism.* Princeton, NJ: Princeton University Press.

Fuller, Matthew, and David Gee. 2008. *Software Studies: A Lexicon.* Cambridge, MA: MIT Press.

Gawer, Annabelle. 2014. "Bridging Differing Perspectives on Technological Platforms: Toward an Integrative Framework." *Research Policy* 43 (7): 1239–49. https://doi.org/10.1016/j.respol.2014.03.006.

Gawer, Annabelle, and Michael A. Cusumano. 2014. "Industry Platforms and Ecosystem Innovation." *Journal of Product Innovation Management* 31 (3): 417–33. https://doi.org/10.1111/jpim.12105.

Gebru, Timnit, Morgenstern, Jamie, Vecchione, Briana, Wortman Vaughan, Jennifer, Wallach, Hanna, Daumé III, Hal, and Kate Crawford. 2021. "Datasheets for Datasets." *ArXiv:1803.09010* [Cs], December. http://arxiv.org/abs/1803.09010.

Geertz, Clifford. 2008. *The Interpretation Of Cultures*. New York: Basic Books.

Genette, Gérard. 1983. *Narrative Discourse: An Essay in Method*. Ithaca, NY: Cornell University Press.

Gillespie, Tarleton. 2010. "The Politics of 'Platforms.'" *New Media & Society* 12 (3): 347–64. https://doi.org/10.1177/1461444809342738.

Gitelman, Lisa. 2008. *Always Already New: Media, History, and the Data of Culture*. Cambridge, MA: MIT Press.

Gitlin, Todd. 1979. "Prime Time Ideology: The Hegemonic Process in Television Entertainment." *Social Problems* 26 (3): 251–66. https://doi.org/10.2307/800451.

Gitlin, Todd. 1982. "Television's Screens: Hegemony in Transition." In *Cultural and Economic Reproduction in Education*. New York: Routledge.

Gitlin, Todd. 2000. *Inside Prime Time: With a New Introduction*. Berkeley, CA: University of California Press.

Godbey, Geoffrey. 1976. "Time Deepening and the Future of Leisure." *Journal of Physical Education and Recreation* 47 (8): 40–42. https://doi.org/10.1080/00971 170.1976.10612341.

Gombrich, E.H. 1999. *The Uses of Images: Studies in the Social Function of Art and Visual Communication*. London and New York: Phaidon Press.

Gomez-Uribe, Carlos A., and Neil Hunt. 2016. "The Netflix Recommender System: Algorithms, Business Value, and Innovation." *ACM Transactions on Management Information Systems* 6 (4): 13:1–13:19. https://doi.org/10.1145/2843948.

Goodin, Robert E., Rice, James Mahmud, Parpo, Antti, and Lina Eriksson. 2008. *Discretionary Time: A New Measure of Freedom*. Cambridge: Cambridge University Press.

Gorak, Jan. 1991. *The Making of the Modern Canon: Genesis and Crisis of a Literary Idea*. London: A&C Black.

Gough, Lyndsay. 2002. "The Drama over Format Rights." *Managing Intellectual Property*. https://www.managingip.com/article/b1kcgvnb171gk1/ the-drama-over-format-rights.

Greengard, Samuel. 2015. *The Internet of Things*. Cambridge, MA: MIT Press.

Greenough, Horatio. 1947. *Form and Function: Remarks on Art, Design, and Architecture*. Berkeley, CA: University of California Press.

Gross, Sabine. 1997. "Cognitive Readings; Or, the Disappearance of Literature in the Mind." Edited by Mark Turner. *Poetics Today* 18 (2): 271–97. https://doi. org/10.2307/1773435.

Guillory, John. 2013. *Cultural Capital: The Problem of Literary Canon Formation*. Chicago, IL: University of Chicago Press. https://www.degruyter.com/document/ doi/10.7208/9780226310015/html.

Gunter, Barrie. 1987. *Poor Reception: Misunderstanding and Forgetting Broadcast News*. New York: Routledge.

Halbwachs, Maurice. 1980. *The Collective Memory*. New York: Harper & Row.

Hall, Stuart. 1999. "Unsettling 'the Heritage', Re-Imagining the Post-Nation Whose Heritage?" *Third Text* 13 (49): 3–13. https://doi.org/10.1080/09528829908576818.

Hallinan, Blake, and Ted Striphas. 2016. "Recommended for You: The Netflix Prize and the Production of Algorithmic Culture." *New Media & Society* 18 (1): 117–37. https://doi.org/10.1177/1461444814538646.

Hands, Joss, Elmer, Greg, and Ganaele Langlois. 2013. "Vol. 14 Platform Politics." *Culture Machine* (blog). https://culturemachine.net/platform-politics/.

Hannerz, Ulf. 1992. *Cultural Complexity: Studies in the Social Organization of Meaning*. New York: Columbia University Press.

Hanseth, Ole, and Kalle Lyytinen. 2010. "Design Theory for Dynamic Complexity in Information Infrastructures: The Case of Building Internet." *Journal of Information Technology* 25 (1): 1–19. https://doi.org/10.1057/jit.2009.19.

Hanson, Clare. 1989. *Re-Reading the Short Story*. London: Palgrave Macmillan.

Harrigan, Pat, and Noah Wardrip-Fruin. 2009. *Third Person: Authoring and Exploring Vast Narratives*. Cambridge, MA: MIT Press.

Hayles, N. Katherine. 2008. *Electronic Literature: New Horizons for the Literary*. The Ward-Phillips Lectures in English Language and Literature. Notre Dame, IN: University of Notre Dame.

Hayles, N. Katherine. 2012. *How We Think: Digital Media and Contemporary Technogenesis*. Chicago, IL: University of Chicago Press.

Helmond, Anne. 2015. "The Platformization of the Web: Making Web Data Platform Ready." *Social Media + Society* 1 (2). https://doi.org/10.1177/2056305115603080.

Herman, David. 2004. *Story Logic: Problems and Possibilities of Narrative*. Lincoln, NE: University of Nebraska Press.

Hesmondhalgh, David. 2012. *The Cultural Industries*. Newbury Park, CA: SAGE.

Hilbert, Martin, and Priscila López. 2011. "The World's Technological Capacity to Store, Communicate, and Compute Information." *Science*, April. https://doi.org/10.1126/science.1200970.

Hilmes, Michele. 2012. *Network Nations: A Transnational History of British and American Broadcasting*. New York: Routledge.

Hilmes, Michele. 2013. *Only Connect: A Cultural History of Broadcasting in the United States*. Boston, MA: Cengage Learning.

Hilmes, Michele, and Jason Jacobs. 2003. *The Television History Book*. London: British Film Institute.

Hilmes, Michele, and Jason Loviglio. 2002. *Radio Reader: Essays in the Cultural History of Radio*. London: Psychology Press.

Hindman, Douglas Blanks, and Kenneth Wiegand. 2008. "The Big Three's Prime-Time Decline: A Technological and Social Context." *Journal of Broadcasting & Electronic Media* 52 (1): 119–35. https://doi.org/10.1080/08838150701820924.

Hinds, Harold E., Ferris Motz, Marilyn, and Angela M.S. Nelson. 2006. *Popular Culture Theory and Methodology: A Basic Introduction*. Madison, WI: Popular Press.

Hobbs, V., and D. Pigott. 1999. "Multimedia Databases: An Approach to Design." *Undefined*. https://www.semanticscholar.org/paper/Multi-media-databases%3A-an-approach-to-design9,525 mm-Hobbs-Pigott/de8b833ee4ae037e7128854879a4a3e9ef9fe7bd.

Hogan, Patrick Colm. 2020. *Style in Narrative: Aspects of an Affective-Cognitive Stylistics*. Oxford: Oxford University Press.

Holt, Jennifer, and Alisa Perren. 2011. *Media Industries: History, Theory, and Method*. Hoboken, NJ: Wiley.

Holt, Jennifer, and Kevin Sanson. 2013. *Connected Viewing: Selling, Streaming, & Sharing Media in the Digital Age*. New York: Routledge.

Horkheimer, Max, and Theodor W. Adorno. 2002. "The Culture Industry: Enlightenment as Mass Deception." In *The Culture Industry: Enlightenment as Mass Deception*, 94–136. Stanford, CA: Stanford University Press. https://www.degruyter.com/document/doi/10.1515/9780804788090-007/html.

Houston, Natalie M. 2017. "Measuring Canonicity: A Network Analysis Approach to Poetry Anthologies." *Undefined*. https://www.semanticscholar.org/paper/Measuring-Canonicity%3A-a-Network-Analysis-Approach-Houston/a3cda0070029707c554ad85e1894e5560b229cd9.

Howe, Samuel Storrs, Parvin, Theodore Sutton, Lloyd, Frederick, Huff, Sanford W., Aldrich,

Virtue, Ethel B. 1914. "Principles of Classification for Ar- chives," in *AHA, Annual Report*, 1: 376-377.

Hristova, Stefka, Slack, Jennifer Daryl, and Soonkwan Hong. 2020. *Algorithmic Culture: How Big Data and Artificial Intelligence Are Transforming Everyday Life*. Lanham, MD: Rowman & Littlefield.

Innis, Harold Adams. 1950. *Empire and Communications*. Oxford: Clarendon Press.

Iriye, A., and P. Saunier. 2009. *The Palgrave Dictionary of Transnational History: From the Mid-19th Century to the Present Day*. London: Palgrave Macmillan.

Jänicke, Stefan, Franzini, Greta, Cheema, Muhammad Faisal, and Gerik Scheuermann. 2015. "On Close and Distant Reading in Digital Humanities: A Survey and Future Challenges." https://doi.org/10.2312/eurovisstar.20151113.

Jaton, Florian. 2021. *The Constitution of Algorithms: Ground-Truthing, Programming, Formulating*. Cambridge, MA: MIT Press.

Jenkins, Henry. 2006. *Convergence Culture: Where Old and New Media Collide*. New York: NYU Press.

Jenkins, Henry. n.d. "Authoring and Exploring Vast Narratives: An Interview with Pat Harrigan and Noah Wardrip-Fruin (Part One)." Henry Jenkins. http://henryjenkins.org/blog/2009/05/an_interview_with_pat_harrigan.html.

Jin, Dal Yong. 2021. *Artificial Intelligence in Cultural Production: Critical Perspectives on Digital Platforms*. New York: Routledge.

Jo, Eun Seo, and Timnit Gebru. 2020. "Lessons from Archives: Strategies for Collecting Sociocultural Data in Machine Learning." *Proceedings of the 2020 Conference on Fairness, Accountability, and Transparency*, January, 306–16. https://doi.org/10.1145/3351095.3372829.

Jockers, Matthew L. 2013. *Macroanalysis: Digital Methods and Literary History*. Champaign, IL: University of Illinois Press.

Kaplan, David M. 2009. *Readings in the Philosophy of Technology*. Lanham, MD: Rowman & Littlefield Publishers.

Karlgren, Jussi. 1990. "An Algebra for Recommendations: Using. Reader Data as a Basis for Measuring Document Proximity." *Cyberjaya:* SYSLAB. Technical Report.

Kathayat, Vinod. 2019. "How Netflix Uses AI for Content Creation and Recommendation." *The Startup* (blog). https://medium.com/swlh/how-netflix9,525 mm-uses-ai-for-content-creation-and-recommendation-c1919efc0af4.

Keen, Suzanne. 2015. *Narrative Form: Revised and Expanded Second Edition*. New York: Springer.

Keinonen, Heidi. 2017. "Television Format as Cultural Technology Transfer: Importing a Production Format for Daily Drama." *Media, Culture & Society* 39 (7): 995–1010. https://doi.org/10.1177/0163443716682076.

Kelleter, Frank. 2017. "Media of Serial Narrative." 2017. Athens, OH: Ohio University Press.

Kenney, Martin, and John Zysman. 2016. "The Rise of the Platform Economy." *Issues in Science and Technology* (blog). https://issues.org/rise-platform9,525 mm-economy-big-data-work/.

Kindt, Tom, and Hans-Harald Müller. 2003. *What Is Narratology?: Questions and Answers Regarding the Status of a Theory*. Berlin: Walter de Gruyter.

King, Katie. 2012. "Women in the Web › Electronic Book Review." https://electronicbookreview.com/essay/women-in-the-web/.

Kitchin, Rob. 2017. "Thinking Critically about and Researching Algorithms." *Information, Communication & Society* 20 (1): 14–29. https://doi.org/10.1080/1369118X.2016.1154087.

Klein, Julie Thompson. 1990. *Interdisciplinarity: History, Theory, and Practice*. Detroit, MI: Wayne State University Press.

Koch, Gertraud. 2017. *Digitisation: Theories and Concepts for Empirical Cultural Research*. New York: Routledge.

Korte, Barbara, Schneider, Ralf, Lethbridge, Stefanie, Korte, Barbara, and Stefanie Lethbridge, eds. 2000. *Anthologies of British Poetry: Critical Perspectives from Literary and Cultural Studies*. Leiden and Boston, MA: Brill. https://brill.com/view/title/29523.

Kosnik, Abigail De. 2016. *Rogue Archives: Digital Cultural Memory and Media Fandom*. Cambridge, MA: MIT Press.

Kramnick, Jonathan, and Anahid Nersessian. 2017. "Form and Explanation." *Critical Inquiry* 43 (3): 650–69. https://doi.org/10.1086/691017.

Kroeber, A.L. 1917. "The Superorganic." *American Anthropologist* 19 (2): 163–213.

Kuttainen, Victoria. 2009. *Unsettling Stories: Settler Postcolonialism and the Short Story Composite*. Newcastle-upon-Tyne: Cambridge Scholars Publishing.

Lakoff, George, and Mark Johnson. 2008. *Metaphors We Live By*. Chicago, IL: University of Chicago Press.

Landau, Neil. 2015. *TV Outside the Box: Trailblazing in the Digital Television Revolution*. New York: Focal Press.

Langlois, Ganaele, Elmer, Greg, McKelvey, Fenwick and Zachary Devereaux. 2009. "Networked Publics: The Double Articulation of Code and Politics on Facebook." *Canadian Journal of Communication* 34 (3): 415-434. https://doi.org/10.22230/cjc.2009v34n3a2114.

Larkin, Brian. 2013. "The Politics and Poetics of Infrastructure." *Annual Review of Anthropology* 42 (1): 327–43. https://doi.org/10.1146/annurev-anthro-092412-155522.

Levine, Caroline. 2006. "Strategic Formalism: Toward a New Method in Cultural Studies." *Victorian Studies* 48 (4): 625–57.

Levine, Caroline. 2015a. *Forms: Whole, Rhythm, Hierarchy, Network*. Princeton, NJ: Princeton University Press.

Levine, Caroline. 2015b. "Forms, Literary and Social." *Dibur Literary Journal*, Form (2). https://arcade.stanford.edu/dibur/forms-literary-and-social.

Levinson, Marjorie. 2007. "What Is New Formalism?" *PMLA* 122 (2): 558–69.

Levi-Strauss, Claude. 1955. "The Structural Study of Myth." *The Journal of American Folklore* 68 (270): 428–44. https://doi.org/10.2307/536768.

Levi-Strauss, Claude. 2008. *Structural Anthropology*. New York: Basic Books.

Lievrouw, Leah A., and Sonia M. Livingstone. 2006. *Handbook of New Media: Student Edition*. Newbury Park, CA: SAGE.

Lifschutz, Vladimir. 2015. "'Series finale': Enjeux et théorie d'un compromis moderne." *TV/Series*, no. 7 (June). https://doi.org/10.4000/tvseries.284.

Linke, Uli. 2015. "Collective Memory, Anthropology Of." In *International Encyclopedia of the Social & Behavioral Sciences*, 181–87. Amsterdam: Elsevier. https://doi.org/10.1016/B978-0-08-097086-8.12036-7.

Lobato, Ramon. 2019. *Netflix Nations: The Geography of Digital Distribution*. New York: NYU Press.

Lomborg, Stine, and Anja Bechmann. 2014. "Using APIs for Data Collection on Social Media." *The Information Society* 30 (4): 256–65. https://doi.org/10.1080/01972243.2014.915276.

Lorusso, Anna Maria. 2015. *Cultural Semiotics: For a Cultural Perspective in Semiotics*. New York: Palgrave Macmillan.

Lotman, Jurij M. 1990. *Universe of the Mind: A Semiotic Theory of Culture*. Bloomington, IN: Indiana University Press.

Lotz, Amanda D. 2007. *The Television Will Be Revolutionized*. New York: NYU Press.

Lotz, Amanda D. 2017. *Portals: A Treatise on Internet-Distributed Television*. Ann Arbor, MI: Michigan Publishing.

Lotz, Amanda D. 2018. *We Now Disrupt This Broadcast: How Cable Transformed Television and the Internet Revolutionized It All*. Cambridge, MA: MIT Press.

Louridas, Panos. 2020. *Algorithms*. Cambridge, MA: MIT Press.

Loviglio, Jason, and Michele Hilmes. 2013. *Radio's New Wave: Global Sound in the Digital Era*. New York: Routledge.

Luhmann, Niklas. 2000. *Art as a Social System*. Stanford, CA: Stanford University Press.

Lyotard, Jean-François. 1984. *The Postmodern Condition: A Report on Knowledge*. Minneapolis, MN: University of Minnesota Press.

Madrigal, Alexis C. 2014. "How Netflix Reverse-Engineered Hollywood." *The Atlantic*. https://www.theatlantic.com/technology/archive/2014/01/how-netflix-reverse-engineered-hollywood/282679/.

Man, John. 2010. *The Gutenberg Revolution*. New York: Random House.

Mandler, J.M. 2014. *Stories, Scripts, and Scenes: Aspects of Schema Theory*. London: Psychology Press.

Manovich, Lev. 1999. "Database as Symbolic Form." *Convergence* 5 (2): 80–99. https://doi.org/10.1177/135485659900500206.

Manovich, Lev. 2001. *The Language of New Media*. Cambridge, MA: MIT Press.

Manovich, Lev. 2011. "What Is Visualisation?" *Visual Studies* 26 (1): 36–49. https://doi.org/10.1080/1472586X.2011.548488.

Marx, Leo, and Merritt Roe Smith. 1994. *Does Technology Drive History?: The Dilemma of Technological Determinism*. Cambridge, MA: MIT Press.

Matallana, Andrea. 2006. *Locos por la radio: Una historia social de la radiofonía en la Argentina, 1923–1947*. Buenos Aires: Prometeo Libros.

Mattern, Shannon. 2016. "Scaffolding, Hard and Soft – Infrastructures as Critical and Generative Structures – Spheres." https://spheres-journal.org/contribution/scaffolding-hard-and-soft-infrastructures-as-critical-and-generative-structures/.

Matthews, Brander. 1901. *The Philosophy of the Short Story*. New York: Longmans, Green, & Co.

McDonald, Kevin, and Daniel Smith-Rowsey. 2018. *The Netflix Effect: Technology and Entertainment in the 21st Century*. New York: Bloomsbury Publishing.

McLuhan, Marshall. 1962. *The Gutenberg Galaxy: The Making of Typographic Man*. Toronto: University of Toronto Press.

McLuhan, Marshall. 1989. *The Global Village: Transformations in World Life and Media in the 21st Century.* Oxford: Oxford University Press.

McLuhan, Marshall. 1994. *Understanding Media: The Extensions of Man.* Cambridge, MA, USA: MIT Press.

McQuillan, Martin. 2000. *The Narrative Reader.* London: Psychology Press.

Merayo Pérez, Arturo, ed. 2007. *La Radio En Iberoamérica: Evolución, Diagnóstico y Prospectiva.* Colección Periodística 21. Sevilla: Comunicación Social.

Mills, Charles Wright. 2008. *The Politics of Truth: Selected Writings of C. Wright Mills.* New York: Oxford University Press.

Misa, Thomas J. 1988. "How Machines Make History, and How Historians (And Others) Help Them to Do So." *Science, Technology, & Human Values* 13 (3/4): 308–31.

Misa, Thomas J., Brey, Philip, and Andrew Feenberg. 2003. *Modernity and Technology.* Cambridge, MA: MIT Press.

Mittell, Jason. 2001. "A Cultural Approach to Television Genre Theory." *Cinema Journal* 40 (3): 3–24.

Mittell, Jason. 2006. "Narrative Complexity in Contemporary American Television." *The Velvet Light Trap* 58 (1): 29–40. https://doi.org/10.1353/vlt.2006.0032.

Miyazaki, Shintaro. 2012. "Algorhythmics: Understanding Micro-Temporality in Computational Cultures | Computational Culture." http://computationalculture.net/algorhythmics-understanding-micro-temporality-in-computational-cultures/.

Miyazaki, Shintaro. 2013. *AlgoRHYTHMS Everywhere: A Heuristic Approach to Everyday Technologies.* Amsterdam: Rodopi. https://doi.org/10.1163/9789401208871_010.

Miyazaki, Shintaro. 2016. "Algorhythmics, Media Archaeology and Beyond." *Medium* (blog). https://medium.com/@algorhythmics/algorhythmics-archaeology9,525 mm-and-beyond-2eff6595e6ab.

Montfort, Nick, and Ian Bogost. 2009. *Racing the Beam: The Atari Video Computer System.* Cambridge, MA: MIT Press.

Moran, Albert. 1998. *Copycat Television: Globalisation, Program Formats and Cultural Identity.* Luton: University of Luton Press.

Moran, Albert, and Justin Malbon. 2006. *Understanding the Global TV Format.* Bristol: Intellect Books.

Moretti, Franco. 2000. "Conjectures on World Literature." New Left Review 1: 54-68.

Moretti, Franco. 2005a. *Graphs, Maps, Trees: Abstract Models for a Literary History.* New York: Verso Books.

Moretti, Franco. 2005b. *Signs Taken for Wonders: On the Sociology of Literary Forms.* New York: Verso Books.

Moretti, Franco. 2013. *Distant Reading.* New York: Verso Books.

Morin, Edgar. 2008. *On Complexity.* New York: Hampton Press.

Morris, Jeremy Wade. 2015. *Selling Digital Music, Formatting Culture.* Berkeley, CA: University of California Press.

Morville, Peter, and Louis Rosenfeld. 2006. *Information Architecture for the World Wide Web: Designing Large-Scale Web Sites*. Sebastopol, CA: O'Reilly Media.

Murphie, Andrew, and John Potts. 2002. *Culture and Technology*. London: Palgrave Macmillan.

Mutschler, Fritz-Heiner. 2018. *The Homeric Epics and the Chinese Book of Songs: Foundational Texts Compared*. Newcastle-upon-Tyne: Cambridge Scholars Publishing.

Nadareishvili, Irakli, Mitra, Ronnie, McLarty, Matt, and Mike Amundsen. 2016. *Microservice Architecture: Aligning Principles, Practices, and Culture*. Sebastopol, CA: O'Reilly Media.

Näser-Lather, Marion, and Christoph Neubert. 2015. *Traffic: Media as Infrastructures and Cultural Practices*. Leiden and Boston, MA: Brill.

Neale, Stephen. 1980. *Genre*. London: British Film Institute.

Newcomb, Horace. 2014. *Encyclopedia of Television*. New York: Routledge.

Nieborg, David B, and Thomas Poell. 2018. "The Platformization of Cultural Production: Theorizing the Contingent Cultural Commodity." *New Media & Society* 20 (11): 4275–92. https://doi.org/10.1177/1461444818769694.

Noble, Safiya Umoja. 2018. *Algorithms of Oppression: How Search Engines Reinforce Racism*. New York: NYU Press.

Nordrum, Amy. 2016. "Researchers Map Locations of 4,669 Servers in Netflix's Content Delivery Network." IEEE Spectrum. August 30, 2016. https://spectrum. ieee.org/researchers-map-locations-of-4669-servers-in-netflixs-content-delivery-network.

Nystrom, Christine L. 1975. *Toward a Science of Media Ecology: The Formulation of Integrated Conceptual Paradigms for the Study of Human Communication Systems*. New York: NYU Dissertation.

O'Connor, Frank. 2011. *The Lonely Voice: A Study of the Short Story*. New York: Melville House.

Odber de Baubeta, Patricia Anne. 2007. *The Anthology in Portugal: A New Approach to the History of Portuguese Literature in the Twentieth Century*. Lausanne: Peter Lang.

Olsson, Jan, and Lynn Spigel. 2004. *Television after TV: Essays on a Medium in Transition*. Durham, NC: Duke University Press.

O'Neil, Cathy. 2016. *Weapons of Math Destruction: How Big Data Increases Inequality and Threatens Democracy*. New York: Crown.

O'Neil, Cathy, and Rachel Schutt. 2013. *Doing Data Science: Straight Talk from the Frontline*. Sebastopol, CA: O'Reilly Media.

Pajkovic, Niko. 2021. "Algorithms and Taste-Making: Exposing the Netflix Recommender System's Operational Logics." *Convergence*. https://doi.org/10.11779,525 mm/13548565211014464.

Pariser, Eli. 2012. *The Filter Bubble: How the New Personalized Web Is Changing What We Read and How We Think.* London: Penguin.

Parry, Milman. 1930. "Studies in the Epic Technique of Oral Verse-Making. I. Homer and Homeric Style." *Harvard Studies in Classical Philology* 41: 73–147. https://doi.org/10.2307/310626.

Parsons, Patrick. 2003. "The Evolution of the Cable-Satellite Distribution System." *Journal of Broadcasting & Electronic Media* 47 (1): 1–17. https://doi.org/10.1207/s15506878jobem4701_1.

Pasler, Jann. 2015. "Writing for Radio Listeners in the 1930s: National Identity, Canonization, and Transnational Consensus from New York to Paris." *The Musical Quarterly* 98 (3): 212–62. https://doi.org/10.1093/musqtl/gdv014.

Patea, Viorica. 2012. *Short Story Theories: A Twenty-First-Century Perspective.* Amsterdam: Rodopi.

Poell, Thomas, Nieborg, David B., and Brooke Erin Duffy. 2021. *Platforms and Cultural Production.* Hoboken, NJ: Wiley.

Postman, Neil. 1970. *The Reformed English Curriculum.* Vol. High School 1980: The Shape of the Future in American Secondary Education. Lanham, MD: Pitman Publishing.

Postman, Neil. 1979. *Teaching as a Conserving Activity.* New York: Dell.

Postman, Neil. 1993. *Technopoly: The Surrender of Culture to Technology.* New York: Vintage Books.

Postman, Neil, and Charles Weingartner. 1971. *The Soft Revolution: A Student Handbook for Turning Schools Around.* New York: Delacorte Press.

Prescott, Lynda. 2016. "The Short Story Anthology: Shaping the Canon." In *The Cambridge History of the English Short*, edited by Dominic Head, 564–80. Cambridge: Cambridge University Press. https://doi.org/10.1017/9781316711712.034.

Price, Kenneth M., and Ray Siemens, eds. 2013. *Literary Studies in the Digital Age: An Evolving Anthology.* New York: MLA Commons.

Propp, V. 2010. *Morphology of the Folktale: Second Edition.* Austin, TX: University of Texas Press.

Rahman, K. Sabeel, and Kathleen Thelen. 2019. "The Rise of the Platform Business Model and the Transformation of Twenty-First-Century Capitalism." *Politics & Society* 47 (2): 177–204. https://doi.org/10.1177/0032329219838932.

Ramsay, Stephen. 2011. *Reading Machines: Toward and Algorithmic Criticism.* Champaign, IL: University of Illinois Press.

Ranganathan, Shiyali Ramamrita. 1950. *Classification, Coding, and Machinery for Search.* Geneva: UNESCO.

Redström, Johan, and Heather Wiltse. 2018. *Changing Things: The Future of Objects in a Digital World.* London: Bloomsbury Publishing.

Reid, Ian. 2017. *The Short Story.* New York: Routledge.

Resnick, Paul, and Hal R. Varian. 1997. "Recommender Systems." *Communications of the ACM* 40 (3): 56–58. https://doi.org/10.1145/245108.245121.

Robinson, John P., and Steven Martin. 2009. "Of Time and Television." *The ANNALS of the American Academy of Political and Social Science* 625 (1): 74–86. https://doi.org/10.1177/0002716209339275.

Rodríguez Ortiz, Raúl. 2019. "Las Tres Etapas Del Radioteatro En Chile: De La Época Dorada al Nuevo Auge de Las Series de Ficción." *INDEX COMUNICACION* 9 (2): 55–73. https://doi.org/10.33732/ixc/09/02Lastre.

Rogers, Richard. 2019. *Doing Digital Methods*. Newbury Park, CA: SAGE.

Rose, Frank. 2012. *The Art of Immersion: How the Digital Generation Is Remaking Hollywood, Madison Avenue, and the Way We Tell Stories*. New York: W.W. Norton & Company.

Rubery, Matthew. 2011. *Audiobooks, Literature, and Sound Studies*. New York: Routledge.

Rubery, Matthew. 2016. *The Untold Story of the Talking Book*. Cambridge, MA: Harvard University Press.

Ryan, Lindy. 2016. *The Visual Imperative: Creating a Visual Culture of Data Discovery*. Burlington, MA: Morgan Kaufmann.

Ryan, Marie-Laure. 2004. *Narrative Across Media: The Languages of Storytelling*. Lincoln, NE: University of Nebraska Press.

Sabin, Roger, Wilson, Ronald, and Linda Speidel. 2015. *Cop Shows: A Critical History of Police Dramas on Television*. Jefferson, NC: McFarland.

Saussure, Ferdinand de. 1986. *Course in General Linguistics*. Chicago, IL: Open Court Publishing.

Sayers, Jentery. 2018. *The Routledge Companion to Media Studies and Digital Humanities*. New York: Routledge.

Scales, Rebecca. 2016. *Radio and the Politics of Sound in Interwar France, 1921–1939*. Cambridge Social and Cultural Histories. Cambridge: Cambridge University Press.

Schnapp, Jeffrey T. 2014. *Knowledge Design: Incubating New Knowledge Forms, Genres, Spaces in the Laboratory of the Digital Humanites; Keynote Delivered Ath the Herrenhausen Conference "(Digital) Humanities Revisited – Challenges and Opportunities in the Digital Age"/ Jeffrey T. Schnapp. [VolkswagenStiftung]*. Hanover: Volkswagen-Stiftung.

Schreibman, Susan, Siemens, Ray, and John Unsworth. 2008. *A Companion to Digital Humanities*. Hoboken, NJ: Wiley.

Schwartz, Barry. 2009. *The Paradox of Choice: Why More Is Less, Revised Edition*. New York: Harper Collins.

Scolari, Carlos A. 2012. "Media Ecology: Exploring the Metaphor to Expand the Theory." *Communication Theory* 22 (2): 204–25. https://doi.org/10.1111/j.14689,525mm-2885.2012.01404.x.

Scott, Allen J. 2000. *The Cultural Economy of Cities: Essays on the Geography of Image-Producing Industries*. Newbury Park, CA: SAGE.

Seaver, Nick. 2017. "Algorithms as Culture: Some Tactics for the Ethnography of Algorithmic Systems." *Big Data & Society* 4 (2). https://doi.org/10.1177/2053951717738104.

Seaver, Nick. 2019. "Knowing Algorithms." In *Knowing Algorithms*, 412–22. Princeton, NJ: Princeton University Press. https://www.degruyter.com/document/doi/10.1515/9780691190600-028/html.

Sepinwall, Alan. 2013. *The Revolution Was Televised: How The Sopranos, Mad Men, Breaking Bad, Lost, and Other Groundbreaking Dramas Changed TV Forever*. New York: Simon & Schuster.

Serling, Rod. 1958. *Patterns: Four Television Plays*. New York: Bantam.

Seruya, Teresa, D'hulst, Lieven, Assis Rosa, Alexandra, and Maria Lin Moniz. 2013. *Translation in Anthologies and Collections (19th and 20th Centuries)*. Amsterdam: John Benjamins Publishing Company.

Seyfert, Robert, and Jonathan Roberge. 2016. *Algorithmic Cultures: Essays on Meaning, Performance and New Technologies*. New York: Routledge.

Shahaf, Sharon, and Tasha Oren. 2013. *Global Television Formats: Understanding Television Across Borders*. New York: Routledge.

Shiller, Robert J. 2017. "Narrative Economics." *American Economic Review* 107 (4): 967–1004. https://doi.org/10.1257/aer.107.4.967.

Shiller, Robert J. 2019. *Narrative Economics: How Stories Go Viral & Drive Major Economic Events*. Princeton, NJ: Princeton University Press.

Simpson, John Andrew. 1989. *The Oxford English Dictionary*. Oxford: Clarendon Press.

Sisson, Patrick. 2020. "The Perfect Virtual Video Store Isn't Netflix. It's DVD.Com." *Vox*. https://www.vox.com/culture/2020/4/23/21230324/netflix-dvd-rental9,525mm-classic-movies.

Slide, Anthony. 1991. *The Television Industry: A Historical Dictionary*. Westport, CT: Greenwood Press.

Smyrnaios, Nikos. 2018. *Internet Oligopoly: The Corporate Takeover of Our Digital World*. Bingley: Emerald Group Publishing.

Smyrnaios, Nikos, and Franck Rebillard. 2019. "How Infomediation Platforms Took Over the News: A Longitudinal Perspective." *The Political Economy of Communication* 7 (1). https://www.polecom.org/index.php/polecom/article/view/103.

Soon, Winnie. 2018. "Executing Liveness: An Examination of the Live Dimension of Code Inter-Actions in Software (Art) Practice." *Leonardo* 51 (5): 530–530.

Soulez, Guillaume. 2011. "La double répétition." *Mise au point. Cahiers de l'association française des enseignants et chercheurs en cinéma et audiovisuel*, 3. https://doi.org/10.4000/map.979.

Soulez, Guillaume, and Kira Kitsopanidou. 2015. *Le levain des médias: Forme, format, média.* Paris: Editions L'Harmattan.

Srinivasan, Ramesh. 2018. *Whose Global Village?: Rethinking How Technology Shapes Our World.* New York: NYU Press.

Srnicek, Nick. 2017a. *Platform Capitalism.* Hoboken, NJ: Wiley.

Srnicek, Nick. 2017b. "The Challenges of Platform Capitalism: Understanding the Logic of a New Business Model." IPPR. https://www.ippr.org/juncture-item/the-challenges-of-platform-capitalism.

Star, Susan. 2010. "This Is Not a Boundary Object: Reflections on the Origin of a Concept." *Science, Technology, & Human Values* 35 (5): 601–17. https://doi.org/10.1177/0162243910377624.

Star, Susan Leigh. 1989. "Chapter 2: The Structure of Ill-Structured Solutions: Boundary Objects and Heterogeneous Distributed Problem Solving." In *Distributed Artificial Intelligence*, edited by Les Gasser and Michael N. Huhns, 37–54. San Francisco, CA: Morgan Kaufmann. https://doi.org/10.1016/B978-1-55860-9,525 mm-092-8.50006-X.

Star, Susan Leigh. 1995. *Ecologies of Knowledge: Work and Politics in Science and Technology.* Albany, NY: SUNY.

Star, Susan Leigh. 1998. "Grounded Classification: Grounded Theory and Faceted Classification." https://www.ideals.illinois.edu/handle/2142/8215.

Star, Susan Leigh, and James R. Griesemer. 1989. "Institutional Ecology, 'Translations' and Boundary Objects: Amateurs and Professionals in Berkeley's Museum of Vertebrate Zoology, 1907–39." *Social Studies of Science* 19 (3): 387–420. https://doi.org/10.1177/030631289019003001.

Star, Susan Leigh, and Karen Ruhleder. 1996. "Steps Toward an Ecology of Infrastructure: Design and Access for Large Information Spaces." *Information Systems Research* 7 (1): 111–34. https://doi.org/10.1287/isre.7.1.111.

Starkey, Guy. 2011. *Local Radio, Going Global.* New York: Springer.

Sterne, Jonathan. 1999. "Television under Construction: American Television and the Problem of Distribution, 1926–62." *Media, Culture & Society* 21 (4): 503–30. https://doi.org/10.1177/016344399021004004.

Steward, Julian Haynes. 1969. *The Concept and Method of Cultural Ecology.* Indianapolis, IN: Bobbs-Merrill.

Steward, Julian Haynes. 1972. *Theory of Culture Change: The Methodology of Multilinear Evolution.* Champaign, IL: University of Illinois Press.

Strate, Lance. 2006. *Echoes and Reflections: On Media Ecology as a Field of Study.* New York: Hampton Press.

Striphas, Ted. 2011. *The Late Age of Print: Everyday Book Culture from Consumerism to Control.* New York: Columbia University Press.

Striphas, Ted. 2012. "What Is an Algorithm? – Culture Digitally." 2012. https://culturedigitally.org/2012/02/what-is-an-algorithm/.

Striphas, Ted. 2015. "Algorithmic Culture." *European Journal of Cultural Studies* 18 (4–5): 395–412. https://doi.org/10.1177/1367549415577392.

Striphas, Ted. 2023. *Algorithmic Culture before the Internet*. New York: Columbia University Press.

Susman, Warren. 1984. *Culture as History: The Transformation of American Society in the Twentieth Century*. New York: Pantheon Books.

Svensson, Patrik, and David Theo Goldberg. 2015. *Between Humanities and the Digital*. Cambridge, MA: MIT Press.

Tabbi, Joseph, ed. 2020. *Post-Digital: Dialogues and Debates from the Electronic Book Review*. London: Bloomsbury Academic.

Taylor, J. Benjamin. 2016. *Extreme Media and American Politics: In Defense of Extremity*. New York: Springer.

Taurino, Giulia. 2022. "The Brokenness in Our Recommendation Systems: Computational Art for an Ethical Use of A.I." In *Disruptive Technologies in Media, Arts and Design*, edited by Alexiei Dingli, Alexander Pfeiffer, Alesha Serada, Mark Bugeja, and Stephen Bezzina, 382:157–68. Lecture Notes in Networks and Systems. Cham: Springer International Publishing. https://doi.org/10.10079,525 mm/978-3-030-93780-5_11.

Thompson, Robert J. 1997. *Television's Second Golden Age: From Hill Street Blues to ER*. Syracuse, NY: Syracuse University Press.

Thylstrup, Nanna Bonde, Agostinho, Daniela, Ring, Annie, D'Ignazio, Catherine, and Kristin Veel, eds. 2021. *Uncertain Archives: Critical Keywords for Big Data*. Cambridge, MA: MIT Press.

Tilson, David, Lyytinen, Kalle, and Carsten Sørensen. 2010. "Digital Infrastructures: The Missing IS Research Agenda." *Information Systems Research* 21 (4): 748–59. https://doi.org/10.1287/isre.1100.0318.

Todorov, Tzvetan. 1969. "Structural Analysis of Narrative." *NOVEL: A Forum on Fiction* 3 (1): 70–76. https://doi.org/10.2307/1345003.

Todorov, Tzvetan. 1976. "The Origin of Genres." *New Literary History* 8 (1): 159–70. https://doi.org/10.2307/468619.

Trouleau, William, Ashkan, Azin, Ding, Weicong, and Brian Eriksson. 2016. "Just One More: Modeling Binge Watching Behavior." In *Proceedings of the 22nd ACM SIGKDD International Conference on Knowledge Discovery and Data Mining*, 1215–24. KDD '16. San Francisco, CA: Association for Computing Machinery. https://doi.org/10.1145/2939672.2939792.

Turner, Graeme, and Jinna Tay. 2009. *Television Studies After TV: Understanding Television in the Post-Broadcast Era*. New York: Routledge.

Ulin, Jeff. 2012. *The Business of Media Distribution: Monetizing Film, TV and Video Content in an Online World*. New York: Routledge.

Uricchio, William. 2011. "The Algorithmic Turn: Photosynth, Augmented Reality and the Changing Implications of the Image." *Visual Studies* 26 (1): 25–35. https://doi.org/10.1080/1472586X.2011.548486.

Van Dijck, José. 2013. *The Culture of Connectivity: A Critical History of Social Media*. New York: Oxford University Press.

Van Dijck, José. 2021. "Seeing the Forest for the Trees: Visualizing Platformization and Its Governance." *New Media & Society* 23 (9): 2801–19. https://doi.org/10.1177/1461444820940293.

Van Arendonk, Kathryn. 2019. "Theorizing the Television Episode." *Narrative* 27 (1): 65–82. https://doi.org/10.1353/nar.2019.0004.

Venkatesan, Raj, and Jim Lecinski. 2021. *The AI Marketing Canvas: A Five-Stage Road Map to Implementing Artificial Intelligence in Marketing*. Stanford, CA: Stanford University Press.

Vitali-Rosati, Marcello. 2016. "What Is Editorialization?" In *Sens Public*. Association Sens Public. https://papyrus.bib.umontreal.ca/xmlui/handle/1866/12972.

Vitali-Rosati, Marcello. 2018. *On Editorialization: Structuring Space and Authority in the Digital Age*. Amsterdam: Institute of Network Cultures.

Wardrip-Fruin, Noah, and Nick Montfort. 2003. *The New Media Reader*. Cambridge, MA: MIT Press.

Warf, Barney. 2012. *Global Geographies of the Internet*. New York: Springer.

Warf, Barney. 2017. *Handbook on Geographies of Technology*. Cheltenham: Edward Elgar Publishing.

Washburn, Sherwood L. 2017. *Classification and Human Evolution*. New York: Routledge.

Wayne, Michael L. 2018. "Netflix, Amazon, and Branded Television Content in Subscription Video On-Demand Portals." *Media, Culture & Society* 40 (5): 725–41. https://doi.org/10.1177/0163443717736118.

Webster, James G. 2005. "Beneath the Veneer of Fragmentation: Television Audience Polarization in a Multichannel World." *Journal of Communication* 55 (2): 366–82. https://doi.org/10.1111/j.1460-2466.2005.tb02677.x.

Weiss, Dennis M., Propen, Amy D., and Colbey Emmerson Reid. 2014. *Design, Mediation, and the Posthuman*. Lanham, MD: Lexington Books.

Wells-Lassagne, Shannon. 2017. *Television and Serial Adaptation*. New York: Routledge.

Wheen, Francis. 1985. *Television: A History*. Century Pub.

Williams, Raymond. 1974. *Television: Technology and Cultural Form*. New York: Routledge.

Williams, Raymond. 1983. *Keywords: A Vocabulary of Culture and Society*. Oxford: Oxford University Press.

Wolf, Mark J.P. 2014. *Building Imaginary Worlds: The Theory and History of Subcrea-tion*. New York: Routledge.

Zapf, Hubert. 2016a. *Literature as Cultural Ecology: Sustainable Texts*. London: Bloomsbury Publishing.

Zapf, Hubert. 2016b. *Handbook of Ecocriticism and Cultural Ecology*. Berlin: Walter de Gruyter.

Index